Working with Traumatic Brain Injury in Schools

Every day, children and adolescents worldwide return to the educational setting having sustained a traumatic brain injury (TBI). The possible negative consequences of TBI range from mild to severe and include neurological, cognitive, emotional, social, and behavioral difficulties. Within the school setting, the negative effects of TBI tend to persist or worsen over time, often resulting in academic and social difficulties that require formal and informal educational assistance and support. School psychologists and other educational professionals are well-positioned to help ensure students with TBI receive this assistance and support.

Working with Traumatic Brain Injury in Schools is a comprehensive practitioner-oriented guide to effective school-based services for students who have experienced TBI. It is primarily written for school-based professionals who have limited or no neurological or neuropsychological training; however, it contains educational information that is useful to professionals with extensive knowledge of neurology and/or neuropsychology. This book is also written for parents and guardians of students with TBI because of their integral role in the transition, school-based assessment, and school-based intervention processes. Chapter topics include: basic brain anatomy and physiology; head injury and severity level classifications; biomechanics of injury; injury recovery and rehabilitation; neurological, cognitive, emotional, behavioral, social, and academic consequences; understanding community-based assessment findings; a framework for school-based assessment (TBI-SNNAP); school-based psychoeducational report writing and school-based interventions; monitoring pharmacological interventions; and prevention. An accompanying website includes handouts, sample reports, and training templates to assist professionals in recognizing and responding to students with TBI.

Paul B. Jantz, PhD, NCSP, is an assistant professor in the school psychology program at Texas State University.

Susan C. Davies, EdD, NCSP, is an associate professor in the school psychology program at the University of Dayton, where she also serves as the program and internship coordinator.

Erin D. Bigler, PhD, ABPP-CN, is a professor of psychology and neuroscience in the Department of Psychology and Neuroscience Center at Brigham Young University, where he also serves as the director of the Magnetic Resonance Imaging (MRI) Research Facility, and an adjunct professor of psychiatry at the University of Utah.

School-Based Practice in Action Series

Series Editors
Rosemary B. Mennuti, EdD, NCSP
and
Ray W. Christner, PsyD, NCSP
Cognitive Health Solutions, LLC

This series provides school-based practitioners with concise, practical guidebooks designed to facilitate the implementation of evidence-based programs into school settings, putting the best practices *in action*.

Assessment and Intervention for Executive Function Difficulties
George McCloskey, Lisa A. Perkins, and Bob Van Divner

Resilient Playgrounds
Beth Doll

Comprehensive Planning for Safe Learning Environments: A School Counselor's Guide to Integrating Physical and Psychological Safety—Prevention through Recovery
Melissa A. Reeves, Linda M. Kanan, and Amy E. Plog

Behavioral Interventions in Schools: A Response-to-Intervention Guidebook
David M. Hulac, Joy Terrell, Odell Vining, and Joshua Bernstein

The Power of Family-School Partnering (FSP): A Practical Guide for School Mental Health Professionals and Educators
Cathy Lines, Gloria Miller, and Amanda Arthur-Stanley

Implementing Response-to-Intervention in Elementary and Secondary Schools: Procedures to Assure Scientific-Based Practices, Second Edition
Matthew K. Burns and Kimberly Gibbons

A Guide to Psychiatric Services in Schools: Understanding Roles, Treatment, and Collaboration
Shawna S. Brent

Comprehensive Children's Mental Health Services in Schools and Communities
Robyn S. Hess, Rick Jay Short, and Cynthia Hazel

Responsive School Practices to Support Lesbian, Gay, Bisexual, Transgender, and Questioning Students and Families
Emily Fisher and Kelly Kennedy

Pediatric School Psychology: Conceptualization, Applications, and Leadership Development
Thomas J. Power and Kathy L. Bradley-Klug

Serving the Gifted: Evidence-Based Clinical and Psychoeducational Practice
Steven I. Pfeiffer

Early Childhood Education: A Practical Guide to Evidence-Based, Multi-Tiered Service Delivery
Gina Coffee, Corey E. Ray-Subramanian, G. Thomas Schanding, Jr., and Kelly A. Feeney-Kettler

Implementing Response-to-Intervention to Address the Needs of English-Language Learners: Instructional Strategies and Assessment Tools for School Psychologists
Holly Hudspath-Niemi and Mary Lou Conroy

Conducting Student-Driven Interviews: Practical Strategies for Increasing Student Involvement and Addressing Behavior Problems
John Murphy

Single Case Research in Schools: Practical Guidelines for School-Based Professionals
Kimberly J. Vannest, John L. Davis, and Richard I. Parker

Working with Traumatic Brain Injury in Schools: Transition, Assessment, and Intervention
Paul B. Jantz, Susan C. Davies, and Erin D. Bigler

Working with Traumatic Brain Injury in Schools

Transition, Assessment, and Intervention

Paul B. Jantz, Susan C. Davies, and Erin D. Bigler

Routledge
Taylor & Francis Group

NEW YORK AND LONDON

First published 2014
by Routledge
711 Third Avenue, New York, NY 10017

and by Routledge
27 Church Road, Hove, East Sussex BN3 2FA

Routledge is an imprint of the Taylor & Francis Group, an informa business

© 2014 Taylor & Francis

The right of Paul B. Jantz, Susan C. Davies, and Erin D. Bigler to be identified as authors of this work has been asserted by them in accordance with sections 77 and 78 of the Copyright, Designs and Patents Act 1988.

Library of Congress Cataloging-in-Publication Data

Jantz, Paul B.
  Working with traumatic brain injury in schools : transition, assessment, and
  intervention / Paul B. Jantz, Susan C. Davies, Erin D. Bigler.
    pages cm — (School-based practice in action; 16)
  Includes bibliographical references and index.
  1. Brain-damaged children—Education. 2. Brain-damaged children—
Psychology. 3. Brain-damaged children—Mental health. 4. Educational
psychology. 5. Educational counseling I. Title.
  LC4580.J32 2014
  371.9—dc23
  2013029734

ISBN: 978-0-415-64253-8 (hbk)
ISBN: 978-0-415-64254-5 (pbk)
ISBN: 978-0-203-08084-9 (ebk)

Typeset in Minion
by Apex CoVantage, LLC

This book is dedicated to those who have sustained a TBI—and to their families and friends. It is also dedicated to those individuals whose goal is to help children with TBI become more successful in the educational setting.

To my husband, Allen Perry, and our "Brady Bunch" of children: Cara, Mia, and Charley Ann; AJ, Jack, and Jeff—Susan.

Contents

List of Figures, Tables, and Case Studies

Figures

Tables

Case Studies

Series Editors' Foreword

We are delighted to see the continued growth of the School-Based Practice in Action Series, which grew out of a discussion between us several years ago while attending a professional conference. At that time, we were each at different points in our careers, yet we both saw and faced the same challenges for education and serving children and families. Acknowledging the transformations facing the educational system, we shared a passion and vision for ensuring quality services to schools, students, and families. This vision involved increasing the strong knowledge base of practitioners together with an impact on service delivery. This would require the understanding of theory and research, although we viewed the most critical element as having the needed resources for bridging empirical knowledge to the process of practice. Thus, our goal for the School-Based Practice in Action Series has been to offer resources for readers based on sound research and principles that can be set directly "into action."

To accomplish this, each book in the series offers information in a practice-friendly manner, and they offer a link to a website to obtain reproducible and usable materials that are a supplement to the content of the book. These resources are designed to have a direct impact on transitioning research and knowledge into the day-to-day functions of school-based practitioners. We recognize that the implementation of programs and the changing of roles come with challenges and barriers, and as such, these processes may take on various forms depending on the context of the situation and the voice of the practitioner. To that end, the books of the School-Based Practice in Action Series may be used in their entirety and present form for a number of practitioners; however, for others, these books will help them find new ways to move toward effective action and new possibilities. No matter which style fits your practice, we hope that these books will influence your work and professional growth.

Working with Drs. Paul Jantz, Susan Davies, and Erin Bigler has been a delightful experience. We are grateful to have had the opportunity to be part of the development of their book, *Working with Traumatic Brain Injury in Schools: Transition, Assessment, and Intervention*. The authors provide a basic theoretical overview of brain anatomy and physiology and skillfully guide the practitioner through the process of implementing useful interventions for children with traumatic brain injury. This book is an excellent comprehensive resource addressing not only academic issues but behavioral, social, and emotional concerns of children as they transition back to school and continue their learning experience. We are pleased to have *Working with Traumatic Brain Injury in Schools* as part of our series.

Finally, we want to extend our thank you to Ms. Anna Moore and Routledge Publishing for their ongoing support of a book series focused on enriching the practice and service delivery within school settings. Their openness to meet the needs of school-based practitioners made the School-Based Practice in Action Series possible. In addition, we must thank Mr. Dana Bliss, whose interest and collaboration made our idea for a book series a reality. We hope that you enjoy reading and implementing the materials in this book and the rest of the series as much as we have enjoyed working with the authors on developing these resources. Best wishes in your work with schools, children, and families.

Rosemary B. Mennuti, EdD, NCSP
Ray W. Christner, PsyD, NCSP
Series Editors, School-Based Practice in Action Series

Acknowledgments

The authors wish to thank Ray Christner and Rosemary Mennuti, series editors, and Anna Moore, our editor at Routledge, for their support. A special thanks goes to Mr. Dana Bliss for suggesting to the lead author that this book be written and to those colleagues who provided editorial feedback and contributions during the writing process: Tracy Abildskov, Steve Auster, Anne Davies, Debbie Ettel, Bobbie Fiori, Christine Hajek, Kristen Ruffer, Jenna Sandlund, Sara Timms, and Lane Valum—and those who provided encouragement throughout the writing process: Elana Bernstein, Sawyer Hunley, and Molly Schaller. Our gratitude is further extended to Jolene Ellis, graduate student at Texas State University, for her feedback, organizational skills, endless correspondence with various entities, and compilation of the index.

1 Traumatic Brain Injury

An Introduction

Traumatic brain injury (TBI) is the leading cause of death and disability in children and young adults worldwide (World Health Organization, 2006). In the United States, it is estimated that each year, for every 100,000 people, 90 will be hospitalized as a result of a TBI and an additional 465 will visit a hospital emergency department (Coronado et al., 2012). Of the school-aged children in the United States who survive their injury, it has been estimated that 1 in 550 will experience a TBI severe enough to result in a long-term disability (Arroyos-Jurado, Paulsen, Ehly, & Max, 2006). The possible negative effects of TBI can range from mild to severe and can include neurological, cognitive, emotional, social, and behavioral difficulties (Jantz & Coulter, 2007). Within the school setting, the negative effects of TBI tend to persist or worsen over time, resulting in academic and social difficulties that require formal and informal educational assistance (Glang et al., 2008).

The transition process from hospital to school, the school-based assessment of TBI-related educational needs, and the development of TBI-related school-based educational interventions are critical to the academic success of students with TBI. Educational professionals working within the school setting (e.g., school psychologists, teachers) are well-positioned to assist students with TBI and their families navigate through these interrelated processes. However, to do so effectively educators and school-based mental health professionals need a basic working knowledge of TBI—including types of injury; mechanisms of injury; injury severity classification systems; initial and ongoing stages of recovery; setting-specific rehabilitation interventions (in-patient and out-patient); common neurological, cognitive, emotional, behavioral, social, and academic consequences; and common community-based assessment practices, neuroimaging techniques, and neuropsychological test batteries. They also need an effective means for collaborating with parents/guardians, medical professionals, and mental health professionals involved in the recovery, assessment, and care of students with TBI. Finally, educational professionals need a good understanding of how to best conduct a school-based assessment of a student with TBI and translate educational and medical data into effective and appropriate TBI-related school-based interventions.

This book is a comprehensive practitioner-oriented guide to effective school-based services for students who have experienced TBI. It is primarily written for school-based professionals who have limited or no neurological or neuropsychological training; however, it also contains information that is useful for professionals with extensive knowledge in neurology and/or neuropsychology. This book is also written for parents/

guardians of students with TBI because of their integral role in the transition, school-based assessment, and school-based intervention processes.

This book provides a glossary of common TBI-related terms on the website that accompanies this book. It also incorporates the TBI School-Based Neuroeducational Needs Assessment Process (TBI-SNNAP). The TBI-SNNAP is an author-developed problem-solving approach to neuroeducational needs assessment and school-based intervention development that is based on the Bransford and Stein IDEAL problem-solving model (1993) and the Heartland Area Education Agency ICEL/RIOT assessment process (2005). A variety of evidenced-based educational interventions grounded in Response to Intervention (RtI) theory are also provided in this book, as well as suggestions regarding educational transition based on current TBI rehabilitation research.

Because a book of this type would be incomplete without a discussion on prevention, information is included on how parents, schools, agencies, and the medical community can develop partnerships focusing on prevention; guidelines for developing and implementing in-service training opportunities for school-based and nonschool-based professionals; state and school-based TBI prevention initiatives; and concussion and helmet awareness programs. In addition to being an indispensable resource for parents/guardians, educational professionals working in the schools, and professionals working outside the school setting, this book is an invaluable supplemental book for graduate level training programs in school psychology, special education, educational leadership, school counseling, child and adolescent psychiatry, and the medical field.

Chapter Overview

This introductory chapter will provide an overview of TBI, including

- prevalence rates;
- costs to society;
- becoming aware of students with TBI;
- special education;
- Section 504 of the Rehabilitation Act of 1973;
- support services in rural communities;
- interdisciplinary roles, functions, and responsibilities; and
- interdisciplinary communication and collaboration.

Prevalence Rates

Overall

It is difficult to determine the true overall number of TBIs occurring every year in the United States and around the world for the following reasons:

Inconsistency in treatment location. Injuries that result in a serious TBI (e.g., motor-vehicle traffic/pedestrian injuries, serious assault injuries, injuries obtained in falls from heights) are most likely to be treated at a hospital emergency department (HED), whereas injuries that result in a less serious TBI (e.g., lacerations to the head from blows, concussions) are more likely to be treated in doctors' offices or outpatient facilities (e.g., clinics, urgent care centers). Because doctors' offices and outpatient facilities are usually not the focus of data collection efforts, TBIs treated at these locations are less likely to be included in reports on the prevalence rate of TBI.

Convenience of data collection. HEDs are the most convenient data collection sites for establishing TBI prevalence rates. This is due to the larger number of visits and their participation in government-sponsored data collection projects. Projects such as the U.S. Department of Health and Human Services Agency for Healthcare Research and Quality's *Healthcare Cost and Utilization Project* (HCUP; 2013), the U.S. Consumer Product Safety Commission's *National Electronic Injury Surveillance System-All Injury Program* (NEISS-AIP; 2013a), and the Centers for Disease Control and Prevention's (CDC) National Center for Health Statistics' *National Hospital Ambulatory Medical Care Survey* (NHAMCS; 2013a) are designed specifically to collect hospital and patient information that includes data on HED visits. Therefore, these three sources tend to be major "go to" sources for statistics on TBI rates. It should be noted, however, that not all hospitals participate in all of these programs and some hospitals do not participate in any. Doctor's offices and outpatient facilities are the least convenient data collection sites for establishing TBI statistics due to the smaller number of visits, greater number of locations, and lack of involvement in government-sponsored data collection projects.

Inconsistency in reporting medical diagnosis of head injuries. Currently there is no agreed upon system in place for determining when a head injury warrants a diagnosis of TBI. For instance, the NEISS-AIP (2013) is a database designed to collect patient information from each participating hospital for *all* nonfatal injuries and poisonings treated in U.S. HEDs. As designed, it "includes only the principal diagnosis and primary body part injured and therefore cannot capture TBIs that were secondary diagnoses. For example, skull fractures, which commonly involve TBI, are listed as fractures of the head and not as TBIs" (CDC, 2011, pp. 1341–1342). Subsequently, an NEISS-AIP-affiliated attending physician treating a patient with a gunshot wound to the head may list the primary diagnosis as a "penetrating gunshot wound to the head" rather than "traumatic brain injury resulting from a penetrating gunshot wound to the head." Another example would be an HED attending physician diagnosing a head injury as a skull fracture rather than TBI.

Inconsistency in TBI terminology/definition. There is no consistency in the terminology or definitions used to describe TBI. For example "head injury is still used synonymously with TBI, but in some cases it refers to injury of other head structures such as the face or jaw" (Lezak, Howieson, Bigler, & Tranel, 2012, p. 180). In this case, an injury to the jaw coded as a "head injury" could inadvertently be included in TBI prevalence rate data. The term "concussion" raises similar issues. That is, although a concussion is defined/considered by some to be a form of mild TBI (mTBI; Lezak et al., 2012) there is controversy as to whether there is a physiological basis for postconcussion symptoms (Evans, 2010; Lee, 2007). Therefore, individuals seeking medical attention in an HED for a concussion may or may not be diagnosed/reported as receiving a TBI.

It should be noted, however, that there is recognition that a "clear, concise definition of traumatic brain injury (TBI) is fundamental for reporting, comparison, and interpretation of studies on TBI" (Menon, Schwab, Wright, & Maas, 2010, p. 1637) and serious attempts are being made to correct these inconsistencies. For example, a panel of experts who made up the Demographics and Clinical Assessment Working Group of the International and Interagency Initiative toward Common Data Elements for Research on Traumatic Brain Injury and Psychological Health recently proposed a consensus definition of TBI. This statement defines TBI as "an alteration in brain function, or other evidence of brain pathology, caused by an external force" (Menon et al., 2010, p. 1638) and it "reflects the understanding that it is the damage to the brain that matters, and not so [*sic*] the damage to scalp or skull" (p. 1638). The panel of experts also provided explanatory notes clarifying each component of the definition.

Failure to recognize symptoms when present.   There are times when TBI can go untreated due to a failure to recognize TBI symptoms. For instance, a parent who is unaware that their young child received a concussion may mistake their child's loss of appetite and complaints of nausea, headache, and fatigue (common signs of a concussion; CDC, 2013b) as the acute onset of a flu virus and fail to seek medical attention. In an extreme case, the symptoms of a more severe TBI may also be mistakenly overlooked. There is also a widespread lack of awareness of TBI among the general public and medical community, as evidenced by current concussion education programs such as the *Heads Up on Concussion* (for health care professionals and youth and high school sports coaches, parents, and athletes), the *Heads Up: Brain Injury in Your Practice* (for primary care settings), the *Heads Up: What to Expect After Concussion* (for patients), the *Facts about Concussion and Brain Injury: Where to Get Help* (for patients), and the *Updated Mild Traumatic Brain Injury Guidelines for Adults* (acute care settings) programs sponsored by the CDC (2013c, 2013d, 2013e, 2013f, 2013g).

The high cost of medical treatment.   It is a well-known fact that medical care is costly. In 2010, approximately 10% of all children under 18 (7.3 million) were without health insurance (Carmen, Proctor, & Smith, 2010). Families who lack sufficient medical insurance or families in poverty may opt to "treat the injury at home" or choose a "wait and see" approach because they cannot afford to take their child to the doctor or HED.

A desire to avoid the involvement of law enforcement or the legal system.   Not all who receive a TBI will seek the aid of the medical community; to do so risks the possibility of unwanted attention from law enforcement officials or the legal system. Examples include: adolescent gang members who do not seek medical attention after receiving a severe beating by rival gang members (involving repeated kicks or blows to the head), because it is considered to be a "gang matter, not a police matter" or they fear retaliation if the assault is reported; nondocumented workers who do not seek medical attention after receiving a blow to the head for fear of being reported to immigration officials; and parents who do not seek immediate medical attention for infants who have been shaken or struck, for fear that the offending party will be charged with a crime.

Infants, Children, Adolescents

Available data indicate that every year in the United States motor vehicle traffic incidents (occupant, motorcyclist, pedal cyclist, pedestrian), falls, assaults, and other external causes (e.g., being struck by or against something) will result in an estimated 1.7 million people arriving in HEDs with TBI (Faul, Xu, Wald, & Coronado, 2010). Of these visits, more than

275,000 will be hospitalized, nearly 52,000 will die from their injury, and over half a million (697,347) will be infants, children, and adolescents between the ages of 0 and 19.

While the majority of 0–19-year-olds who arrive at the HED will be treated and released to go home (631,146), the greater the age at the time of the injury, the more likely the injury will result in hospitalization or death. For example, adolescents ages 15–19 are twice as likely to be hospitalized and 1.5 times more likely to die as a result of their injury than are infants and children ages 0–14 (Faul et al., 2010; Shi et al., 2009). These higher rates for adolescents ages 15–19 are likely due to this age groups' increasing propensity to engage in high-risk activities—such as not wearing a seat belt when riding in a car driven by someone else, riding in a vehicle driven by someone who has been drinking alcohol, being involved in a physical fight, carrying a weapon, engaging in competitive contact sports, and using drugs and alcohol (CDC, 2010, 2011; Johnston, O'Malley, Bachman, & Schulenberg, 2011; Shi et al., 2009). Regardless of the age group, males are two to three times more likely to receive a TBI than are females.

Sports and Recreation Injuries

According to the CDC (2011), every year in the United States approximately 2.6 million children and adolescents ages 4–19 will visit an HED for sports- and recreation-related injuries. Of these visits, approximately 7% of the injuries (182,000) will be TBIs. Of these, almost three quarters (136,500) will occur among males and 71% will occur among children and adolescents ages 10–19. The reason the majority of sports- and recreation-related TBIs occurs among ages 10–19 is likely due to any or all of the following:

Physical maturation. As children in this age group mature, there is a noticeable increase in their strength, weight, and speed. When combined with motion-oriented sports (e.g., basketball, hockey) or recreation activities (e.g., sledding, ice-skating) these increases can result in a greater amount of momentum and force of impact, thereby increasing the chance of injury (CDC, 2011; Proctor & Cantu, 2000). For example, consider the difference in increased risk of injury that occurs when a 170-pound high school quarterback is tackled behind the line of scrimmage by an opposing 250-pound tight end during the opponent's homecoming game—compared to two 50-pound 8-year-olds in a similar situation during a game of peewee football on a Saturday afternoon.

High-risk activities. For this age group there is an increased involvement in off-ground sports (e.g., gymnastics, rodeo) or recreation activities (e.g., horseback riding, trampolining) that combine momentum, speed, mass, and height, that can lead to TBI, as is the case when a gymnast falls during a routine on the pommel horse or uneven bars or a person falls to the ground while executing a backflip on the neighbor's trampoline. There is also increased involvement in high-risk wheeled sports (e.g., freestyle biking, freestyle skiing) and recreation activities (e.g., skateboarding) that encourage and value stunts and tricks, also increasing risk of TBI, as is the case when a participant falls during a freestyle biking, half-pipe routine.

Risk rating. In rank order, the top five sports and recreation activities that account for the majority of nonfatal TBI-related HED visits under the age of 19 are: bicycling, football, playground activities, basketball, and soccer (CDC, 2011). The top five, rank-ordered sports and recreation activities for males and females ages 10–19 are shown in Table 1.1.

Table 1.1 Top five, rank-ordered activities accounting for nonfatal TBI hospital emergency department visits for males and females ages 10–19

Sex/Rank	Age group (yrs)				
	≤ 4 No. (%)	5–9 No. (%)	10–14 No. (%)	15–19 No. (%)	≤ 19 total No. (%)
Male					
1	Playground 3,187 (35.3*)	Bicycling 5,997 (23.6)	Football 8,988 (20.7)	Football 13,667 (30.3)	Football 24,431 (19.9)
2	Bicycling 1,608 (17.8)	Playground 4,790 (18.9)	Bicycling 8,302 (19.1)	Bicycling 4,377 (9.7)	Bicycling 20,285 (16.5)
3	Baseball 656 (7.3)	Baseball 2,227 (8.8)	Basketball 4,009 (9.2)	Basketball 4,049 (9.0)	Playground 9,568 (7.8)
4	Scooter riding 460 (5.1)	Football 1,657 (6.5)	Baseball 3,061 (7.0)	Soccer 3,013 (6.7)	Basketball 9,372 (7.6)
5	Swimming 429 (4.8)	Basketball 1,133 (4.5)	Skateboarding 2,613 (6.0)	ATV riding 2,546 (5.6)	Baseball 8,030 (6.5)
Other	2,680 (29.7)	9,558 (37.7)	16,476 (37.9)	17,488 (38.7)	51,284 (41.7)
Total	9,020	25,362	43,449	45,140	122,970
Rate† (95% CI)	86 (61–112)	248 (182–313)	410 (316–504)	417 (323–512)	292 (225–360)

Female

1	Playground 2,297 (47.8)	Playground 3,455 (30.3)	Bicycling 2,051 (12.2)	Soccer 2,678 (16.0)	Playground 7,136 (14.2)
2	Bicycling 775 (14.4)	Bicycling 2,361 (20.7)	Basketball 1,863(11.1)	Basketball 2,446 (14.6)	Bicycling 5,928 (11.8)
3	Baseball 321 (6.0)	Baseball 541 (4.7)	Soccer 1,843 (11.0)	Gymnastics§ 1,513 (9.1)	Soccer 4,767 (9.5)
4	Trampolining 261¶(4.8)	Scooter riding 525 (4.6)	Horseback riding 1,301 (7.7)	Softball 1,171 (7.0)	Basketball 4,615 (9.2)
5	Swimming 257 (4.8)	Swimming 504 (4.4)	Playground 1,041 (6.2)	Horseback riding 1,028 (6.2)	Horseback riding 2,853 (5.7)
Other	1,275 (23.7)	4,006 (35.2)	8,724 (51.9)	7,872 (47.1)	25,011 (49.7)
Total	5,386	11,391	16,824	16,709	50,310
Rate[†] (95% CI)	54 (34–74)	117 (87–146)	167 (130–203)	163 (122–204)	126 (96–155)

Data: National Electronic Injury Surveillance System—All Injury Program, United States, 2001–2009.

Note: Reprinted from "Nonfatal traumatic brain injuries related to sports and recreation activities among persons aged <19 years—United States, Surveillance Summaries, 2001–2009." U.S. Department of Health and Human Services, Centers for Disease Control and Prevention (CDC, 2011), *Morbidity and Mortality Weekly Report (MMWR)*, 60, pp. 1337–1342.

Abbreviations: ATV = all-terrain vehicle; CI = confidence interval.
[*] Percentages might not sum to 100% because of rounding.
[†] Per 100,000 population.
[§] Includes cheerleading and dancing.
[¶] Estimate might be unstable because the coefficient of variation is > 30%.

Costs to Society

The costs associated with TBI are both monetary and human. A recent study (Kayani, Homan, Yun, & Zhu, 2009) estimated that in Missouri during 2005 the direct costs for TBI-related HED visits and hospitalizations were $111 million. In its report to Congress on mTBI, the National Center for Injury Prevention and Control (2003) reported that the costs associated with the treatment of mTBI were $17 billion each year. The economic costs associated with TBI for 2010 were estimated to be $76.3 billion (Coronado, McGuire, Faul, Pearson, & Sugerman, 2012). In 2003, based on data reported by the Healthcare Cost and Utilization Project using the KID database compiled in 2000, it was estimated that 50,658 children in the United States under the age of 18 were hospitalized for a TBI-related injury at a cost of more than $1 billion in inpatient charges, making it the fifth most expensive hospital diagnosis for children (Schneier, Shields, Hostetler, Xiang, & Smith, 2006).

The human costs of TBI are difficult, if not impossible, to measure. While some of the consequences of TBI (social, emotional, neurological, cognitive, and behavioral indicators) may be measured in terms of a score on an assessment instrument or by comparing performance to an established norm group, the costs of those consequences to the individual or to those with whom he/she comes in contact are not easily quantified. It is difficult, if not impossible, to measure the costs of the personal, familial, or collegial grief/loss that can occur in an instant, but last a lifetime. It is also difficult, if not impossible, to measure the costs associated with a change in personality; short-term memory loss; partial paralysis; interpersonal conflict; parental stress; feelings of helplessness or hopelessness that comes with 24-hour care; decreases in academic performance; withdrawal from friends and family; or uncontrollable headache, fatigue, or nausea. While these costs (and a myriad of others) may not be easy to measure, they are not hard to imagine. Those who experience them will tell you the cost is high.

Becoming Aware of Students With TBI

How a student with TBI comes to the attention of school professionals (e.g., psychologist, school counselor, teacher) varies. For example, parents/guardians can inform school professionals at prearranged formal meetings, which generally occur at or about the time the student is returning to school; under less formal circumstances (e.g., during back-to-school-night meetings, during encounters at grocery stores); or during the background medical history portion of a special education eligibility evaluation interview, when the school psychologist asks: "Has your child ever received a head injury?" or "Has your child ever been admitted to the hospital?" or "Has your child ever had a concussion?" Community and hospital professionals (e.g., medical professionals, physical therapists, licensed psychologists, speech-language pathologists) involved in the care of students with TBI can also inform school professionals after obtaining parent permission to do so. When this happens, it is done when the students transition from hospitals or rehabilitation centers back into the school setting.

There are times when a school professional may become aware of a student's TBI through personal interactions with the student. For example, the student may inform school professionals that he/she has sustained a TBI in a "life history" or "what I did over the summer" writing sample; a teacher may notice that a recently arrived transfer student from another state is complaining of severe headaches and frequently appears to "daydream" in his 9th-grade math class; or a football coach may notice that during strength-training exercises a student has significant left-sided weakness and on the football field he doesn't seem to "see" his opponent whenever his opponent comes from the left side. While these latter two examples are not in-and-of-themselves indicative of TBI, they can be of significant enough concern to cause the school professional to begin asking the student questions or begin consulting with the school psychologist or nurse—who then interviews the parent/guardian. Finally, there are also times when school professionals become aware of a student's TBI prior to his/her arrival at school via local newspaper articles, TV news reports, or third-party report by persons "in the know."

Special Education

According to the Technical Assistance Coordination Center child count data (http:// tadnet.public.tadnet.org/pages/712), more than 6.5 million students across the United States between the ages of 3 and 21 are receiving special education services under a special education disability category. Of these, approximately 25,000 students were receiving services under a special education category of Traumatic Brain Injury. This number, however, does not reflect the number of students with TBI who were receiving special education services under a different special education category (e.g., Other Health Impaired); did not meet minimal special education eligibility criteria, but still had educational, behavioral, or emotional deficits/needs; or sustained a TBI, but were never brought to the attention of the special education multidisciplinary assessment team.

The Individuals with Disabilities Education Improvement Act of 2004 (IDEIA 04) obligates all public schools receiving federal funding to identify, locate, and evaluate all children with disabilities, ages birth–21, who are in need of special education services or early intervention; regardless of the severity of their disabilities. Known as "child find" (IDEIA 04; U.S. Federal Register, 2006, p. 46764), this process includes children with disabilities who are homeless, wards of the state, highly mobile (including migrant children), and/or children with disabilities attending private schools (including religious schools). Child find also stipulates that children who are suspected of having a disability and in need of special education be identified, located, and evaluated, even if they are advancing from grade to grade.

Within IDEIA 04, and related to the child find provision, is a provision that allows for "early intervention services." These early intervention services apply specifically to infants and toddlers with disabilities from birth through the age of 2 who:

> are experiencing developmental delays, as measured by appropriate diagnostic instruments and procedures in 1 or more of the areas of cognitive development, physical development, communication development, social or emotional development, and adaptive development; or have a diagnosed physical or mental condition that has a high probability of resulting in developmental delay. (IDEIA 04, 2005, p. 100)

Early intervention covers a wide variety of services, including family training, counseling, and home visits; special instruction; speech-language pathology and audiology services; sign language and cued language services; occupational therapy; physical therapy; psychological services; service coordination services; medical services for diagnostic or evaluation purposes; early identification, screening, and assessment services; health services necessary to enable the infant or toddler to benefit from the other early intervention services; social work services; vision services; assistive technology devices and assistive technology services; and transportation and related costs that are necessary to enable an infant or toddler and their families to receive any of these services.

TBI became an official special education disability category in 1990, when the 1975 Education for All Handicapped Children Act (EHA) was reauthorized by the U.S. Congress and became the Individuals with Disabilities Education Act (IDEA; 1990). The official special education definition for TBI was codified in 1992 and reads:

> *Traumatic brain injury* means an acquired injury to the brain caused by an external physical force, resulting in total or partial functional disability or psychosocial impairment, or both, that adversely affects a child's educational performance. The term applies to open or closed head injuries resulting in impairments in one or more areas, such as cognition; language; memory; attention; reasoning; abstract thinking; judgment; problem-solving; sensory, perceptual, and motor abilities; psycho-social behavior; physical functions; information processing; and speech. The term does not apply to brain injuries that are congenital or degenerative, or to brain injuries induced by birth trauma.
>
> (U.S. Department of Education, 1992, p. 44802)

Once infants, children, or adolescents with TBI are identified through child find, schools are obligated under IDEIA 04 to locate and evaluate them in order to determine if there is a need for special education and related services designed "to meet their unique needs and prepare them for further education, employment, and independent living" (IDEIA 04, §601(d)(1)(a), p. H.R. 1350–1355) or a need for early intervention services designed to "meet the developmental needs of an infant or toddler with a disability" (IDEIA 04, §632(4)(c), p. H.R. 1350–1399). If, following a multidisciplinary team evaluation in the area of suspected disability, it is determined by the Individualized Family Service Plan (IFSP) team (age < 3) or the Individualized Education Program (IEP) team (ages 3–21) that the infant, child, or adolescent needs services, services must be provided at no cost to the family. Early intervention services for infants and toddlers are delineated by an IFSP and special education and related services are outlined in an IEP. Although infants and toddlers with TBI receive early intervention services under the umbrella of IDEIA 04, they do not receive a special education classification label. Children and adolescents with TBI receive services under the Traumatic Brain Injury special education label, beginning at age 3. It should be noted that although child find is designed to identify, locate, and evaluate children with disabilities as early as birth in order to help ensure their unique needs are met and the infant is prepared for further education, employment, and independent living, many parents/guardians of infants with TBI do not think to contact school child find personnel at the time of the injury; nor is the medical community under any legal obligation to notify public schools when an infant receives a TBI.

Underrepresentation in Special Education

Given that each year in the United States more than 44,000 school-aged children and adolescents (5–19) are hospitalized as a result of TBI (Faul et al., 2010), it is likely that the approximately 25,000 K-12 students who receive special education services each year under a Traumatic Brain Injury disability category (Technical Assistance Coordination Center, 2011) greatly underrepresents the true number of students with TBI who require special education and/or related services. Possible reasons for underidentification include:

Age at the time of injury. Depending on the age of the child at the time of the TBI, parents/guardians may not yet be thinking about their child's educational needs. Therefore, they may not seek out services available under IDEIA 04. Consider for example the parents of a ten-month-old infant who sustains a moderate TBI after a 3-foot fall from a patio deck onto a concrete sidewalk. As their infant leaves the hospital and begins her course of improvement/rehabilitation, it is likely that her parents will not be thinking about her entering school in five years. However, when the time does come, their daughter may have been meeting major milestones within reasonably expected time frames and appearing to learn without difficulties. In consequence, because she appears to be functioning normally, her parents/guardians may not think it is important to inform school professionals that she sustained a TBI five years earlier (see Case Study 6.1— Josiah; Moderate TBI). The effects of age of injury on outcome will be discussed in greater detail in chapters 5, 6, and 7.

Measurable learning difficulties may be delayed. To be eligible for special education under IDEIA 04, a student's TBI must have an adverse effect on educational performance. However, there are times when the adverse effect of TBI on educational performance may be delayed. For example, it may take months before the cumulative effects of less severe short-term memory difficulties or unrelenting headaches begin to have an adverse effect on a student's academic progress. There are also times when it may take years before the effects become apparent, as can be the case when early damage to a later maturing region of the brain occurs. For example, a student in kindergarten might sustain damage to the frontal regions of the brain (one of the last areas to mature); however, the effects of the injury might not become evident until later grades when the effects of the early injury (failure to acquire foundational sequential decision-making competencies) result in impaired planning and organization skills. In cases like these, a student may not immediately demonstrate the required "adverse effect on educational performance" that otherwise qualify the student for special education services.

Misclassification/Misattribution. At the time of their TBI, some students may have already been receiving services under a special education category (e.g., significant learning disability). In these cases, some special education multidisciplinary teams may feel that the student would not benefit by changing the classification to TBI. In other cases, a student's TBI-related behavior may be misattributed to other causes (see chapter 4) and the child may be misclassified under a different classification category (e.g., emotionally disturbed).

Other. Although figures are not available for any of the following, a portion of those hospitalized will (a) sustain a severe enough TBI that they will not be able to return to/enter the educational system, (b) will return/enter with no significant adverse effect on educational performance, or (c) will have their educational needs met with a Section 504 Accommodation Plan (see below).

Section 504 of the Rehabilitation Act of 1973

In the United States, Section 504 of the Rehabilitation Act of 1973 (Section 504) was established, in part, to protect the rights of individuals with disabilities. It applies to all programs and activities that receive federal financial assistance, including federal funds. Under Section 504, schools that receive funds from the U.S. Department of Education are required to provide a free and appropriate education (FAPE) to qualified school-age individuals with a disability in their jurisdiction, regardless of the nature or severity (http://www2.ed.gov/about/offices/list/ocr/docs/edlite-FAPE504.html#note1). A student with a disability under Section 504 has a physical or mental impairment which substantially limits one or more major life activities (e.g., learning), has a record of such an impairment, or is regarded as having such an impairment. It is important to note, however:

> in public elementary and secondary schools, unless a student actually has an impairment that substantially limits a major life activity, the mere fact that a student has a "record of" or is "regarded as" disabled is insufficient, in itself, to trigger those Section 504 protections that require the provision of a free appropriate public education (FAPE). (http://www2.ed.gov/about/offices/list/ocr/504faq.html, Q 37)

A student is determined to qualify under Section 504 by a team of knowledgeable individuals, including the parents, who are familiar with the student and his/her disability. If a student with TBI meets the eligibility requirements for Section 504, he/she will be entitled to reasonable accommodations or the reasonable modification of policies, practices, or procedures, and a Section 504 Accommodation Plan will be developed. The following are examples of possible accommodations for students with TBI (U.S. Department of Education, 2010):

- arranging for a health care and emergency plan;
- providing extended school year/time;
- furnishing memory/organizational aids;
- providing alternative testing;
- initiating tutoring programs;
- educating staff and peers about TBI; and
- implementing an academic monitoring process.

All students with TBI who meet the eligibility requirements under IDEIA 04 also meet the eligibility requirements for Section 504; however, a student can meet eligibility for Section 504 but not IDEIA 04.

Support Services in Rural Communities

Compared to families living in urban and suburban areas, families in rural communities often do not have ready access to hospital trauma departments, neurological rehabilitation centers, mental health services, and/or residential treatment centers. In addition, when these services are available, they often have inadequate staffing, equipment, and poor transportation services (Galynker et al., 2000; Gamm, Hutchison, Dabney, & Dorsey, 2010). Further complicating factors include geographic barriers, resource constraints, and a shortage of qualified medical professionals and other essential personnel (Bray, 2001; Office of Technology Assessment, 1989; Stamas, 1997; Williams, Ehrlich, & Prescott, 2001). Despite these shortcomings, research indicates that TBI demographics, injury severity variables, neuropsychological abilities, and rehabilitation outcomes are generally similar to urban areas (Johnstone et al., 2003; Mazurek et al., 2011). One possible advantage students with TBI have living in rural settings, as opposed to students living in urban or suburban settings, is that rural settings may provide students with TBI more opportunities to get away from daily pressures and live at a more relaxed pace that accommodates fatigue (Jones & Curtin, 2010).

Interdisciplinary Roles, Functions, and Responsibilities

Depending on the TBI severity level, students who return to school often experience a predictable range of educational and social-emotional difficulties (Fulton, Yeates, Taylor, Walz, & Wade, 2012). The medical community, neuropsychological/psychological community, educational community, and parents/guardians play important roles, serve important functions, and have unique responsibilities during the transition, school-based assessment, and educational intervention of these students. While it would be inappropriate to dictate the role, function, and responsibility of each of these groups, some general assumptions regarding these can be made.

Medical Community

The general educational role of medical professionals in the transition, school-based assessment, and educational intervention for students with TBI is to provide parents/ guardians and school-based multidisciplinary teams with useful information regarding the medical nature of a student's TBI. That is, they can provide medical reports and supporting medical records that describe and define the nature of a student's injury (including any physical injuries not related to the brain). Their general educational function is to identify an injury to the brain and officially indicate that the student sustained a TBI. In general, their educational responsibility is to provide supporting documentation, in nontechnical, jargon-free language. They also have a general responsibility to make themselves available for consultation and, if necessary, attend multidisciplinary team meetings.

Neuropsychological and Psychological Community

The general educational role of neuropsychological and psychological professionals in transition, school-based assessment, and educational intervention processes is to provide parents/guardians and school-based multidisciplinary teams with useful information regarding the TBI-related neurological, cognitive, and social-emotional strengths, weaknesses, and limitations of the student. Their general educational function is to identify how these strengths, weaknesses, and limitations are related to the student's TBI and how they might affect a student's ability to learn in the educational setting. Similar to the medical community, their educational responsibility is to provide supporting documentation, in nontechnical, jargon-free language, and their more general responsibility is to make themselves available for consultation and, if necessary, attend multidisciplinary team meetings.

Parents/Guardians

The general educational role of parents/guardians in the transition, school-based assessment, and educational intervention processes is to inform schools that their infant, child, or adolescent sustained a TBI, provide insight into pre-TBI functioning, and assist school-based multidisciplinary teams in the development of educational interventions. Their general educational function is to help school-based multidisciplinary teams understand pre-injury life for the student in the areas of neurological, cognitive, social-emotional, and overall educational functioning.

Schools and School Personnel

The school, and those professionals working within the school, plays a crucial role in facilitating a student's transition to the educational setting from the hospital/rehabilitation facility, assessing the educational impact of a student's injury, and providing evidence-based interventions (Harvey, 2006). The general role of the school/school professionals in the transition, school-based assessment, and educational intervention for students with TBI is twofold. One role is to help students with TBI transition into the educational setting in the most efficient manner. The other role is to determine, within the guidelines of IDEIA 04/Section 504, whether or not the neurological, cognitive, and/or social-emotional consequences of a student's TBI are adversely affecting the student's ability to be successful within the educational setting. The function of the school/school professionals is to help students with TBI access appropriate educational services within the school setting and to provide educationally-focused social, emotional, and behavioral support. In general, their responsibilities include collaborating with other professionals, parents/guardians, and agencies; providing thorough and timely evaluations; and developing appropriate interventions designed to help students with TBI become more successful in their education.

Interdisciplinary Communication and Collaboration

Depending on the severity level of the TBI, a student with TBI may be simultaneously receiving injury-related services from a number of different community-based disciplines. These services may be specifically designed to address TBI deficits (e.g., training to enhance memory deficits), TBI-related physical injuries obtained at the time of injury (e.g., physical therapy for a torn rotator), or both. Therefore, a student with TBI could be under the care of a psychiatrist, neurologist, neuropsychologist, psychologist, speech pathologist, physical therapist, and/or an occupational therapist. Once students have entered/reentered the educational setting they may also receive school-based services from a school psychologist, school counselor, speech-language pathologist, occupational therapist, physical therapist, and/or special education teacher. In order to reduce redundancy of services and avoid any ethical/legal problems in the delivery of services, communication/collaboration between all professional disciplines involved in helping a student with TBI is critical. To be effective, communication/collaboration needs to involve two-way consultation, dialogue, and exchange of relevant student information. In an ideal world, communication/collaboration between service providers is frequent and robust; in the real world, this is not always the case. While it is the responsibility of each professional involved to ensure that communication/collaboration occurs with other disciplines, this will only happen when there is awareness by each professional that additional service-providers are involved. The importance of interdisciplinary communication/collaboration and guidelines for those involved (including parents/guardians) will be further discussed in chapters 8 and 10.

2 Brain Anatomy and Physiology

By enclosing the brain within the skull, cushioning it with fluid, and stabilizing it with supporting connective membranes, nature has provided a unique way of protecting the human brain from injury. Without this protective system, it is quite easy to imagine the damage that could occur. For example, if this system were not present to hold the brain in place, consider the amount of damage that would occur to a marathon runner's brain as it bounced around inside the skull for 26.2 miles. Although this protective system does a good job of protecting the brain during normal day-to-day activity, as will be discussed in chapter 3, it is not very effective in preventing injury to the brain during the forces that accompany more significant events (e.g., falls, motor vehicle accidents). To fully appreciate the nature of TBI-related neurological, cognitive, emotional, behavioral, social, and academic consequences, it is helpful to understand basic brain anatomy and the brain-skull interface.

Chapter Overview

This chapter will provide an overview of

- basic brain anatomy;
- brain protection.

Basic Brain Anatomy

Although the gross anatomy of the human brain is relatively straightforward, a discussion of every major structure of the brain is beyond the scope of this book. However, a brief examination of the brainstem (medulla, pons, midbrain), cerebrum (frontal lobe, temporal lobe, parietal lobe, occipital lobe), limbic structures (amygdala, hippocampal formation, hypothalamus), and cerebellum is warranted. Additionally, at the cellular level the brain is extremely complex, so discussion will be limited to the physical structure of neurons and basic neuron communication (action potentials). For those interested in gaining a more in-depth understanding of brain anatomy at both the gross and cellular level, there exist many textbooks that discuss the complexities of the brain, and the Internet provides many reputable webpages as well (see the website for a list).

Gross Brain Anatomy

The human brain, while being one of the larger human organs, is actually quite small. In fact, the entire average adult brain (including the brainstem and cerebellum) would fit rather nicely inside a 4.5 × 5.5 × 6.5-inch box. Although small, the brain is much heavier than one would expect; with the average adult brain weighing about 3 pounds and the average newborn's brain weighing approximately three quarters of a pound. From a global perspective, the brain is comprised of the brainstem, cerebrum, limbic structures, and cerebellum.

The brainstem. The brainstem consists of three parts (in ascending order): the medulla, the pons, and the midbrain (Figure 2.1). It is located at the upper end of the spinal cord, at a level beginning approximately where the upper lip meets the base of the nose and extending to approximately the top of the eyeball. The average brainstem is approximately 3 inches in length and ranges in diameter from about 0.5 inches (medulla) to 1.25 inches (pons). The *medulla* is involved in maintaining vital body functions, such as breathing and heart rate. The *pons* is involved in motor control, movement, posture, some sensory analysis, and levels of consciousness (including sleep). The *midbrain* is involved in vision, visual reflexes, hearing relay, some auditory reflexive responses, eye movement, body movement, and voluntary motor function.

The cerebrum. Also known as the "cortex," the cerebrum is the largest part of the brain, accounting for approximately 82% of the total brain mass. The cerebrum is divided

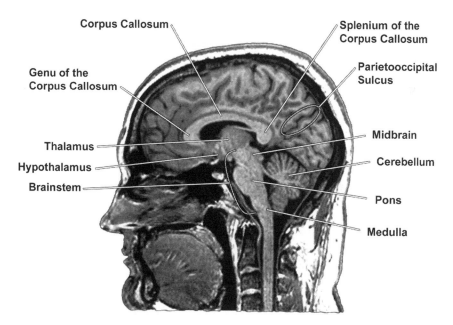

Figure 2.1 T1-weighted MRI scan obtained in the sagittal plane showing the cerebellum, thalamus, hypothalamus, parietooccipital sulcus, and parts of the brainstem and corpus callosum.

01. **Caudate nucleus**
02. **Central sulcus**
03. **Cingulate gyrus**
04. **Corpus Callosum**
05. **Frontal lobe**
06. **Frontal pole**
07. **Insular Cortex**
08. **Internal capsule**
09. **Longitudinal fissure**
10. **Occipital lobe**
11. **Parietal lobe**
12. **Postcentral gyrus**
13. **Precentral gyrus**
14. **Putamen**
15. **Sylvian fissure**
16. **Temporal lobe**
17. **Temporal pole**

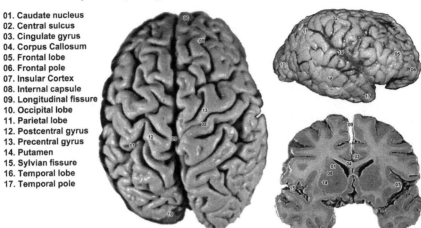

Figure 2.2 Postmortem axial, sagittal, and coronal view of major cerebral landmarks.

down the center (lengthwise from the front of the brain to the back of the brain) into two hemispheres (right and left) by a deep valley called the *longitudinal fissure* (Figure 2.2). Each hemisphere is comprised of four large areas or "lobes"—the *frontal lobe, temporal lobe, parietal lobe,* and *occipital lobe* (Figure 2.3). The two hemispheres are connected to each other by a major bundle of nerves known as the *corpus callosum,* which allows the left and right hemispheres to exchange information (Figure 2.1; Figure 2.2; Figure 2.4; Figure 2.11). The surface of the cerebrum looks like it has folded back upon itself and formed bumps (*gyri*), grooves (*sulci*), and deep valleys (*fissures*). With the understanding that the four lobes of the cerebrum span across both the right and left hemispheres, for the purpose of clarity, each lobe will be discussed from the perspective of a single hemisphere.

Frontal lobe (FL). The FL takes up the forward half of the hemisphere, from the middle of the ear to the forehead (Figure 2.3), and is the largest of the four lobes: the area of the FL can be covered by a human hand. The front edge of the FL sits directly behind the forehead and the back edge ends at a point that would be approximately equal to an imaginary vertical plane connecting the middle of the ears. The back edge of the FL is separated from the parietal lobe by the vertically running *central sulcus.* The bottom edge of the FL is separated horizontally from the temporal lobe by the horizontally running *lateral (Sylvian) fissure.* Situated just in front of the central sulcus is an important, vertically aligned bump of brain called the *precentral gyrus* (also referred to as the *motor cortex*). The FL is involved with reasoning, planning, parts of speech, movement, emotions, disinhibition, and problem solving. The precentral gyrus is involved in various aspects of movement.

Parietal lobe (PL). The PL sits directly behind the FL, beginning on the backside of the central sulcus. The front edge of the PL begins with a bump of brain next to the central sulcus called the *postcentral gyrus* (also called the *somatosensory cortex*); however, the back edge of the PL (on the outside surface, called the *lateral surface*) does not have a clearly

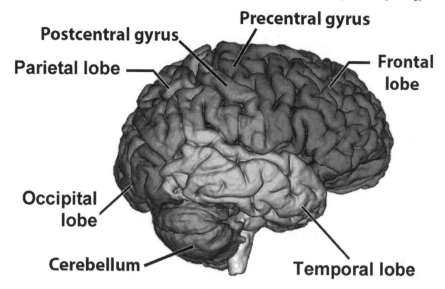

Precentral gyrus

Postcentral gyrus

Parietal lobe

Frontal lobe

Occipital lobe

Cerebellum

Temporal lobe

Figure 2.3 Sagittal view of the lobes of the cerebrum including important gyri and sulci.

visible landmark separating it from the rear-most lobe of the brain (occipital lobe). Rather, the back edge of the PL is determined by drawing an imaginary line between two landmarks (*parietooccipital sulcus* and *preoccipital notch*). On the inner face of the PL (the part toward the center of the brain directly adjacent to the opposite hemisphere, called the *medial surface*) the back edge is determined by the parietooccipital sulcus. The bottom of the parietal lobe is partially determined by the lateral (Sylvian) sulcus on the front end and is determined at the rear by an imaginary extension of the lateral sulcus. The PL can be covered by the palm of the hand. The PL is involved with sensory feedback for movement, spatial orientation, attention, recognition, and perception of stimuli. The postcentral gyrus is involved in various aspects of somatosensory experience (sensations of temperature, pain, light touch, and proprioception—a sense of where your body is in space).

Temporal lobe (TL). The TL sits beneath the rear and lower-front section of the FL, beneath the lateral (Sylvian) fissure, and beneath the occipital lobe under a continuation of the lateral fissure. The rear-most edge of the TL is not clearly bounded by visible landmarks, rather it joins together at a confluence of the parietal lobe and the occipital lobe in an area referred to as the *parietal-temporal-occipital association area*. The front-most edge of the TL (called the *temporal pole*) wraps inward toward the center of the brain, under the front-most part of the FL where the medial surface of the TL lies adjacent to the midbrain. The medial aspect of the TL houses two critical structures of the *limbic system*—the *hippocampus* and *amygdala*, to be discussed below. The TL is involved with memory, perception and recognition of auditory stimuli, and speech.

Occipital lobe (OL). The OL sits at the very back of the hemisphere. The rear edge of the OL sits directly in front of the back of the skull. The front edge of the OL does not have clearly visible landmarks. The OL is involved in visual processing and visual perception.

The Limbic Structures

Also known as the "limbic system" or "emotional brain," the limbic structures are located deep within the cerebrum (Figure 2.4; Figure 2.1). Although there are some who do not believe there is a limbic "system" (Brodal, 1981; Kotter & Stephan, 1997; Nieuwenhuys, 1996), there is a general consensus that there are at least three important interconnected limbic structures: the amygdala, the hippocampal formation, and the hypothalamus. There are two amygdalae, hippocampal formations, and hypothalami—one in each hemisphere. For clarity, these structures will be discussed from the perspective of a single hemisphere.

Amygdala. The amygdala is located toward the front, top, inside portion of the TL at approximately the level of the ear. It is almond-shaped and about 1 inch in length. The amygdalae are involved with emotion, emotional memory, fear response, and the perception of emotions in other people.

Hippocampal formation (HF). The HF is located just behind the amygdala and is made up of the *hippocampus proper,* the *dentate gyrus,* and the *subiculum.* It is about 1.5 inches long. The HF is involved with learning, memory, spatial navigation, and control of attention. It is intimately connected with the amygdala and thought to be essential for emotional memory.

Hypothalamus. The hypothalamus is located at approximately the level of the eyeball (Figure 2.1). It is situated slightly above and in front of the midbrain and rests just inside the two tracts of the optic nerve. The hypothalamus is approximately the size of an almond and is directly connected to the *pituitary gland.* The hypothalamus is involved with monitoring thirst, hunger, hormone concentrations, body temperature, sleep cycles, regulating pulse, blood pressure, and breathing, emotional feelings, sexual development and functioning, and responses to pain and pleasure.

The Cerebellum

Also known as the "little brain," the cerebellum is located just behind the middle to lower part of the brainstem, at the level of the medulla and pons, and rests just above the base of the skull (Figure 2.1; Figure 2.3; Figure 2.11). The cerebellum looks somewhat like a bean cut in half lengthwise and laid open like butterfly wings, therefore, it is comprised of two bean-shaped hemispheres (right and left). The average cerebellar hemisphere is approximately $0.5 \times 2.0 \times 2.5$ inches. The surface of the cerebellum is folded back on itself many, many times forming bumps (gyri), grooves (sulci) and deep valleys (fissures). As a result, the combined surface area of the cerebellum is similar to that of the cerebral cortex. Although the cerebellum is very small, accounting for approximately 10% of brain mass, it is believed that up to 80–85% of all human neurons are found in the cerebellum (Azevedo et al., 2009; Herrup & Kuemerle, 1997; Lange, 1975). The cerebellum is involved with the regulation and coordination of movement, posture, and balance. The cerebellum is now thought to be vitally important to all aspects of cognition including memory, executive functioning, and language—it may truly be a "little

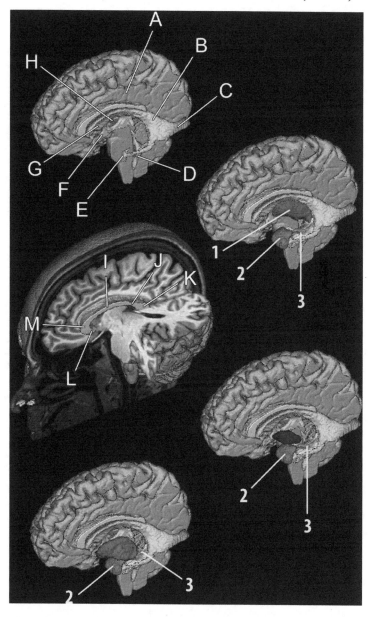

Figure 2.4 Three-dimensional cutaway of the brain showing the thalamus (1), amygdala (2), and the hippocampal formation (3). Also shown are: cingulate gyrus (A), atrium of the lateral ventricle (B), posterior horn of the lateral ventricle (C), fourth ventricle (D), temporal horn of the lateral ventricle (E), preoptic recess of the third ventricle (F), anterior horn of the lateral ventricle (G), massa intermedia (H), body of corpus callosum (I), isthmus of corpus callosum (J), splenium of corpus callosum (K), rostrum of corpus callosum (L) and genu of corpus callosum (M).

Adapted from Lezak, M. D., Howieson, D. B., Bigler, E. D., & Tranel, D. (2012). *Neuropsychological Assessment*, 5th Edition. New York, NY: Oxford University Press.

brain"—evidence particularly supporting this hypothesis is found in children with congenital hydrocephalus who have virtually no cerebrum, but do have an intact cerebellum (Lezak et al., 2012; Tedesco et al., 2011).

Cellular Brain Anatomy

All of the preceding major brain structures are directly, or indirectly, connected to each other through a vast network of interconnecting nerve cells, called *neurons*. Neurons are supported and facilitated by another type of brain cell called a *glial cell*. A variety of different types of glial cells provide a range of different support services to neurons including (a) facilitating synaptic functioning—the process and structures involved in the chemical (*neurotransmitter*) exchange of information between neurons, (b) neural signaling—the neuronal processes involved with the transfer of information to and from the external environment, (c) providing structural support, (d) providing nutritional and scavenger functions, and (e) providing neuronal insulation (Araque & Navarrete, 2010; Fellin, 2009; Lezak et al., 2012). Excluding the brainstem and a few structures deep within the cerebrum (diencephalon, basal ganglia), but including the cerebellum, it is estimated there are more than 125 billion neurons in the human brain (Azevedo et al., 2009; Lezak et al., 2012). Roughly 20% of neurons in the brain are located in the outer one-quarter inch of the cerebrum, which is called the "*cerebral cortex*" or "*neocortex*." With billions of neurons involved in brain functioning, the possible number of interconnections is staggering.

In order to help understand how brain tissue is damaged during a TBI (discussed in chapter 3), it is important to understand the basic physical structure of a neuron, including the cell body, axon, dendrites, and axon collaterals (branches). It is also important to understand how neurons are functionally connected and how they communicate with each other.

Physical structure of neurons. The majority of neurons are made up of a cell body, an axon (often with several collaterals), dendrites, and a terminal button (Figure 2.5).

Although there are variations in the size, shape, and function, these basic components are common to all neurons. A typical *cell body* of a neuron, called a *soma*, contains the nucleus (and other components) and comes in many different shapes and sizes. Extending from the cell body are at least one, but typically numerous, relatively short, tube-like structures called *dendrites*. An individual dendrite can be compared to a tree without leaves; that is, it has a trunk (coming out of the cell body) with branches that split off into more branches called *dendritic arborizations*. Dendrites receive information from other neurons at locations called *axodendritic synapses* found on the trunk and/or branches of the dendrite. Also extending from the cell body of the neuron is a single, tube-like structure called an *axon*. Although each neuron in the brain only produces a single axon, the axon frequently branches off into multiple segments called *collateral axons*. The end of each axon, or *axon collateral*, terminates in a knob-like structure called a *terminal button*. Axons, especially longer axons, frequently have insulating sausage-shaped "sheaths" of fat and protein (*myelin*) separated by a tiny space (called the *node of Ranvier*) that insulate the axon, and speed electrical impulses along its length. Myelin sheaths in the brain are formed by glial cells called *oligodendrocytes*.

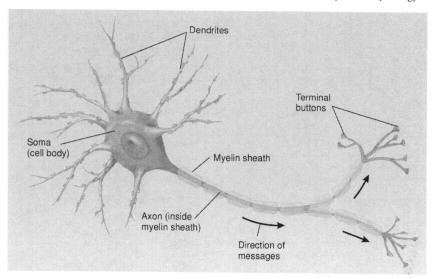

Figure 2.5 Schematic of a multipolar neuron showing the main parts of a neuron.

Neurons can be multipolar, bipolar, or unipolar. A *multipolar neuron* (the most common) has one axon that ends in one or more terminal buttons (and may also have collateral axons ending in terminal buttons), but it has multiple individual dendrites extending from all over the cell body (Figure 2.5). A *bipolar neuron* has one axon that ends in one or more terminal buttons (and may also have collateral axons ending in terminal buttons) but it only has one individual dendrite extending from the opposite end of the cell body from the axon (Figure 2.6). A *unipolar neuron* has a short tube extending from the cell body that splits into two branches, one branch ends in a dendrite and the other branch ends in one or more terminal buttons (Figure 2.6). A unipolar neuron has no dendrites protruding from the cell body. Bipolar neurons are typically found in the sensory systems and unipolar neurons are typically found in the somatosensory systems.

For simplicity, neurons are frequently depicted by an artist's illustration (such as in Figure 2.5). Unfortunately, while such illustrations are easy to understand, they can be misleading when it comes to representing the truly fragile nature of a neuron (Figure 2.7). To get an idea of just how fragile a neuron is, it is helpful to compare it to a human hair. The average diameter of a human hair is approximately 0.18 millimeters, or 0.007086ths of an inch. With this in mind, consider that the average diameter of a neuron's axon is approximately 3/10,000ths of a millimeter (0.0003 mm) or 0.000011811ths of an inch. The average length and diameter of a neuron's cell body is approximately 3/100ths of a millimeter (0.03 mm), or 0.001181ths of an inch, and the average length of a single neuron's axon is approximately 1.0 millimeters, or 0.039370ths of an inch (Lezak et al., 2012).

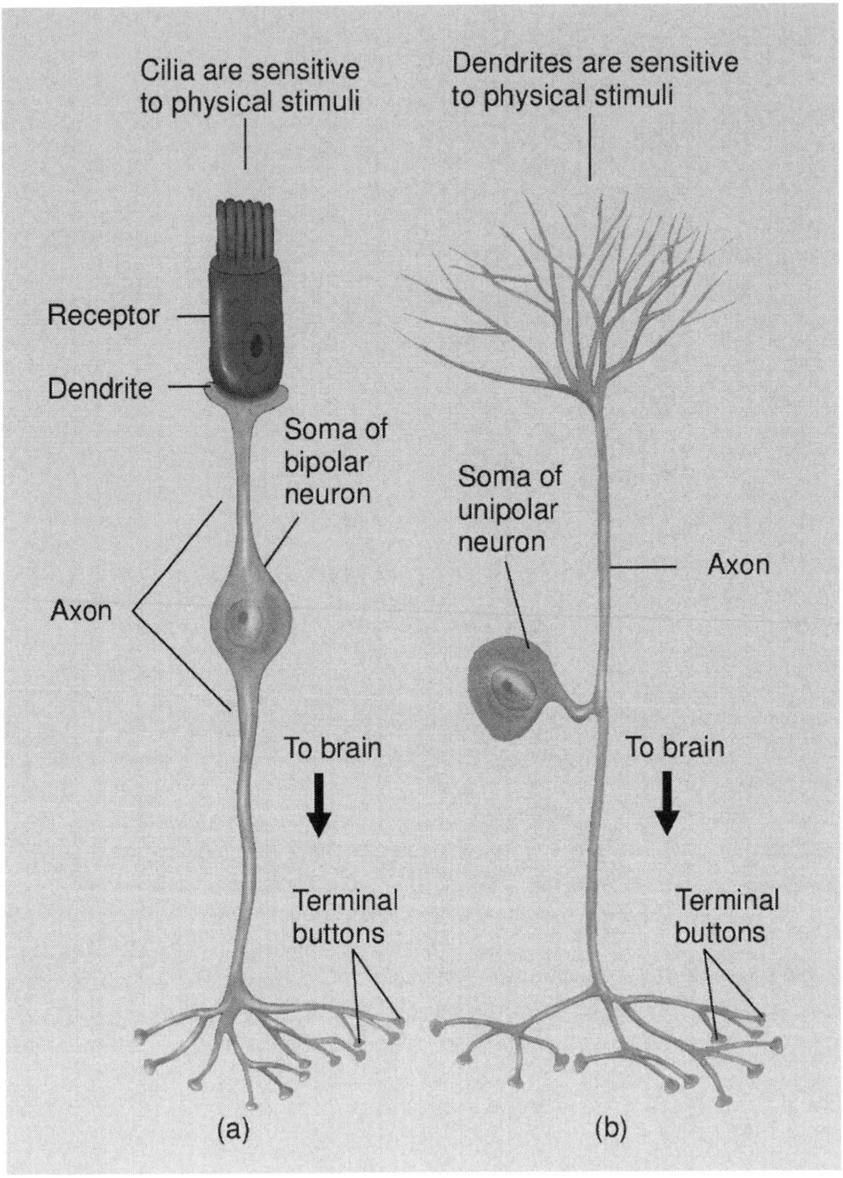

Figure 2.6 Neurons. (a) A bipolar neuron, primarily found in sensory systems. (b) A unipolar neuron, found in the somatosensory system.

Carlson, N. R., *Physiology of Behavior*, 9th Edition. © 2007. Printed and electronically reproduced by permission of Pearson Education, Inc., Upper Saddle River, New Jersey.

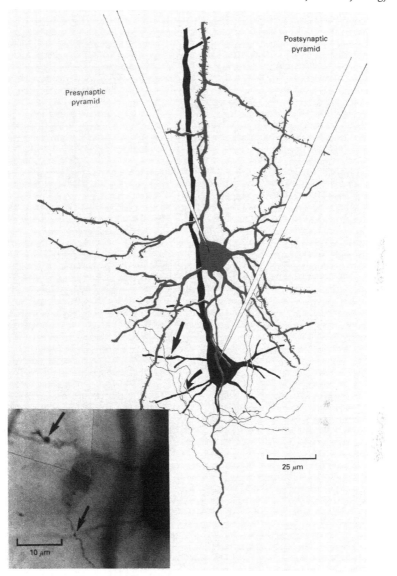

Figure 2.7 Neurons from the neocortex of a rat. Reconstruction of a pair of connected pyramidal cells in layer V of the rat motor cortex. For clarity, only part of the axons and some of the dendrites are shown. Two buttons from axon collaterals of the presynaptic pyramid closely appose basal dendrites of the postsynaptic pyramid (arrows). The inset photomontage shows the labeled buttons of the presynaptic axon (arrows) in close proximity to the labeled dendrites of the postsynaptic pyramid. Note the extremely fragile nature of the photographed neurons compared to the sturdy appearance depicted in the drawing of the neurons. The dark area in the center of the photograph is the soma of the neuron and the squiggly lines are dendrites.

From Deuchars, J., West, D. C., & Thomson, A. M. (2004) Relationships between morphology and physiology of pyramid-pyramid single axon connections in rat neocortex in vitro. *Journal of Physiology*, *478*(3), 423–435. © 1994.

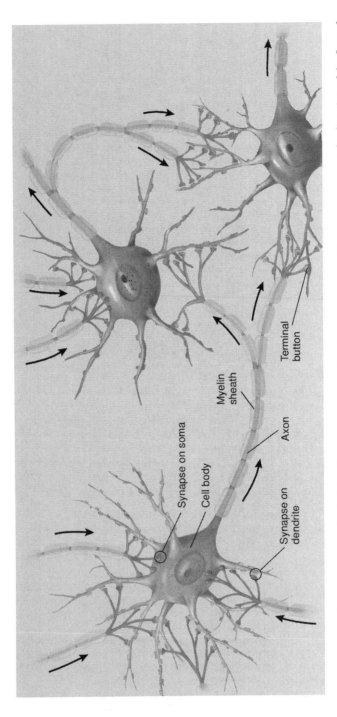

Labels on figure: Synapse on soma · Cell body · Myelin sheath · Axon · Terminal button · Synapse on dendrite

Figure 2.8 Schematic of neuron communication showing synaptic connections between neurons. The arrows represent the direction of the flow of information.

Carlson, N. R., *Physiology of Behavior*, 9th Edition. © 2007. Printed and electronically reproduced by permission of Pearson Education, Inc., Upper Saddle River, New Jersey.

Neuron communication. Neurons "talk" to each other using electrical and/or chemical signals. Electrical communication occurs as an electrical impulse sent along the length of an axon or as an electrical change in the membranes of adjacent neurons. Electrical impulses along axons are called *action potentials* (AP). APs are almost always generated at the end of the axon nearest to the cell body, although they can be produced anywhere along the axon. A *resting membrane potential* is always present, and an AP will not occur until a certain membrane potential threshold is reached. A variety of physiological influences, either excitatory or inhibitory, occur at the cellular level that may influence how an AP fires, but in normal circumstances they are generated only when needed. An AP is considered to be "all-or-none," and once triggered for release cannot be stopped, and the AP will travel the length of the axon to a predetermined destination (usually the terminal bud/button). As the AP travels the length of the axon, it does not increase or decrease in size (strength), but remains constant. If an AP reaches a branch in an axon (axon collateral), it will split (Figure 2.8), but will not increase or diminish in size (strength).

Individual neurons will always generate the same size AP, which lasts approximately 1 millisecond and can travel as fast as 197 feet per second (approximately 134 miles per hour). Once the AP reaches the axon terminal, it communicates with another neuron's dendrites either electrically, by interacting with the new neuron membrane across an *electrical synapse* known as a *gap junction,* or chemically, by triggering the release of *neurotransmitter molecules* across a gap called a *chemical synapse* (for more information on chemical synapse function see chapter 4, p. 60). Chemical communication is not always limited to a chemical synapse exchange. Chemical communicators known as *neuromodulators* can be secreted by a neuron in large numbers and travel great distances to receptor sites on other neurons. The functions of neurotransmitters/neuromodulators are varied and beyond the scope of this book, but include the excitation or inhibition of neurons, regulation of synaptic transmission, and neuronal growth.

Brain Protection

Whereas most people have never seen a living human brain, when asked to imagine what a living brain looks like, they tend to rely on their most familiar point of reference—pictures or artist's renditions found in textbooks and research articles. Therefore, when asked, most people are inclined to think of the brain as being a firm, almost rubber-like object, that if removed from the skull, would maintain its shape without difficulty. In reality, nothing could be farther from the truth. The consistency of a living human brain is much like a soft-boiled egg, or that of butter left out on the table that has just begun to soften; therefore, if removed from the skull it would have difficulty maintaining its shape for long.

Collectively, it takes three things to maintain the structural integrity of the living brain: bone (*skull*), tissue (*meninges*), and pressurized fluid (*cerebrospinal fluid* [CSF]). These three things also help protect the brain from injury. Paradoxically, however, while these three things are generally effective in protecting the brain from most traumas, as will be seen in chapter 3, these systems are also most often responsible for injury to the brain. To best understand how these protective systems interface with the brain each will be examined below.

Skull

The human skull is actually made up of two sets of bones—the eight bones of the cranial vault (cranium) and the 14 bones of the face (including the mandible). Only the cranial vault (CV) will be discussed as it is most closely situated to the brain and most likely to cause direct injury. The CV is covered by the scalp (Figure 2.9), which is made up of five layers: skin (including hair and sebaceous glands), subcutaneous connective tissue (a dense tissue containing blood vessels, nerves, arteries), galea aponeurotica (a fibrous sheet), loose areolar connective tissue (contains emissary veins that drain blood from sinuses in the dura mater to veins outside the skull), and pericranium (a membrane over the skull). The scalp is the first layer of protection for the brain, providing a limited amount of cushioning from bumps and blows to the head.

Beneath the scalp is the bone of the CV, which completely surrounds the brain. The CV is the next layer of protection for the brain. At birth the CV is made up of six unfused bones approximately 0.5–1.0 mm (0.001968 to 0.039370 inches) thick (Holck, 2005). It also has two soft spots called *fontanelles;* one on the top front portion of the CV and one on the top rear of the CV. Within one to two months the soft spot at the back of the infant's head will close, eventually becoming solid bone. The soft spot at the front of the infant's head and the *cranial sutures*—strong, fibrous, elastic tissues connecting the cranial bones—will close and harden into solid bone by 9–18 months of age; however, the bone will not begin to develop the characteristic three-layer construction (*inner table, diploe, outer table*) found in adults until the age of 3–4. The fused CV is 4–8 mm (0.157480 to 0.314960 inches) thick for a young child and about 10 mm thick for an adult (0.393700 inches).

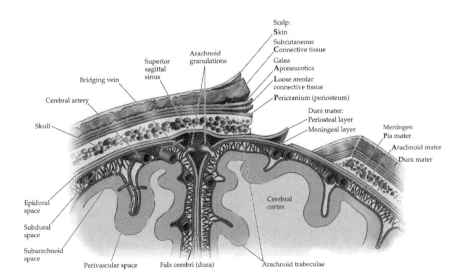

Figure 2.9 Layers of protection for the brain.

From: Blumenfeld: *Neuroanatomy Through Clinical Cases*, Second Edition, Sinauer Associates, Inc., Sunderland, MA 2010.

The CV contains holes (*foramina*) that allow cranial nerves, the spinal cord, and blood vessels to enter and exit the CV. The largest hole (*foramen magnum*) is at the base of the skull, located at approximately the point where the spinal cord meets the medulla. The inside of the base of the CV is made up of bony ridges that divide it into three sets of matching compartments (*fossae*)—a left and right *anterior (front) cranial fossa,* a left and right *middle cranial fossa,* and a left and right *posterior (rear) cranial fossa* (Figure 2.10; Figure 3.3).

The inside surface of the CV and its fossae, although smooth, contains bumps, edges, and ridges designed to fit around various parts of the bottom and sides of the brain (Figure 2.10; Figure 3.3). The brain fits snugly inside the CV and the ridges and bumps (in conjunction with the meninges and cerebrospinal fluid—see below) help hold the brain in place. If the inner table of the skull were too smooth, the brain would slosh around with any kind of movement, such as jumping or running. In addition to

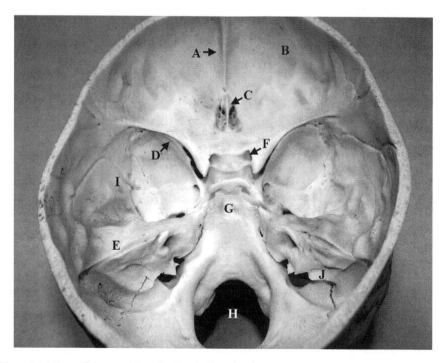

Figure 2.10 Base of the cranial vault. The skull cap has been removed, exposing the inner surface of the base of the cranial vault, with the various anatomic structures and the three cranial fossa clearly defined. The uneven surface of each fossa is clearly observable. The general location of the hippocampus (medial wall of the middle cranial fossa) and where the base of the frontal lobe is located (anterior cranial fossa) are depicted. A = frontal crest; B = anterior cranial fossa; C = crista galli with cribiform plate beneath; D = sphenoid bone; E = petrous temporal bone; F = clinoid bone and area of the sella turcica; G = clivus; H = foramen magnum; I = middle cranial fossa; J = posterior cranial fossa.

the skin, the CV helps provide another layer of protection for the brain by shielding it (to some extent) from external bumps and blows to the head.

Tissue (Meninges)

Inside the CV lies the next layer of protection for the brain, the meninges. The meninges are made up of three successively layered, interconnected membranes (*meninx*)—dura mater, arachnoid, and pia mater (Figure 2.9).

Dura mater. The outermost membrane of the meninges, the dura mater (DM), is a relatively tough, fibrous membrane that surrounds the entire brain and adheres to the inside of the CV. At the level of the midbrain the DM splits. Part of the DM (the *tentorium cerebelli*) tucks under the bottom of the cerebral hemisphere and continues around the midbrain, creating an opening called the *tentorial notch*. It also forms a layer over the cerebellum that separates the bottom of the occipital lobes and the top of the cerebellum (Figure 2.11). The DM also continues down the brainstem and exits through the foramen magnum. Once it leaves the foramen magnum it continues on down the spinal column. At the top of the CV the DM tucks into the longitudinal fissure all the way down to approximately the level of the corpus callosum, forming a thin layer (called the *falx cerebri*—Figure 2.11) that separates the left and right cerebral hemispheres. At the points where the DM tucks, it forms channels (called *sinuses*) that allow for veins and the flow of CSF. The DM helps provide another level of protection to the brain from external bumps and blows to the head by helping to support the brain and hold it in place.

Arachnoid. The middle membrane of the meninges, the *arachnoid,* adheres to the inner surface of the DM; however it does not adhere to the membrane below it, the *pia mater* (Figure 2.9). The arachnoid is a delicate cobweb-like gauze-like membrane, hence its name. Between the arachnoid and the pia mater is a space called the *subarachnoid space* which is made up of web-like processes (called *arachnoid trabeculae*). The arachnoid trabeculae act as bridging supports and attach to the arachnoid membrane above and the pia mater below (except over the sulci). Within the subarachnoid space, the walls of the arachnoid trabecular form little compartments (called *subarachnoid cisterns*) that are filled with CSF. These cisterns also provide natural pathways for intracranial arteries, veins, and cranial nerves. The arachnoid and arachnoid space help provide another level of protection to the brain from external bumps and blows to the head by providing additional cushioning and some supportive structure.

Pia mater. The innermost membrane, the pia mater, is an extremely delicate membrane that adheres directly to the surfaces of the gyri and sulci of the cerebral hemispheres and the cerebellum. It also surrounds each fine, nourishing blood vessel that penetrates the surface of the brain, creating a tiny space around the blood vessel called the *perivascular space.* The pia mater is impermeable to fluid, and acts to contain the CSF in the subarachnoid space, thereby helping in the protection of the brain from external bumps and blows by working together with the arachnoid, dura mater, and CSF.

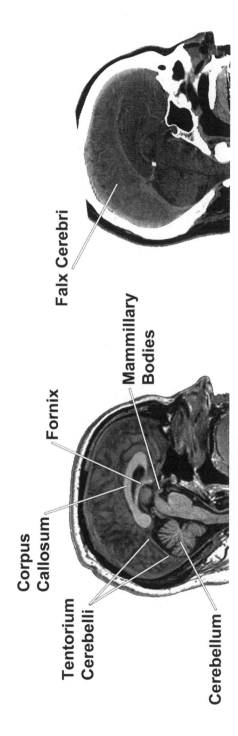

Figure 2.11 T1-weighted MRI scan (left) and CT scan (right) obtained in the sagittal plane showing the falx cerebri. The T1-weighted MRI scan also shows the tentorium cerebelli, cerebellum, fornix, and mammillary bodies.

Fluid

CSF is a clear fluid found within and around the outside surface of the brain and spinal cord. Most CSF is produced by glandular-like structures called *choroid plexus*—located within the *ventricular system* of the brain. CSF is defused from arterial blood and is reabsorbed by veins. The ventricular system consists of four ventricles and their connecting passages (Figure 2.4; Figure 2.12).

The largest ventricles are called the *lateral ventricles* (LV). There are two LV shaped much like a boot spur—one in the left cerebral hemisphere and one in the right cerebral hemisphere. Following the boot spur analogy, one spur of the LV begins at a level just beneath the bottom front of the corpus callosum (called the *genu of the corpus callosum*— Figure 2.1; Figure 2.4). It immediately begins to enlarge somewhat and curves back, down, and outward before moving forward again ending in the other spur, located in the front-middle portion of the temporal lobe. The very beginning portion of the top spur is called the *anterior horn of the lateral ventricle* and the very ending point of the lower spur is called the *inferior horn of the lateral ventricle*. At the point that the top spur of the LV begins to curve forward again to form the lower spur of the LV, it also extends backward to form a horn-like part that expands backwards into the occipital lobe called the *posterior horn*.

On the bottom-inside, toward the front of each LV are small openings known as *interventricular foramen* (also known as the *foramen of Monroe*). These openings allow for CSF to drain out of the LV into a third narrow oblong ventricle. At the bottom back end of the *third ventricle* there is a small connecting tube known as the *cerebral aqueduct* which allows CSF to drain into the *fourth ventricle*. The third ventricle is situated in the vertical center plane of the brain (i.e., the midline) and is surrounded by a structure

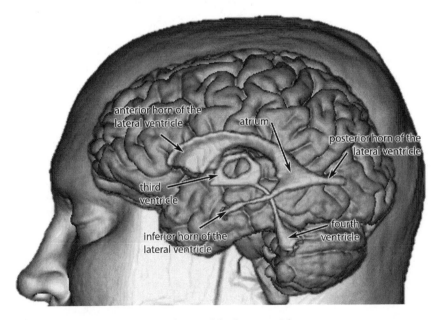

Figure 2.12 Three-dimensional sagittal view of the four ventricles.

called the *thalamus*. The *fourth ventricle* is a diamond-shaped ventricle located inside the brainstem reaching the length of the pons and partly into the medulla. A portion of the top, back side of the diamond-shaped fourth ventricle backs up against the cerebellum. There are two small tube-like foramen coming out of the wide part of the diamond-shaped fourth ventricle called the *foramina of Luschka*. Off the beginning of each foramina of Luschka is an opening called the *foramen of Magendie*. The bottom of the fourth ventricle drains into the spinal canal.

Production and absorption of CSF is a constant process resulting in CSF being completely replaced approximately every six hours. The majority of CSF is contained within the brain and if an outside portion of the brain fails to develop, such as with a developmental disorder affecting the cerebral cortex, or shrinks (as happens in old age), or if a piece of brain is removed (e.g., surgical removal of the temporal lobe to stop temporal lobe epilepsy), the *choroid plexuses* produce enough extra CSF to compensate for the missing brain mass; expanding the ventricle to bring intracranial pressure into balance, thereby helping the brain remain in its correct location. Passive expansion of the ventricle in response to brain injury or a failure to develop is referred to as *hydrocephalus ex vacuo*. Developmentally or in response to injury, obstruction of CSF flow due to infection or hemorrhage may occur. If this happens, there is abnormal expansion of the ventricle because the CSF pressure exceeds the space occupied by brain tissue and the CSF pressure compresses the tissue. This is referred to as *obstructive hydrocephalus*. Also, abnormal production of excessive CSF may also produce hydrocephalus.

3   Traumatic Injuries to the Brain

TBI is a complex phenomenon involving an intricate succession of pathological events, time-related physiological and structural changes/degeneration at the neuronal level, and time-related biochemical/neurochemical changes—all of which are interrelated and linked to the degree of cranial vault (CV) damage, the manner in which the initial injury occurred during the injurious event, and the severity of the resulting injury.

Chapter Overview

This chapter will provide an overview of

- head injury classifications;
- biomechanics of injury;
- hemorrhaging; and
- injury severity.

Head Injury Classifications

The human brain is capable of being injured with or without the structural integrity of the CV being compromised. As a result, any injury to the head that also results in an injury to the brain is generally classified in one of two ways: as an open/penetrating head injury or as a closed/nonpenetrating head injury. In this book an open/penetrating head injury is referred to as a penetrating head injury (PHI) and a closed/nonpenetrating head injury is referred to as a closed head injury (CHI).

Penetrating Head Injury (PHI)

A PHI is defined *as an injury to the head in which an object pierces the cranial vault (and at least the dura mater), or a blunt force impact from an object fractures the cranial vault in such a manner that bone fragments pierce at least the dura mater.* There are three different subtypes of PHI: penetrating, perforating (through-and-through), and tangential (Erdogan, Gonul, & Seber, 2002; Harcke, Levy, Getz, & Robinson, 2008). Penetrating generally refers to an injury in which an object enters (but does not exit) the CV/meninges. An example of this type of PHI is a knife wound that penetrates a distance of 1 inch into the CV. Perforating (through-and-through) generally refers to an injury in which the object enters into, and passes completely through, the CV, creating an identifiable entry and exit wound. An example of this type of PHI is a bullet that enters the middle of the forehead and exits the CV behind the ear. Tangential generally refers to an injury in which an object strikes the CV with a glancing blow and enough force that cranial bones are broken inwardly, tearing the dura mater (called a complex depressed skull fracture). The object itself may also penetrate at least the dura mater. An example of this type of PHI is an injury obtained during an earthquake in which the corner of a 2" × 6" brick falls from the top of a two-story building and strikes a glancing blow to the back of a pedestrian's head with enough force to penetrate one quarter of an inch into the brain.

Closed Head Injury (CHI)

A CHI is defined as *an injury to the head from either a blunt force impact that does not pierce the dura mater, or as a result of the sudden acceleration/deceleration of the brain within the intact cranial vault.* CHI can include injuries in which the CV is cracked (called a linear [or hairline] skull fracture) or depressed (called a depressed skull fracture; Figure 3.3), however the dura mater is not penetrated.

There are two subtypes of CHI: contact force and inertial force—acceleration/deceleration. A *contact force* (CF) injury happens when a stationary (or relatively stationary) person's head is struck by a moving object, such as when a hockey puck flies into the stands and strikes a spectator in the forehead. An *inertial force—acceleration/deceleration* (IF) injury happens when a person's moving head (acceleration) comes in contact with a nonmoving object (deceleration). An example of IF would be when a person falls from a ladder (acceleration) and strikes their head against the pavement (deceleration).

Biomechanics of Injury

Damage to the brain is a result of rapid deformation of the brain, successive pathological events (e.g., a loss of CSF, followed by a drop in CSF pressure, followed by a collapsed ventricle), and time-related physiological and structural changes/degeneration at the neuronal level, e.g., swelling of the terminal stump of disconnected axons (Ivancevic, 2009; Lezak et al., 2012; Mazzeo, Beat, Singh, & Bullock, 2009; Smith & Meaney, 2000). In addition, time-related biochemical/neurochemical changes occur that affect the synthesis and/or release of neuroprotective and/or autodestructive chemical compounds, e.g., acetylcholine (Gennarelli & Graham, 2005). Time-related changes are correlated with injury severity and can take place within minutes, hours, days, months, or even years (Lezak et al., 2012).

Regardless of the nature of the injury (i.e., PHI or CHI), damage to the brain will consist of primary and secondary damage. *Primary damage* (PD) is the immediate damage caused by the mechanical forces involved at the time of the injury. Examples of PD include axonal shearing/tearing, destruction of brain tissue, bleeding outside of brain tissue (*hemorrhage*), bleeding inside brain tissue (*contusion*), leaking CSF, and a drop in intracranial pressure (ICP). *Secondary damage* (SD) is delayed damage that is a direct result of PD. Examples of SD include cerebral swelling (*edema*); movement of brain tissue, CSF, and blood vessels away from their usual position inside the CV (*brain herniation*); lack of blood flow to tissue (*ischemia*); blood clotting (*coagulopathy*); obstruction of the blood supply (*infarction*); fever (*pyrexia*); partial lack of oxygen to tissue (*hypoxia*); total lack of oxygen to tissue (*anoxia*); increased ICP; cell death (*necrosis*); programmed cell death (*apoptosis*); and infection.

There are two interrelated ways in which the neuron and its axon(s) can be injured during TBI: *neuronal membrane damage* (NMD) and *traumatic axonal injury* (TAI). Both are common to PHI and CHI. NMD occurs at the cellular level, and is the result of either primary or secondary damage. NMD involves a complex array of pathophysiological and structural changes in the neuronal membrane (e.g., distortion of ion channels; Bigler & Maxwell, 2012a) and results from the wide spectrum of biomechanical forces involved in PHI and CHI. TAI affects the white matter (axons) of the brain and encompasses all of the possible cellular-level injuries associated with axonal shearing in PHI or CHI (Lezak et al., 2012). There are two types of TAI—primary axotomy and secondary axotomy. *Primary axotomy* occurs immediately at the time of injury and results from tearing and shearing forces, whereas *secondary axotomy* begins within one hour (as swelling occurs in the nerve axon and in surrounding brain tissue) and evolves over the next days or months (Bigler & Maxwell, 2012a; Lezak et al., 2012; Tang-Schomer, Patel, Baas, & Smith, 2010). Primary and secondary damage from TAI can take the form of internal and external disturbances at the cellular level that lead to necrosis (cell death) and apoptosis (programmed cell death/"suicide").

While there is damage common to both PHI and CHI, there is also damage unique to each (Lezak et al., 2012).

Penetrating Head Injury

The extent of PD resulting from a PHI is typically *focalized* in nature. That is, the PD tends to be limited to the site of the injury and the pathway of the penetrating object. However, it is possible for PD to be more *diffuse* as well; damaging the brain some distance from the pathway of the object (Barach, Tomlanovich, & Nowak, 1986). In addition, the PD is highly correlated with such factors as the object's angle of approach, kinetic energy, mass, velocity, and shape (Barach et al., 1986; Kazim, Shamim, Tahir, Enam, & Waheed, 2011). For example, PD caused by a clothes iron sliding off an ironing board, glancing off the back of the head, and causing a small bone fragment to penetrate the dura mater (*tangential PHI*) is much different than the PD caused by an industrial explosion in which a one-half-inch piece of metal rod penetrates the forehead, travels through the brain, and exits out the rear of the head (*perforating PHI*). The nature and extent of PD is likewise dependent on the depth of penetration and/or inertial force of the penetrating object (Lezak et al., 2012). For example, in the case of a PHI caused by a gunshot—the most common form of PHI (Faul et al., 2010)—the bullet will create a temporarily expanding cavity which stretches and distorts brain tissue, resulting in the laceration of blood vessels and the destruction of brain tissue and neurons near the wound tract due to pressure waves generated by the bullet (Barach et al., 1986). "This temporary cavity then collapses upon itself only to re-expand in progressively smaller undulating wave-like patterns. Every cycle of temporary expansion and collapse creates significant surrounding tissue injury to the brain" (Kazim et al., 2011, p. 397). The bullet will also compress brain tissue in its path resulting in a permanent cavity and—depending on the bullet's proximity to a ventricle—the bullet's pressure waves may also cause the CSF to expand rapidly in all directions with equal force (following the laws of hydraulics), damaging surrounding brain tissue (Barach et al., 1986). In the case of a PHI in which the object/projectile penetrates the meninges and enters into the brain tissue beneath, the object/projectile will carry with it bits of foreign material (e.g., hair, skin, bone, and, possibly, object fragments such as wood splinters, metal fragments, and glass) capable of causing additional PD (tissue/vascular damage) and the potential for infection (secondary damage). There will also be a change in intracranial pressure and bleeding in the meninges and bruising/swelling in brain tissue. In the case of a perforating PHI, PD will also include damage at the exit sight. When a PHI only involves the meninges, PD will be limited to the immediate exterior point of impact (skin and bone) and will include hemorrhaging in the related layer of the meninges (discussed below). Depending on the nature and force of the impact it may also include contusion of underlying brain tissue, edema, and axonal shearing/tearing. Secondary PHI damage may include cerebral swelling, brain herniation, ischemia, hypoxia, anoxia, infarction/necrosis, and/or infection, and will depend on the nature and extent of the primary damage.

Closed Head Injury

As described below, the extent of PD and SD resulting from a CHI can be focalized and/or diffuse depending on the nature and force of the injury.

Contact force. PD from a contact force (CF) injury is typically the result of a rapid sequence of events (Goldsmith & Plunkett, 2004; Lezak et al., 2012). First, there is an inward depression of the bone of the CV at the point of impact and the outward bending of bone immediately adjacent to the point of impact. Second, as the bone of the CV moves inward, the kinetic energy of the blow is transmitted by a pressure shockwave through the brain. Third, the shockwave rebounds off the inside bone on the side of the CV opposite the point of impact, and begins traveling back throughout the brain. This entire process can be easily understood if one envisions the familiar slow motion film of a pebble dropping into a still glass of water. First the rock enters the water causing the water around the rock to push downward, outward, and upward; at the same time sending concentric shockwaves outward from the rock (point of impact). These shockwaves travel across the water (and down toward the bottom of the glass), strike the sides of the glass (and the bottom of the glass), and rebound back in toward the point of impact. If the impacting force of a CF injury is significant enough, bone will fracture at the point of impact (linear skull fracture), thereby releasing some of the kinetic energy (Lezak et al., 2012) and potentially lessening the force of the initial shockwave and its rebound wave. If the impacting force is sufficient enough to result in a depressed skull fracture, the injury will be classified as a PHI and will include the additional PD described above. PD can also include compression of brain tissue beneath the point of contact, contusion of the scalp, and tearing of the pia mater (the innermost meninges that attaches directly to the brain).

Inertial force. PD from an inertial force (IF) injury is the result of translational (linear) acceleration or angular acceleration, followed by rapid deceleration (Agrawal & Mahapatra, 2012). *Translational (linear) acceleration* occurs when all parts of the brain move in a straight line along the brain's center of gravity. An example of this would be when a basketball player is knocked to the floor during a drive to the basket and she slides across the floor, striking the top of her head against the supporting pole of the basketball hoop (*rapid deceleration*). *Angular acceleration* occurs when the brain moves along its center of gravity and also rotates around its center of gravity. *Angular deceleration* occurs when the head suddenly comes to a halt (Figure 3.1); for example, when a running person trips, falls forward, and strikes their forehead against a concrete park bench. Angular acceleration injuries resulting from impacts to the side of the head produce more severe injuries than do angular acceleration injuries resulting from impacts to the front or back of the head (Yoganandan et al., 2009). PD from CHI can take the form of tissue compression, contusion, swelling, hemorrhaging, and vascular tearing. SD from this type of CHI can include hemorrhaging, herniation, and swelling.

A PD phenomenon common to IF injury is *contrecoup damage* (Kim & Gean, 2011); damage that occurs opposite the site of initial impact damage (called *coup* damage) and generally consists of contusions (Figure 3.2). Although there are numerous theories as to what happens to cause contrecoup damage, a popular theory (Drew & Drew, 2004) is that when a head in motion strikes a nonmoving object, the less dense brain is displaced in the opposite direction from the blow by the denser CSF moving in the direction of the blow, resulting in contrecoup damage (see Drew & Drew, 2004, for a review of this and other theories).

Inertial force acceleration/deceleration injuries are well-known to cause *diffuse brain injury* (DBI). This is because brain structures connect to each other and the CV in different ways and brain tissue varies in consistency (Andriessen, Jacobs, & Vos, 2010). Consequently, during acceleration/deceleration different parts of the brain move at different speeds which cause shearing, tearing, and compression of tissue. Diffuse brain injury is widespread damage to axons and blood vessels and damage due to hypoxia, ischemia, and brain swelling (Andriessen et al., 2010).

A common CHI phenomenon occurring in motor vehicle accidents that involve a side impact is *diffuse axonal injury* (DAI; Yoganandan et al., 2009). DAI, a subset of TAI, involves immediate, widespread, primary damage to the axons. It can involve increasingly severe damage to white matter, depending how deep the effects go. That is, it can include only regions of white matter at the interface between the gray and white matter of the lobes or it can extend "deeper" to include damage to the corpus callosum, or it can extend even deeper to include damage to areas of the brainstem (Adams et al., 1989; Gentry, 1994). Damage can include disruptions of the axon axolemma (covering) and tearing/shearing of the axon away from the body of the neuron.

The Role of the Cranial Vault Base and the Falx Cerebri in Primary Damage

Contrary to intuition, the human brain does not rest directly on the base of the CV; rather, it floats just above the base, suspended in CSF. In addition, the brain is held in place by the meninges and CSF pressure, and to some degree, the brainstem. As a result, under normal circumstances the brain is well-protected from significant movement and damage during any daily bumps, shifts, and/or quick rotations. However, during the rapid deformation of the brain that occurs in an IF injury, the base of the CV and the meninges (especially the falx cerebri) can become agents of significant damage to the temporal and frontal lobes, the corpus callosum, and an area called the *cingulate*

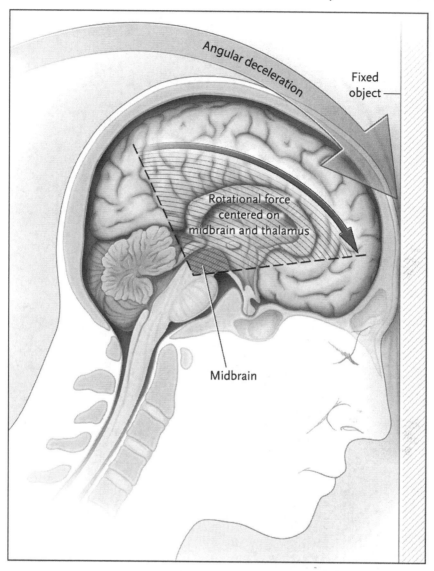

Figure 3.1 Biomechanical schematic showing how TBI results from a rotational motion of the cerebral hemispheres in the anterior–posterior plane, around the fulcrum of the fixed-in-place upper brainstem. Note how angular deceleration of the brain (thick arrow) occurs when a head suddenly comes to a halt when striking a fixed object. Note that the thin arrow shows how the brain rotates around its center of gravity (midbrain), while also moving along its center of gravity (angular acceleration).

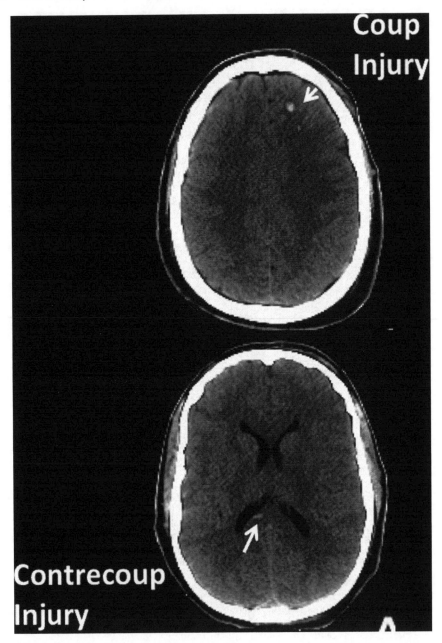

Figure 3.2 CT scans illustrating coup-contrecoup injury. CT of adolescent involved in a head-on collision in which face and forehead struck steering wheel, window, and dashboard producing a coup injury (left frontal hemorrhage noted in upper CT scan [white dot]) and contrecoup injury (hemorrhage in the posterior corpus callosum on the opposite right side [white dot]).

gyrus—located just above the length of the corpus callosum (Bigler, 2007; Bigler & Maxwell, 2012a).

The best way to understand how the base of the CV can damage the brain during an IF injury is to recall that the brain is indirectly connected to the base of the CV by way of the successively layered, interconnected, pia mater-arachnoid-dura mater membranes (Figure 2.9). That is, starting with the brain and moving in an outward direction, the brain is directly attached to the inner surface of the pia mater; the majority of the outer surface of the pia mater is directly attached to the arachnoid trabeculae; the arachnoid trabeculae are directly attached to the inner surface of the arachnoid membrane; the outer surface of the arachnoid membrane is attached to the inner surface of the dura mater; and finally. the outer surface of the dura mater is attached to the inner surface of the base of the CV. In this way, the successive, indirect connection of meningeal membranes (and the CSF in the arachnoid space) "holds" the brain in place within the CV. As the brain shifts about and deforms during an IF injury, the combined interconnected meningeal membranes tug at the various delicate blood vessels of the brain, rupturing them, and causing bleeding (Lezak et al., 2012).

The structure of the CV base has three form-fitting depressions called the *anterior (front) cranial fossa, middle cranial fossa,* and *posterior (back) cranial fossa* (Figure 2.10; Figure 3.2). These fossae help keep the brain in place by "cupping" around the bottom portions of the frontal lobes, temporal lobes, and the cerebellum. In addition, in order to further keep the brain in place and give the dura mater better purchase, the surface of the base of the fossae have ridges that conform to the various gyri on the bottom of the frontal lobes, temporal lobes, and cerebellum. The anterior cranial fossa also has two wing-shaped bones (named the lesser sphenoid bones; Figure 3.3).

Given the cupping construction of the CV base and the "roughness" of the individual fossae, it is easy to envision the bottom of the frontal and temporal lobes scraping along the rough surfaces of the anterior and middle cranial fossae as the brain distorts and bounces around during a rapid acceleration/deceleration IF injury. It is also easy to envision the forward-most portions of the frontal and temporal lobes (called the *frontal and temporal poles*) lifting away from these surfaces and slamming back down as the brain returns to its original position in the anterior cranial fossae. The cerebellum is less likely to receive this sort of damage because it is prevented from movement by the tentorium cerebelli and the brainstem.

The *falx cerebri* is a tough sheet of sickle-shaped dura membrane that extends partway down between the cerebral hemispheres (Figure 2.11). It attaches along the length of the top of the CV and attaches in the front to a small bony ridge (called the *crista galli*) that runs down the middle of the anterior cranial fossa. In the rear, it attaches to the top surface of the tentorium cerebelli, just above the middle of the cerebellar hemispheres. Although the falx cerebri is designed to keep the two cerebral hemispheres from moving sideways, it can also damage the brain due to its unique design. Because the falx cerebri is sickle-shaped, the centermost portion does not extend down all the way between the two hemispheres to touch the corpus callosum. As a result, the middle portion of the corpus callosum is left uncovered and unprotected against movement while both ends are protected. Therefore, should a hemisphere be pushed toward the center of the brain, as occurs with some types of secondary damage (e.g., herniation due to hemorrhaging) and during a sideways IF injury, the falx cerebri will act as a fulcrum point, restraining

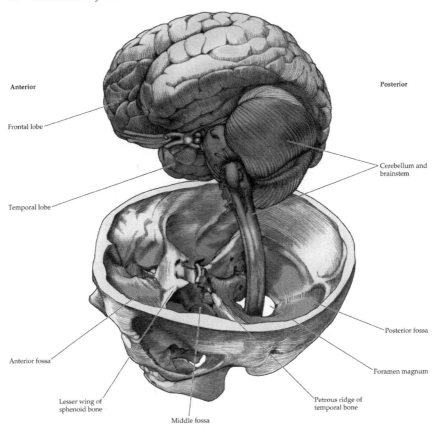

Anterior   Posterior

Frontal lobe

Cerebellum and
brainstem

Temporal lobe

Posterior fossa

Anterior fossa

Foramen magnum

Lesser wing of
sphenoid bone

Petrous ridge of
temporal bone

Middle fossa

Blumenfeld 2e *Neuroanatomy*
Blum2e_05.04
Sinauer Associates
11/13/09

Figure 3.3 Illustration showing how the brain rests inside the cranial vault. It is easy to see from this illustration how the bottom of the frontal and temporal lobes are vulnerable to injury as the brain distorts and bounces around during a rapid acceleration/deceleration inertial force injury. It is also easy to see how well the brainstem and cerebellum are secured in place and protected against inertial force injury.

the ends of the corpus callosum but allowing the center portion to pass beneath the center portion of the falx cerebri. This will result in focal shear-strain effects on the axons of the corpus callosum and associated vasculature (Bigler & Maxwell, 2012a). It will also set in motion a neuropathological process that can damage the neuronal structure and ultimately lead to cell death (Farkas & Povlishock, 2007).

Age-Related Injury Mechanisms

There are developmental aspects of anatomy and physiology that allow for injury mechanisms not found in adults. These include cranial vault bone development; brain water content and myelination; head size in relation to body and neck muscle weakness;

face-to-cranium ratio; face development; and body size (Pinto, Porettie, Meoded Tekes, & Huisman, 2012).

Cranial vault development. As noted earlier in chapter 2, it takes between 9 and 18 months for the soft spots and cranial sutures of an infant's head to close and begin hardening, thereby allowing these bones to move, rather than fracture. While this can be helpful, it can be detrimental as well. For example, if swelling or bleeding occurs as a result of a contact force injury, the free-floating plates will allow the head to increase in size; however the free-floating bone is also more easily driven into dura and brain tissue. Structurally, it is not until 3–4 years of age that the bone of the CV develops the three-layer system found in adults (i.e., inner table, diploe, outer table). Prior to age 3–4, the bone of the cranial vault is made up of very thin, but relatively strong, laminated (*lamellar*) layers of bone (Holck, 2005). This lamellar construction and thinner thickness allows the cranial vault to remain flexible, allows for a greater level of bone deformity without fracturing, and results in better impact absorption from blows (without breaking). While this is helpful during minor bumps to the head, it can be damaging during more significant contact force injuries. That is, a bone fracture helps to dissipate the kinetic energy of a blow, thereby reducing the effects of the pressure shock wave coursing through the brain, however, greater bone malleability acts to push bone inward, misshaping the brain and causing vascular hemorrhaging and TAI.

Unique to infants and children (up to age 3, and rarely after age 8) is a phenomenon called *growing skull fracture* (Iyer, Saxena, & Kumhar, 2003). A growing skull fracture is a rare complication in which the fracture line of a skull fracture increases in size. It is the result of a lacerated dura, the formation of a cystic mass filled with CSF, and the ongoing pulsation of CSF that accompanies the rapidly growing brain volume in this age group.

Brain water content and myelination. The white matter of the neonatal brain contains significantly less *myelin* (fatty insulation on nerve axons) than that of an adolescent or adult brain, resulting in a less dense brain. In addition, the neonatal brain is made up of approximately 89% water, compared to approximately 77% water for adults. This lower density and higher water content results in a "softer" brain that is more susceptible to greater distortion during an inertial force (acceleration/deceleration) injury (Pinto et al., 2012).

Head size in relation to body and neck muscle weakness. Until approximately the age of 8, children's heads are much larger and heavier in relation to their body size than are the heads of adults. In addition, their neck muscles are much weaker, allowing the head to more easily "flop around" during the sudden rotational forces in IF injuries. Therefore, young children are more vulnerable to injury.

Face-to-cranium ratio and face development. Infants and young children (toddlerhood) have a significantly smaller face-to-cranium ratio than do adolescents and adults (CDC, 2013h; Meschan, 1975). This results in the forehead slightly protruding over the vertical plane of the chin and creates a "top-heavy" body. The combination of being top-heavy and having a protruding forehead allows for an increased opportunity for injury during a fall. Finally, the fulcrum point of a toddler compared to an adolescent or adult when struck by a car is much different (Pinto et al., 2012, Fig. 1, p. e2). For example, the front bumper of a car will strike a toddler, who is lower to the ground, at the level of the shoulder (pinning the arm and hand against the body) or head, whereas an adolescent or adult is much more likely to be struck at the level of the waist or knees without pinning the arm and hand against the body.

Children often sustain a TBI in ways not typical of adolescents or adults. That is, they are particularly susceptible to injury from nonaccidental trauma, physical abuse, shaking, being run over by vehicles, and pulling heavy objects such as television sets onto themselves (Duhaime, Holshouser, Hunter, & Tong, 2012). Secondary damage can result from bleeding (*subdural hematoma*—see below) and *aneurysms* (enlargement of a blood vessel, usually an artery) in the underlying brain tissues.

Hemorrhaging

When the vasculature of the head and brain are ruptured, bleeding will occur in the form *hemorrhaging* or *hematoma* (a collection of blood that usually clots). These typically take the form of an epidural hematoma, subdural hematoma (acute, subacute, chronic), subarachnoid hemorrhage, intracerebral hemorrhage, and/or contusion (Figure 3.4).

Epidural hematoma (EDH). EDH–also called an *extradural hematoma*—is a form of primary damage that occurs as a consequence of a CV fracture at the initial site of a CF injury. An EDH is caused by a ruptured blood vessel (usually an artery) that rapidly bleeds into the space between the CV and the dura mater. The bleeding is rapid because arteries leave the heart under high pressure. This rapid bleeding causes a collection of blood (*hematoma*) that takes on a classic "lens" or "bean" shape. (Figure 3.4). As the hematoma increases in size it *compresses* brain tissue and causes a rapid increase in *intracranial pressure* (ICP). This compression and ICP damages the brain at the neuronal and cellular level along the length of the hematoma. If the hematoma is large enough, it will push the brain (*herniate*) toward the opposite side of the injury (Figure 3.4), causing contrecoup damage (*contusion* and *compression injury*). If the hematoma is situated in line with one of the ventricles, it can collapse the ventricle as it expands, causing compression of the surrounding brain tissue (Figure 3.4). Epidural hematomas occur within minutes or hours and generally require emergency neurosurgery in order to remove the blood clot and release the ICP. If left untreated, epidural hematomas are usually fatal.

Subdural hematoma (SDH). SDH is a form of primary damage that occurs as a consequence of the rapid deformation of the brain during an IF injury. An SDH can occur at the coup or contrecoup site, when a blood vessel connecting the dura mater to the surface of the brain (usually a vein called *a bridging vessel*) ruptures and blood fills the space between the dura mater and the arachnoid (*subdural space*). This bleeding causes a hematoma that takes on a classic "crescent" shape (Figure 3.4). As the hematoma increases in size—in addition to the primary damage associated with an epidural hematoma—it causes further damage by tearing more bridging vessels as the brain is forced away from the dura mater. With an SDH, the subdural space is filled at the rate of the bleeding of the ruptured blood vessel. As a result, an SDH caused by a ruptured

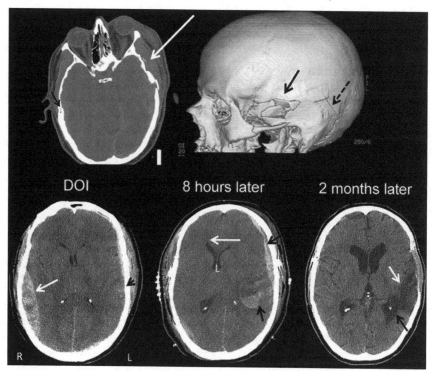

Figure 3.4 CT scans illustrating primary and secondary damage, brain hemorrhages, skull fractures, ventricle compression, and midline shifting.

Note: all four axial CT scans are in the radiological orientation, meaning the right side of the image is the left side of the brain and vice versa. The top right 3-D CT shows the left side of the patient's head. The axial CT on the top left is the acute CT emergently performed that shows the left depressed and comminuted (splintered and crushed) temporal bone fracture (white arrow) and a linear fracture on the right side of the skull (black arrow). Top right is the 3-D CT reconstruction of the left depressed skull fracture (black arrow). Note that posteriorly from the last indentation of the depressed fracture that the fracture becomes nondepressed and linear (dotted arrow). Bottom left CT depicts the position and size of a large epidural hematoma (white arrow) on the initial day-of-injury (DOI) scan. The epidural hematoma was removed, but this allowed the blossoming of intraparenchymal hemorrhaging on the left (bottom black arrow, middle scan) in association with subarachnoid and subdural blood (top black arrow, middle scan). In fact, on the DOI scan the hemorrhaging in this area did not initially appear ominous (black arrow). Approximately two months postinjury, prominent left temporal encephalomalcia is evident (white arrow) combined with generalized volume loss of brain parenchyma (tissue). This series of scans also illustrates primary and secondary damage, ventricle compression, and midline shifting. In this case, the depressed skull fracture on the left side of the head and the epidural hematoma both represent sites of primary damage. The encephalomalcia and generalized volume loss of brain parenchyma (resulting in an expanded left atrium of the lateral ventricle—black arrow, bottom right CT scan) represent secondary damage. In the 8-hour CT scan, compression of the anterior horn of the left lateral ventricle is evident as the brain shifts to the right (white arrow) in association with subarachnoid and subdural blood (top black arrow, middle scan). Finally, in the 8-hour CT scan, it is seen how the intraparenchymal hemorrhaging on the left (bottom black arrow) has resulted in a complete compression of the left atrium of the lateral ventricle.

vein will form much more slowly than one caused by a ruptured artery. This is because blood in a vein is under significantly less pressure than an artery; it is moved through the vein by gravity, the contraction of skeletal muscles, and one-way valves that prevent backflow. Therefore, when cut, a vein will "ooze" blood. Blood in an artery, on the other hand, is under pressure; it moves through the artery by a combination of force generated by the heart muscles and expansion/contraction of the arterial wall. When an artery is cut, it will "squirt" blood each time the heart beats. There are three types of SDH—acute, subacute, and chronic. An *acute subdural hematoma* generally occurs as a result of a severe head injury and is identified within two days of injury. Even though it generally involves slower bleeding venous blood, an acute SDH typically involves a greater number of vessel ruptures. In consequence, if left untreated, acute subdural hematomas can quickly become fatal. A *subacute subdural hematoma* is generally identified within three days to three weeks postinjury and a *chronic subdural hematoma* is identified more than three weeks following injury. Similar to an SDH is a phenomenon called *subdural hygromas,* in which CSF, instead of blood, leaks into the subdural space. Although not near as significant, on certain neuroimaging scans these collections of CSF are difficult to differentiate from SDH (Gharahbaghian, Schroeder, Mittendorff, & Wang, 2011).

Subarachnoid hemorrhage (SAH). SAH is a form of primary damage that occurs as a consequence of the rapid deformation of the brain during an IF injury. It is a result of a ruptured blood vessel (usually an artery) in the subarachnoid space (Figure 3.4). The blood from the ruptured blood vessel rapidly bleeds into the subarachnoid space, which is normally filled with CSF. However, unlike an EDH, in which the blood pools and clots, the bleeding from an SAH does not remain primarily in the area around the sight of injury; rather it spreads diffusely through the subarachnoid space. Therefore, although bleeding is rapid, there is a much slower increase in ICP, because the blood needs time to increase the pressure within the pulsating arachnoid space. An SAH can cause *cerebral vasospasm,* which is a narrowing in a blood vessel that results in a decrease in blood flow, causing damage or death to parts of the brain (Kim & Gean, 2011).

Intracerebral hematoma. Intracerebral hematoma, also known as *intraparenchymal hematoma,* is a form of primary damage caused by IF injuries in which tears in large blood vessels result in heavy bleeding within the brain tissue (Figure 3.4).

Contusion. Contusion is a form of primary damage generally caused by CF injuries in which small blood vessels rupture within the brain tissue (Figure 3.2). Contusion can occur at the coup or contrecoup site. They are generally found where there are sharp edges or ridges in the CV (e.g., the cranial fossae).

Injury Severity: Medical Settings

In medical settings, injury severity level is used to select treatment options, estimate the risk of injury complication, and predict outcome (e.g., survival, level of postinjury impairment). Medical professionals typically classify TBI along a descriptive severity continuum, and placement is determined by a number of interrelated factors. Although there is variation in the criteria and methodology used to determine severity level, most approaches consider the following: level of altered consciousness, postinjury memory disruption, and anatomical damage. In addition, depending on the suspected, or actual, nature of the anatomical damage to the head or brain, neuroimaging may be incorporated in the decision-making process.

Level of Altered Consciousness

Posner, Saper, Schiff, & Plum (2007) define *consciousness* as "the state of full awareness of the self and one's relationship to the environment" (p. 5). Using this definition, *level of altered consciousness* can be used to refer to a *continuum of awareness* ranging from its mildest form, *confusion* (where some degree of consciousness is retained), to its most severe form, *permanent vegetative state* (where there is *total loss of consciousness* [TLOC]).

Confusion. Confusion is a state of altered level of consciousness, wherein the individual is temporarily perplexed, and unable to make sense about such things as time, place, person, and/or event. Confusion typically begins immediately after a blow to the head; however, its onset can also be delayed for up to several minutes (American Academy of Neurology, 1997). In addition, confusion can last anywhere from moments to hours.

Coma. Coma is a sleep-like state, in which a person has a TLOC, is unable to be aroused, is unresponsive to all external stimuli, exhibits no understandable words, is not aware of inner needs (e.g., hunger), and lies with eyes closed (Posner et al., 2007). Although the person may grimace and demonstrate stereotyped withdrawal reactions in response to noxious external stimuli (e.g., pain), there is no defensive movement to block the localized noxious stimuli. In other words, a person in a coma does not show evidence of awareness of self or the environment. The defining characteristic of coma is the absence of spontaneous eye opening or sleep/wake cycles. Coma rarely persists longer than two to four weeks without the individual beginning to awaken. If there is a return to sleep/wake cycles, spontaneous eye-opening, blinking, roving eye movement, and startle reflex, but there is a continued unawareness of self or environment, the condition changes to what is known as a *vegetative state.* If the vegetative state continues longer than 30 days, the individual is considered to be in a *persistent or chronic vegetative state.* If this state continues for 12 months (in the case of TBI etiology), the individual is considered to be in a *permanent vegetative state,* which can last for many years. Sometimes during the transition to or from coma a person can enter into a *minimally conscious state* in which the person has severely impaired consciousness with minimal but definite behavioral evidence of self or the environment. A person in a minimally conscious state may follow simple commands, answer "yes/no" using gesture or vocalization, have intelligible verbalization, and/or engage in purposeful behavior. The condition may be permanent as well.

On the milder end of the continuum, altered consciousness can include a *brief loss of consciousness* (BLOC) which can last from moments to hours, as is often the case in mTBI. Although by definition BLOC is a coma (due to unawareness of self or environment), it is generally not referred to as such, rather it is referred to as being "knocked out," being "knocked unconscious," or "experiencing a brief loss of consciousness." It is important to note that TBI can occur without BLOC or TLOC; but at some point in time, an individual will always experience some level of altered consciousness as described above—especially with CHI. In addition, injury severity designation is not always contingent upon a BLOC. For example, a person can sustain a severe TBI without BLOC, which is frequently the case with a PHI (Granacher, 2008). It is also widely recognized that mTBI can occur without BLOC (Lezak et al., 2012).

An almost universally employed measure that assesses all levels of altered consciousness is the *Glasgow Coma Scale (GCS)* (Teasdale & Jennett, 1974). The GCS is a simple, easily scored measure that assesses an injured person across three domains: ability to open eyes, ability to communicate verbally with others, and ability to move limbs. It is scored by domain (1–4 points for eye opening; 1–6 points for motor response; 1–5 points for verbal response) and produces a summed score ranging from 3–15 points. The higher the score, the less severe the TBI; therefore, scores of 13–15 points are considered to indicate a mild TBI, 9–12 points indicate a moderate TBI, and 3–8 points indicate a severe TBI. Although the GCS is perhaps the most widely used measure for TBI severity, and it has shown usefulness in early care decision-making and outcome prediction, it is subject to inherent limitations that complicate its use (Sherer, Struchen, Yablon, Wang, & Nick, 2008). For example, the use of recreational drugs and/or alcohol can affect a person's ability to respond; as can intubation, sedation for agitation, and facial injuries—all of which can result in a lowered GCS score. In addition, because the GCS can be administered repeatedly over time, there is no agreement as to which GCS should be used to classify severity level: the GCS taken at the scene or in route to the hospital, the best/worst first 24-hour score, the best first 24-hour motor score, or the GCS obtained six hours after injury (Lezak et al., 2012). Further complicating this decision is the fact that some individuals deteriorate en route, in the emergency department, or in the intensive care unit.

Postinjury Memory Disruption

Postinjury memory disruption, also known as *posttraumatic amnesia* (PTA), is common following TBI. There are two types of PTA, anterograde amnesia and retrograde amnesia. As it pertains to TBI, *anterograde amnesia* (AA) refers to the inability to form new memories immediately following the injury. That is, individuals with TBI-induced AA will not be able to recall, or will have extreme difficulty recalling, new life events beginning at the moment of their injury. For example, after falling from a tree and striking his head on the pavement, an adolescent boy would not recall—or would have extreme difficulty recalling—getting up from the pavement, speaking with a paramedic at the scene of the injury, or being taken to the hospital. AA can last from minutes to weeks (and more rarely, months); therefore, an individual may believe he is meeting a doctor for the first time, despite ongoing daily contact. As the individual improves over time, AA may involve partial memories, rather than continuous memories, or there may be a waxing and waning of memory formation. For example, an individual may remember the name of a neurologist, but not remember what that person does, or how he/she has come to know that person. A person who has experienced AA may never recall the period during which they experienced the AA. *Retrograde amnesia* (RA), as it pertains to TBI, refers to the inability to recall events or information prior to the time of injury. Depending on the injury severity, RA can apply to moments, days, weeks, or months prior to the trauma. RA tends to be temporally bound, usually affecting the most recently acquired memories prior to the injury; sparing factual information from the past. For example, an individual with RA might not remember the details of how he/she was injured, or what was happening just prior to the injury, but can recall his/her name, date of birth, street address, or pet's name. A person who has experienced RA may never recall the details just prior to the TBI.

The extent and duration of PTA is commonly assessed using the *Galveston Orientation and Amnesia Test* (*GOAT;* Levin, O'Donnell, & Grossman, 1979). The GOAT is a mental health status examination that assesses confusion and amnesia. It has eight questions that measure orientation to time, place, and person and two questions that assess memory before and after the injury event. Based on a patient's response, points are assigned to each of the 10 questions and the total number of error points (if any) is deducted from 100 possible points. The higher an individual scores on the GOAT, the less atypical memory impairment he/she is considered to have. Scores of 76–100 are considered as normal, 66–75 as borderline, and ≤65 as impaired or still in a state of PTA.

The following guidelines are also used when PTA is used to estimate TBI injury severity: PTA < 5 minutes (very mild); 5–60 minutes (mild); 1–24 hours (moderate), 1–7 days (severe), 1–4 weeks (very severe), and > 4 weeks (extremely severe).

Anatomical Damage

It is believed by many that, regardless of the severity level, TBI always involves some level of anatomical damage to the brain. In order to establish the full extent of actual or suspected anatomical damage, and to help with medical planning and intervention procedures, medical professionals often rely on the use of imaging technologies like x-ray and computed tomography (CT). *X-ray* is often used at the time of admittance to the emergency department because it is cheap, readily available, and useful in obtaining gross information about the presence of a major CV fracture or metal fragments/objects within the CV. *CT,* a form of x-ray, is frequently used in the emergency department evaluation process because it is relatively quick and is particularly sensitive in detecting masses, fractures, and hemorrhages. Less often, but increasingly more frequently, advanced neuroimaging techniques (e.g., *magnetic resonance imaging—MRI*) are being utilized as their benefit in treatment and intervention are realized. When CT or MRI technology is used in the assessment of TBI, it is not unusual to obtain a scan of the brain on the day of injury (DOI), following any surgical intervention, and again at 4–6 weeks postinjury.

To better understand the long-term anatomical damage from all severity levels of TBI, medical and research personnel are now using advanced neuroimaging technologies such as *fluid attenuated inversion recovery sequence* (FLAIR), *gradient recalled echo* (GRE), *proton density sequence* (PD), *susceptibility weighted imaging* (SWI), *diffusion tensor imaging* (DTI), *functional MRI* (fMRI), *resting state fMRI* (rsfMRI), and *voxel-based morphometry* (VBM).

Injury Severity: Educational Settings

Within the educational setting, a designation of TBI severity level is not required for a student to receive services under the Individuals with Disabilities Education Improvement

Act of 2004 (IDEIA 04) or to receive accommodations under Section 504 of the Rehabilitation Act of 1973 (Section 504). In fact, IDEIA 04 does not prescribe what documentation, if any, is required for determining that a student is eligible for special education under the TBI category. To qualify for special education services under IDEIA 04, the student only needs to meet the federal definition (chapter 1) and show that he/she meets the eligibility criteria for special education. Individual states, however, may require specific documented proof of TBI (e.g., hospital discharge summary) or require the presence of a licensed professional who is qualified to make the diagnosis on the multidisciplinary evaluation team. To qualify for Section 504 accommodations, the student need only be determined to have a physical or mental impairment that substantially limits one or more major life activities (learning), have a record of such impairment, or be regarded as having such an impairment. Again, individual states may require specific documentation or specialized evaluation team membership.

Injury Severity: Classifications

Since 1974, when Teasdale and Jennett first introduced the GCS, TBIs have been classified into one of three categories (mild [mTBI], moderate, or severe). In order to best understand TBI severity classifications, it is important to recognize that they are on a continuum, and two people with the same severity classification will experience different strengths, limitations, and/or outcomes. For example, a person on the mildest end of the mTBI severity spectrum may experience transient neurological changes that spontaneously resolve within minutes, hours, or days, while a person on the most serious end of the mTBI spectrum may continue to experience symptoms for more than a year.

Mild Traumatic Brain Injury

It is estimated that, in the United States and worldwide, approximately 80% of all TBIs will be classified as a mild traumatic brain injury (mTBI; CDC, 2013i; Corrigan, Selassie, & Orman, 2010). The mTBI category can be thought of as having two subcategories: uncomplicated and complicated. An *uncomplicated mTBI* is an mTBI that is not accompanied by intracranial primary or secondary damage on the DOI, as measured by neuroimaging technology. A *complicated mTBI* is an mTBI that presents with neuroimaging evidence of intracranial abnormalities on DOI. Although research on outcome differences between the two subcategories is mixed (see Lange, Iverson, & Franzen, 2009, for a review) the distinction remains, as advanced neuroimaging technologies (e.g., magnetization transfer imaging [MTI], susceptibility weighted imaging [SWI]) are beginning to reveal neuronal damage not previously revealed by older neuroimaging technologies (e.g., CT) (Bigler & Maxwell, 2012a).

As noted above, providing a definitive definition for an mTBI is challenging. For the purpose of this book, mTBI is subsumed under the consensus definition for TBI developed by a panel of experts who made up the Demographics and Clinical Assessment Working Group of the International and Interagency Initiative toward Common Data Elements for Research on Traumatic Brain Injury and Psychological Health. It states that TBI is *"an alteration in brain function, or other evidence of brain pathology, caused by an external force"* (Menon et al., 2010, p. 1638, italics added).

Concussion. At the mildest end of the mTBI continuum is concussion (Bigler & Maxwell, 2012b; Prigatano & Gale, 2011). As early as the thirteenth century (Strauss & Savitsky, 1934), concussion, and its effect, has been the subject of formal discussion. In 1910, Bennet formally classified a subgroup of concussion, in which there was no loss of consciousness, as being a milder form of concussion. Since that time, the definition and classification of concussion has been the subject of debate. What has been primarily disputed is whether or not any or all of the following must be present for an injury to be considered to be a concussion: a loss of consciousness, PTA, and/or neuroimaging evidence of anatomical damage. What has not been debated, even since the earliest discourse, is that concussion has an immediate onset and requires either a direct blow to the head or a significant acceleration/deceleration of the brain. Complicating the classification of concussion is the uncertainty regarding how long neurocognitive or neurobehavioral effects last beyond the acute phase (hours to days) and how to measure these (Bigler, 2012).

While the majority of individuals who sustain an mTBI will be on the least severe end of the mTBI continuum, the remainder will fall along the more severe end. For these individuals, CT scans will most likely show linear or depressed fractures, subdural or epidural hematomas, microhemorrhaging, contusion, edema, and/or DAI. They will also most likely experience persistent amnesia, seizures, headache, vomiting, and neurologic deficits (e.g., working memory impairment, slowed processing) that can last for years (Lezak et al., 2012). In addition, mTBI brings unique challenges to differential diagnosis of neuropsychiatric conditions. For example, the relationship between mTBI and posttraumatic stress disorder (PTSD) is complex and controversial (Bryant, 2011). However, there are times when an individual who has sustained an mTBI may awaken from their initial coma to traumatic circumstances. For example, as Bryant notes (2011), during an automobile accident, some individuals may not remember the point of impact that caused their mTBI; however, upon regaining consciousness they are fully aware of extraction from the vehicle and associated injury pain which can lead to them reporting distressing memories of their experience at a later date. This experience can increase the risk of developing PTSD, although differentiating between PTSD, postconcussive symptoms, and premorbid psychiatric disorders (e.g., depression, anxiety, adjustment difficulties) can be difficult due to overlap of symptoms. In addition, sometimes sustaining an mTBI can provide a causative explanation for behaviors that were previously undiagnosed, further complicating differential diagnoses. For example, a child, parent, or school professional may misattribute symptoms of attention deficit hyperactivity disorder (ADHD) or academic difficulties (such as learning disabilities) to mTBI due to the temporal correlation.

Moderate Traumatic Brain Injury

An approximate 10% of all TBIs in the United States and worldwide will be classified as being moderate (CDC, 2013i; Corrigan et al., 2010). The guidelines frequently used for determining a moderate TBI are a loss of consciousness for 1–24 hours, PTA for 1–24 hours, abnormal brain imaging results, and a GCS of 9–12 or a coma of no longer than within six hours of admission. The nature and duration of TBI symptoms and consequences vary widely and commonly include, but are not limited to, difficulties with everyday living, headaches, memory problems, loss of initiative, and/or loss of spontaneity. In addition, it is not uncommon for significant cognitive difficulties (e.g., short-term memory difficulties, slowed processing speed) to continue up to six months postinjury. While most individuals with moderate TBI will be able to function independently and return to work or school, they will likely experience affective, behavioral, and learning problems (e.g., muted or flattened affect or empathy, temper outbursts, impulsivity, difficulty with self-monitoring) that impair their ability to flourish.

Severe Traumatic Brain Injury

An approximate 10% of all TBIs in the United States and worldwide will be classified as being severe (CDC, 2013i; Corrigan et al., 2010). Common classification guidelines for a severe TBI are a loss of consciousness for > 24 hours, PTA for > 24 hours, abnormal brain imaging results, and a GCS of ≤ 8 or a coma of > 6 hours duration after admission. Individuals who have suffered a severe TBI, and survived, do not return to premorbid levels of social functioning and rarely function independently. They also typically experience a range of significant cognitive and motor deficits, severe executive dysfunction, and emotional or psychiatric disorders. Those individuals at the most serious end of the severe TBI continuum usually die or remain in either a persistent vegetative state or a minimally conscious state.

4 TBI Recovery and Rehabilitation

I do not use the term "recovery" when discussing brain injuries. Brain damage that is severe enough to alter the level of consciousness even momentarily, or to result in even transient impairment of sensory, motor, or cognitive functions, is likely to leave some residual deficit. In cases where the damage is more than mild, the use of the word "recovery"—which implies restoration or return to premorbid status—when discussing a patient's progress can give the patient and family false hope, delay practical planning, and may cause unnecessary anxiety and disappointment.

—Muriel Deutsch Lezak, (footnote in Lezak, 1995, p. 283)

The complicated neuronal makeup of the human brain, combined with the infinite number of ways in which the brain can be injured, cause recovery and rehabilitation following TBI to be a complex process that is not fully understood. TBI recovery and rehabilitation are closely related to the nature of the injury (e.g., PHI), the injury severity level, and the availability of medical treatment at the time of the injury. They are also complicated by myths, misconceptions, and misattribution of causality (Hooper, 2006a; McClure, 2011). As a result, *recovery*, the extent to which an individual returns to pre-injury levels of functioning, and *rehabilitation*, the application of interventions designed to assist an individual in the recovery process, are sometimes misunderstood by medical professionals, educational professionals, and parents/guardians.

Chapter Overview

This chapter will provide a general overview of the recovery and rehabilitation processes and introduce factors that can influence these. This chapter will contain discussions on

- TBI recovery;
- mechanisms of recovery;
- TBI rehabilitation;
- factors affecting recovery and rehabilitation;
- myths and misconceptions about TBI recovery and rehabilitation;
- misattribution of causality; and
- some final words about recovery.

TBI Recovery

Recovery is perhaps one of the most misconstrued aspects of TBI. This is because when it comes to TBI-induced functional impairment; it is human nature to assume the logic of Tweedledum and Tweedledee in Lewis Carroll's classic children's story *Through the Looking-Glass, and What Alice Found There* (Carroll, 1872):

> "I know what you're thinking about," said Tweedledum: "but it isn't so, nohow."

> "Contrariwise," continued Tweedledee, "if it was so, it might be; and if it were so, it would be; but as it isn't, it ain't. That's logic." (p. 74)

Thus for many, in the absence of observable evidence indicating the presence of TBI impairment, logic will dictate that impairment does not exist. One example of this logic is: if a student who is known to have sustained a TBI returns to school able to walk and talk without difficulty, then logic dictates that the student has "recovered" from his/her TBI. Another example is: if a student returns to school following a TBI able to recite the alphabet without error, then logic dictates that the student has recovered from his/her TBI and any exhibited inability to spell words correctly is not related to the TBI; rather, the student is "faking" or "just rushing through the work."

Maintaining an accurate appreciation of the extent to which a student has returned, or will return, to pre-injury levels of functioning following a TBI is critical during the transition from the medical/rehabilitation setting to the educational setting. If students, parent/guardians, or educational professionals do not hold an accurate understanding of TBI recovery, it can easily lead to one or more of the following for any of these individuals:

- reluctance to be involved in the transition process;
- inaccurate appraisals of ability and/or potential;
- negation or minimization of reported limitations or deficits;
- erroneous, premature, or unsuccessful attempts to resume pre-injury educational activities (including sports and physical education classes);
- resistance to educational intervention efforts;
- setting unreasonable or unattainable goals;
- unrealistic levels of expected participation;
- self-blame for lack of progress;
- inappropriate comparison to peer performance;
- feelings of frustration, helplessness;
- feelings of hopelessness, low self-esteem, depression, or anxiety;
- incorrect responses to inappropriate behaviors or social interactions;
- misattributions and/or misconceptions of behaviors; and
- "one-size-fits-all" or "cookie cutter-approaches" based on previous experiences with TBI.

Gaining an accurate appreciation of recovery begins with understanding that moderate and severe TBI typically produces irreversible primary damage to the brain, as well as some degree of functional impairment to the individual. That is, neural cells and/or blood vessels are irreversibly damaged or destroyed, and the function they performed either ceases completely or continues at a less efficient level.

Within mTBI, however, there is variability. For the majority of those who sustain an mTBI, symptoms diminish within minutes to hours to days, leaving no lasting measurable consequences, and the person returns to their previous baseline activities without further difficulty (Bigler, 2012). This is because most mTBIs only stretch and/or compress axons disrupting metabolic and synaptic functioning, and as long as an axon is not stressed beyond its tolerance level (its unique and individualized tensile strength), it will return to normal functioning (Ottens et al., 2006). In addition, a quick, noncomplicated recovery following an mTBI can be explained from an evolutionary perspective. mTBIs have been occurring for eons, especially from things like simple falls or fisticuffs. Through evolutionary processes, it appears that over hundreds of thousands of years, the human brain has adapted to most mTBIs, if they occur once or at least sparsely. If you examine the gradient of recovery following an mTBI, there is a quick recovery of the motor reflexes and motor control that are needed for escape or fight or flight reactions. This is then followed by the return of cognitive efficiency. However, because cognitive networks are much more substantial than motor reflex and motor control networks, they take a bit longer to physiologically come back online. This can be somewhat compared to a computer "rebooting" after it crashes. The more simplified computer programs required to maintain the underlying computer processes return quickly, while the more complex video programs required to display the desktop take a significantly longer time to reload. Furthermore, since the industrial revolution, head injuries occurring from mechanical devices, explosions, motor vehicle accidents, etc. have produced more severe mTBIs to which our brains have not adapted. Therefore, these injuries result in vague, ill-defined, persisting symptoms. For these more severe mTBIs, advanced neuroimaging techniques—e.g., gradient recalled echo imaging (GRE; including susceptibility-weighted imaging [SWI]) along with diffusion tensor imaging (DTI)—provide evidence of irreversible damage at the cellular level of the neuron (e.g., microbleeding due to blood vessel damage, diffuse axonal injuries [DAI]) that is not evident on conventional magnetic resonance imaging or computed tomography taken on the day of injury (see Shenton et al., 2012 for a review; Figure 4.1)

These advanced neuroimaging technology results also challenge conventional wisdom that mTBI symptoms resolve rapidly (3–10 days postinjury) and completely in all cases, with no residual deficits (see Slobounov, Gay, Johnson, & Zhang, 2012 for a review). As it currently stands, whether or not an individual "recovers completely" from mTBI is a matter of subjective opinion.

Regardless of the severity level of TBI, there are clinicians and researchers who question if recovery has really occurred (Stein, 1999). This is especially true if recovery has been measured based on the attainment of a recovery goal, rather than the means by which the goal was attained (e.g., regaining the ability to walk [goal] vs. walking with assistance [means]) or if the assessment instrument used to measure goal attainment was not sensitive to subtle deficits. With moderate and severe TBI, however, it is widely accepted among medical professionals and neuropsychologists that "full recovery" is highly unlikely, and "recovery" will be an ongoing lifetime process of deficit compensation and improvement toward pre-injury levels of functioning.

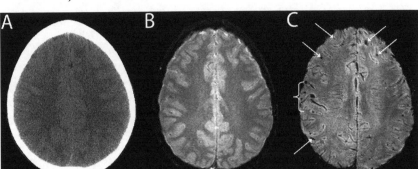

Figure 4.1 Side-by-side neuroimaging comparison showing mTBI hemorrhagic lesions. This 12-year-old male had sustained a concussion in a skate-boarding accident. Eyewitness accounts estimate LOC to be approximately 7 minutes, but in the ER the patient was alert and not amnesic. However, because of the positive LOC a CT scan was performed (A), followed by the more routine GRE sequence (B) which revealed only a hint of hemosiderin deposition (a paramagnetic byproduct in white matter left over from bleeding considered to be an indicator of diffuse axonal injury; Silver, McAllister, & Yudofsky, 2011), however, the susceptibility-weighted sequence (C) clearly demonstrated multiple foci of hemosiderin deposition (see arrows).

Reproduced by permission from Jill Hunter, M.D., Texas Children's Hospital, Houston, Texas.

It is important to recognize that TBI recovery is a process along a continuum. Even though on occasion recovery may appear to happen very rapidly, it does not happen abruptly. For example, while it may appear that with the opening of his/her eyes (an abrupt event) an individual who has lost consciousness as a result of a blow to the head may suddenly appear to move from a state of unconsciousness (a sign of coma) to a state of wakefulness (a sign of possible recovery from a coma state), this is not the case. Prior to opening his/her eyes, there has been a cascade of neurological and physiological events occurring leading up to the act of eye-opening. Furthermore, although the individual's eyes are now open, he/she has not yet returned to a pre-injury state of functioning. That is, prior to losing consciousness, the individual was coherent, able to make decisions, and able to respond willfully to his/her immediate environment. However, upon returning to a state of wakefulness following a loss of consciousness (no matter how brief), the individual will be confused and unresponsive to his/her immediate environment for a period of time.

When the term "*spontaneous recovery*" is used in reference to TBI, it does not mean that an individual suddenly changes from having an impairment to suddenly being impairment free; instead, it means that an observable behavior (sign) has resolved over time without the aid of an intervention, or it has resolved before a reasonably expected time frame after an intervention has been implemented. Also, while it may appear that a TBI symptom or sign has disappeared (resolved), this can be deceptive (as noted in the loss of consciousness example above).

TBI recovery can be measured in terms of the degree of restoration or adaptation of anatomical structures, return to pre-injury levels of functioning, and medical improvement (i.e., how well the person is progressing away from dependency on medical interventions). In conjunction with these measures, three time-related stages of recovery (acute stage, subacute stage, chronic stage) are frequently referenced, although definitions of what constitutes a stage will vary. For example, in one instance, the acute stage may be defined as lasting from one to six days and the chronic stage will be defined as beginning at six months postinjury (Henry et al., 2011). In other instances the acute stage may be defined as lasting up to six months (High, Roebuck-Spencer, Sander, Struchen, & Sherer, 2006) and the chronic stage may be defined as beginning three months postinjury (Gupta & Taly, 2012). In this book these stages are defined in a medical context as follows:

Acute Stage

Depending on the seriousness of the injury, the acute stage lasts from a few minutes to hours to days. The acute phase technically begins immediately upon the traumatic injury. For those TBIs requiring medical attention, the acute stage is generally first documented with the arrival of emergency personnel at the scene of the injury or with the individual's arrival in the emergency department of the hospital. The medical goal during this time is to stabilize the individual and minimize or prevent secondary injury. How this is accomplished will be determined by the severity of the brain injury, the injury type (e.g., PHI), any accompanying TBI complications (e.g., hematoma, imbedded objects), and any accompanying injuries (e.g., severe burns, broken bones, and, in particular, cardiovascular and/or pulmonary injuries). Typical activities (in no particular order) during the acute stage may include, but are not limited to, any of the following:

- controlling bleeding;
- maintaining body fluid levels;
- obtaining neuroimages of the brain;
- administering antiseizure and antibiotic medication, especially with any penetrating injury;
- placing the individual on a ventilator;
- elevating the head and torso;
- inducing mild-to-moderate hypothermia;
- surgery to remove objects;
- surgery to monitor and/or reduce intracranial pressure (ICP) from hematomas, hemorrhages, herniation, and/or edema;
- surgery to insert a peripherally inserted central catheter (PICC) line (used to administer intravenous fluids and medications); and
- surgery to insert a shunt to drain excess cerebral spinal fluid (CSF) or blood.

During the acute stage, neuropsychological status is either showing rapid changes and variability or persistent profound deficits.

Subacute Stage

The subacute stage of recovery lasts from days to weeks. For those individuals requiring medical attention, the length will depend on other injuries and the level of coma. The subacute stage is generally considered to begin once the individual has been medically stabilized. The medical goals during this time are to monitor stability and/

or improvement; treat any new medical complications; prevent or minimize secondary damage; initiate early rehabilitation; and plan for, and prepare, the individual for participation in post-hospital rehabilitation. It is also common—by the very nature of experiencing a TBI in a fall, accident, or assault—that other injuries, especially internal non-neurological and orthopedic, occur, which may influence TBI outcome and likewise need treatment. For example, any pulmonary injuries may affect oxygenation to the brain and any excessive bleeding may also deprive the brain of sufficient oxygenated blood. Typical activities during the subacute stage may include, but are not limited to, any of the following:

- treating and preventing muscle contractions;
- treating infections;
- having hospital-based specialists (e.g., physical therapists, occupational and speech therapists, neuropsychologists, neurologists, social workers) conduct evaluations and assessments to determine the need for ongoing treatment and future medical or rehabilitative needs;
- developing realistic transition goals;
- educating family members/caregivers about current and future medical and/or rehabilitative needs;
- evaluating and monitoring ongoing cognitive improvement/decline;
- evaluating and monitoring ongoing physical improvement/decline; and
- starting early cognitive and physical rehabilitation efforts.

During the subacute stage, the neuropsychological status continues to show rapid changes and variability or persistent profound deficits.

Chronic Stage

The chronic stage of recovery begins a few months postinjury and for those individuals who have been under medical care, the medical goal is to prepare the individual for discharge from the hospital. The goal may also include preparation for continued medical and rehabilitative support services. Typical activities during the subacute stage may include, but are not limited to, any of the following:

- having hospital-based specialists conduct final discharge evaluations and assessments;
- meetings with families and long-term care or rehabilitation agency personnel;
- meetings with families and educational professionals to begin the transition process from the medical setting to the educational setting; and
- weaning medications and medical routines.

During the chronic stage neuropsychological status is mostly stable.

Mechanisms of Recovery

The function of the brain is to process information and carefully work out different biological responses (Araque & Navarrete, 2010). When damage occurs to the brain as a result of a TBI, the processing of information becomes compromised. If information processing is compromised significantly enough, it can lead to a total loss of function and biological responses. Exactly how the brain compensates for damaged tissue, or lost function, following a TBI is not fully understood; however, it is associated with something called "plasticity" or "neuroplasticity." To understand the mechanisms of brain recovery and the concept of neuroplasticity, it is helpful to briefly discuss the brain's complex communication processes.

Neuronal Networks

The brain contains billions of neurons organized into many interconnected regions, each of which is comprised of functional neuronal networks. Each brain region influences other regions depending on the input and output of their connecting pathways (Johansen-Berg & Rushworth, 2009). In order to optimize functional efficiency, brain regions are believed to contain strong, locally segregated, but tightly connected, clustering patterns (called *small-world networks*) that have short connecting white matter path lengths within the network (Micheloyannis et al., 2006; Watts & Strogatz, 1998; Yan & He, 2011). Although brain regions have their own unique connections, it is not unusual for them to share some common connections with other brain regions (Johansen-Berg & Rushworth, 2009; Sepulcre, Sabuncu, & Johnson, 2012). This is accomplished through centrally located *hubs* (sometimes called *hub nodes*) that connect widely distributed networks allowing for fast transport and efficient integration of information across networks (Sepulcre et al., 2012; van den Heuvel, Mandl, Stam, Kahn, & Hulshoff Pol, 2010). The anatomical connections that make up the various brain networks represent potential connections that are determined by neuromodulators (see below) that permit information to flow via different paths (Bargmann, 2012).

Neuron Communication

Brain networks and regions communicate with each other in different ways at the neuronal level, one of which is via bundles of white matter (neuronal axons), called *fibers* (Figure 4.2). There are three major classifications of white matter fibers: projection fibers, association fibers, and commissural fibers (Carpenter & Sutin, 1983). *Projection fibers* convey signals from the cerebral cortex (outermost layer of brain) to distant locations deep within the brain and vice versa. An example of a projection fiber is the *corona radiata*.

Association fibers interconnect various cortical regions within the *same* hemisphere. There are two types: long association fibers and short association fibers. *Long association fibers* interconnect cortical regions in different lobes within the same hemisphere, and *short association fibers* interconnect adjacent gyri and are sometimes called "*u-fibers.*" An example of a long association fiber is the *superior longitudinal fasciculus* which interconnects the occipital lobe and the frontal lobe. *Commissural fibers* interconnect matching cortical regions of *both* hemispheres. An example of a commissural fiber is the *corpus callosum* (Figure 2.1; Figure 2.2; Figure 2.4).

Brain networks and regions also communicate at the neuronal level via specialized areas called *synapses* (Carpenter & Sutin, 1983). As shown in Figure 2.8, synapses

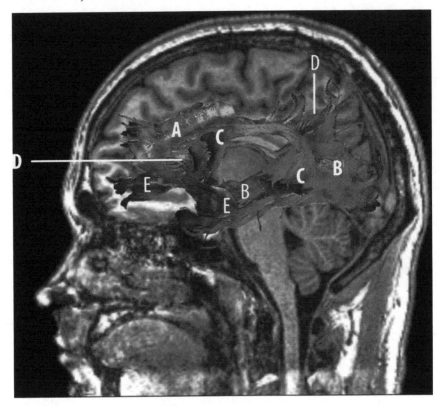

Figure 4.2 Diffusion tensor imaging tractography of white matter fibers: cingulum bundle (A), inferior occipitotemporal fasiculus (B), arcuate fasiculus (C), occipitofrontal fasiculus (mostly hidden, D) and uncinate fasiculus (E).

can occur between axon and axon (*axo-axonic synapse*), axon and dendrite (*axo-dendritic synapse*), and axon and neuron body (*axo-somatic synapse*). In some cases communication between neurons occurs via *electrical synapses* without the presence of chemical neurotransmitters. Instead, communication occurs directly with other neurons via direct electrical coupling at specialized areas called *gap junctions*. In most cases, however, communication between neurons occurs by means of neurotransmitters and neuromodulators via chemical synapses. At *chemical synapses,* action potentials trigger the release of chemical neurotransmitters from the *presynaptic terminal.* These neurotransmitters then diffuse across the *synaptic gap (cleft)* to bind with neurotransmitter receptors on the *postsynaptic membrane* of the receiving neuron. *Neuromodulators* are chemicals released by a neuron (synaptically or nonsynaptically) that work in conjunction with neurotransmitters. Neuromodulators influence neurotransmitters' effect on a receiving neuron (Mendoza & Foundas, 2008). They are capable of diffusing three-dimensionally throughout the brain via the CFS, by a process called *volume transmission,* and they are capable of affecting many different neurons by activating extra-synaptic receptors (Agnati, Zoli, Stromberg, & Fuxe, 1995; Bach-Y-Rita, 2003). Neurotransmitters are capable of directly eliciting an action potential in a nerve cell, whereas neuromodulators are not; they are only capable of altering the behavioral response of a nerve cell to the neurotransmitter to which they are associated (Mendoza & Foundas, 2008). As a result, the influence of neuromodulators on neuronal functioning is much slower than that of neurotransmitters. Neuromodulators, however, are capable of changing the composition of a neuronal circuit, allowing it to either recruit new neurons or exclude previous participants. That is, neuromodulators allow networks to engage in different patterns of activity (Bargmann, 2012).

Plasticity/Neuroplasticity

TBI results in cell death and/or deafferentation, both of which are correlated with injury severity (Lezak et al., 2012; Munoz-Cespedes, Rios-Lago, Paul, & Maestu, 2005). *Cell death* (*necrosis* or *apoptosis*) is the result of a cascade of pathophysiological and structural changes that occur in response to internal and external disturbances of the neuron. *Deafferentation* refers to the interruption or loss of afferent pathways or signals. *Afferent* pathways or signals are "any type of fiber connection or information coming into a nerve cell or body of cells" (Mendoza & Foundas, 2008, p. 657).

Each cellular component of a neuron plays an important role in the functioning of that neuron. Because neurons do not function as isolated units (Fingelkurts, Fingelkurts, & Kahkonen, 2005), each neuron in turn plays an important role in the functioning of other neurons within its brain area or network. These brain areas or networks play an important role in the functioning of any other brain area or network with which they are associated. Therefore, when neurons experience cell death or deafferentation, there is a significant ripple effect on the operating efficiency of "downriver" signal recipients. That is, the operating efficiency of every healthy neuron, brain area, or brain network "downstream" from the damaged or dead neuron is compromised to some degree. An example of this is *diaschisis*, which is a loss of function or neuronal signaling in a neuronally connected brain area some distance from the damaged brain area.

Following TBI, the brain responds to cell death and deafferentation by reorganizing its structure, function, and connections (Cramer et al., 2011). This is often referred to as "plasticity" or "neuroplasticity," although specific definitions vary greatly. *Neuroplasticity* can occur at the molecular, synaptic, cellular, or network level. That is, synapses can change their form and structure, dendrites and spines can grow or contract, axons can change their trajectory, neurotransmitters can be modulated, and/or synaptic activity can be increased or decreased (Nudo, 2006). Neuroplasticity can be both adaptive and maladaptive (Cramer et al., 2011). Neuroplasticity is considered to be *adaptive* when it results in a gain in function. An example of adaptive neuroplasticity is when network reorganization in a damaged brain area allows an undamaged brain network to "take over" a lost function. Neuroplasticity is considered to be *maladaptive* when it results in negative consequences. An example of maladaptive neuroplasticity is the new onset of seizures or spasticity (Bach-Y-Rita, 2003; Nudo, 2006). Neuroplasticity is believed to occur via any of the following processes (DeFina et al., 2009; Munoz-Cespedes et al., 2005):

- *unmasking,* the process by which previously dormant neuronal pathways become functional after a damaged/dead neuron no longer sends sufficient inhibitory signals to the neurons controlling that pathway;

- *long-term potentiation* or *long-term depression,* in which existing synapses become strengthened (potentiated) or weakened (depressed);
- changes in the excitability of neuronal membranes;
- changes in the anatomical structure of neurons (e.g., *axonal sprouting,* where new axons sprout on surviving neurons that share common terminal fields—these new axons take over for damaged neurons [Ramirez, 2001]);
- reorganization or reweighting of functional interactions in existing brain region networks;
- recruitment of new brain areas into the damaged network;
- use of alternate networks not usually involved in the task performance; and
- sensory substitution in which a region previously dedicated to receiving the sensory input of one modality becomes capable of processing a new kind of sensory input (e.g., auditory areas taking over visual areas).

TBI Rehabilitation

In order to better understand current views on TBI rehabilitation, a brief review of the history of TBI rehabilitation is warranted. Although TBI has been occurring since before recorded time, rehabilitative efforts specifically directed toward the treatment of TBI do not appear to have been documented until World War I, at which time the first programs dedicated to treating soldiers with TBI are believed to have been created in Germany and Austria (Boake & Diller, 2005). These innovative programs recognized the connection between TBI and neuropsychological impairment; as a result, they used neurological assessment of memory, vigilance, visual-spatial perception and reasoning, and speech and language as a means to identify impairments. They then taught compensatory strategies in speech, writing, and reading that took advantage of unimpaired skills. The primary goal of rehabilitation at the time was to prepare the individual to return to the workforce. Prior to World War II, there was only one official hospital in the United States dedicated to treating war veterans with TBI. Treatment in this New Jersey hospital mainly consisted of public school speech teachers providing patient-specific daily instruction and exercises in conversation, reading, and writing (Boake & Diller, 2005). Following World War II, rehabilitative centers with a focus on compensatory training, functional prognosis, and medical complications were established in various countries throughout the world. These programs often consisted of multidisciplinary teams of psychologists and speech-language pathologists who worked with cognitive and communication disorders (Boake & Diller, 2005). In the Soviet Union, rehabilitation of war veterans with TBI concentrated on compensatory strategies for motor planning, visual planning, and executive functions. In the United Kingdom, work with war veterans who had TBI led to the understanding that the duration of posttraumatic amnesia (PTA) was a good predictor of return to work. In addition, it also revealed the prevalence and risks of posttraumatic seizure disorders and a range of other complications following TBI (Boake & Diller, 2005). The 1950s and 1960s saw a rise in the number of treatment centers worldwide and the emergence of psychological rehabilitative services grounded in behaviorism, behavior-conditioning, and psychoanalysis. The 1980s brought the addition of cognitive neuropsychology

(Mazaux & Richer, 1998). In the 1990s a shift in health care toward efficiency and reduced costs led to shorter rehabilitation periods, and rehabilitative efforts began to include the subjective experience of the patient in addition to the objective measures of functional limitations (Boake & Diller, 2005). The 1990s also saw the focus of rehabilitation treatment shift from abstract cognitive remediation and inpatient rehabilitation programs to a more ecological approach emphasizing home-based therapy focused on daily living situations and work skills (Mazaux & Richer, 1998). Twenty-first-century TBI rehabilitation and intervention is evolving as a result of the renewed attention on TBI brought about by military conflicts in Afghanistan and Iraq and advances in neuroimaging technology.

As noted earlier, the extent to which a person returns to pre-injury levels of functioning depends on many contributing factors. While rehabilitation following TBI is a regularly administered practice, there is controversy surrounding its effectiveness in the recovery process (Institute of Medicine, 2011; Munoz-Cespedes et al., 2005). This is due in part to difficulties in separating the effects of rehabilitation from those of spontaneous recovery (Brasure et al., 2012). It is also due in part from inconsistent outcomes following rehabilitation efforts. For example, a recent study by Sandhaug, Andelic, Vatne, Seiler, and Mygland (2010), found that more than one half of the individuals with moderate TBI who received specialized, inpatient rehabilitation continued to have cognitive residual disability at discharge. In addition, a large number of individuals with severe TBI continued to remain functionally impaired at discharge. While there are additional factors contributing to the controversies surrounding rehabilitation, they are beyond the intent of this chapter and therefore will not be covered.

Rehabilitation can occur in one or all of the following settings: the trauma hospital, an inpatient rehabilitation facility, or an outpatient rehabilitation facility (Kronkosky Charitable Foundation, 2012; Mazaux & Richer, 1998).

The Trauma Hospital

In addition to the medical procedures described previously under the acute stage of recovery, acute rehabilitation generally takes place during coma and arousal states. Rehabilitative interventions can include the prevention/minimization of complications (e.g., bed sores, muscle atrophy, respiratory) and sensory stimulation designed to accelerate arousal. Rehabilitation that takes place in the trauma hospital is generally referred to as *acute rehabilitation*.

Inpatient Rehabilitation Facility

Once an individual is discharged from the trauma hospital, if there is a significant need for ongoing rehabilitation, he/she will be sent to an inpatient facility. Rehabilitative interventions are typically aimed at facilitating and accelerating recovery of physical and cognitive impairments and compensating for disabilities. They can also include psychosocial adjustment (i.e., self-acceptance of impairment). Rehabilitative interventions can include physical therapy, occupational therapy, speech and language therapy, and neuropsychological therapy. Rehabilitation efforts in an inpatient facility are generally referred to as *subacute rehabilitation*.

Outpatient Rehabilitation Facility

Should an individual require continued rehabilitation support following discharge from an inpatient rehabilitation facility, these services are generally available through an outpatient rehabilitation facility. Rehabilitative interventions typically include outpatient therapy designed to help the individual gain physical, domestic, and/or social independence; reduce handicaps; and reenter the community. They also help the individual return home, obtain financial independence, return to work/school, participate in social relationships, and engage in leisure activity. If necessary, psychosocial rehabilitation continues with the emphasis on helping the individual realize that nothing will be as it was before the TBI, learning to live with permanent impairments, accepting life as it currently is, and working on coping with the reality of having sustained a life-altering injury. Rehabilitative interventions can include outpatient therapy to maintain or enhance recovery; home health services for continuation of rehabilitation in the home setting; community reentry programs to prepare for a return to independent living, work, or school; and independent living programs. Rehabilitation efforts in an outpatient rehabilitation facility are referred to as *postacute rehabilitation.*

Factors Affecting Recovery and Rehabilitation

In addition to the severity of injury, there are a number of factors that can influence an individual's recovery and/or rehabilitation following TBI. These include access to health insurance; differences in health insurance benefits; access to, and availability of, inpatient and outpatient rehabilitation services; duration and quality of rehabilitation services; availability of transportation to facilities; language barriers (Arango-Lasprilla & Kreutzer, 2010; Ashley, O'Shanick, & Kreber, 2009); pre-injury age, education, race, ethnic status, marital status, employment status, substance abuse history, and psychiatric history (High, Boake, & Lehmkuhl, 1995); the amount and type of practice during rehabilitation and the years of neurological therapy experience of rehabilitation therapists (Kimberley Samargia, Moore, Shakya, & Lang, 2010); emotional functioning of caregivers (Sander, Maestas, Sherer, Malec, & Nakase-Richardson, 2012); prejudicial attitudes of qualified health care professionals (Redpath et al., 2010); and the rehabilitation referral decision-making process of practitioners (Foster, Tilse, & Fleming, 2004).

Discussing each of these factors in depth is beyond the intent of this chapter; however, the "take-away" message is that past and present research indicates that TBI recovery and rehabilitation is a very complex process, which is influenced by more than just injury severity. Therefore, it is important that the reader recognize and incorporate this knowledge into their assessment process when examining recovery and rehabilitation outcome. Three contributing factors worth noting, however, are discussed below. If the reader is interested in the other factors they are encouraged to read the research articles noted above.

Access to Health Insurance

The costs associated with the medical care of TBI are high. Data from 2004 on the costs associated with TBI in Europe indicate the average cost was approximately equal to that of the United States (Berg, Tagliaferri, & Servadei, 2005). For comparison, 2006 data on TBI-associated hospitalization costs for treating 58,000 children under the age of 20 in the United States amounted to $2.56 billion in hospital charges alone (HCUP Kids' Inpatient Database, 2006). For a wide variety of reasons, many people worldwide do not have access to health insurance. Without adequate medical health insurance, the cost of medical treatment in the United States is well beyond the reach of the majority of people (U.S. Department of Health and Human Services, 2011). In addition, those without health insurance often have significantly shorter lengths of stay in the hospital setting (Mainous, Diaz, Everett, & Knoll, 2011). It is therefore likely that those individuals without insurance who are receiving medical treatment for TBI will also spend less time in medical settings, which in turn will most likely impact their rehabilitation and recovery.

Differences in Health Insurance Benefits

Even for those individuals fortunate enough to have health insurance, coverage will vary depending upon their insurance policy guidelines. In 2009, 74% of the 59.2 million private sector employees in the United States enrolled in employer-sponsored health insurance programs were required to meet an annual deductible, and 73% had a co-pay amount for visits (Davis, 2011). It is also not unusual for health insurance policies to require the insured to pay up to 20% of the costs of surgery and hospital stays. With the increasing high cost of medical care since the 1990s and the shift in health care at that time toward efficiency and reduced costs (Boake & Diller, 2005), it is likely these factors will impact recovery and rehabilitation of TBI.

Availability of and Access to Services

Before a person with TBI can take advantage of inpatient and outpatient services, these services must first be available. To those living in rural communities, rehabilitation services may not be available or of sufficient quality to ensure maximum benefit following TBI. In addition, even when quality services are readily available, individuals with TBI may have difficulty accessing these services. For example, if they are dependent upon caretakers (i.e., they are unable to function independently), the caretaker may not have adequate transportation or the ability to take time off of work.

Myths and Misconceptions About Recovery and Rehabilitation

Myths and misconceptions about TBI recovery abound. Myths and misconceptions have been shown to be held by the general public (Guilmette & Paglia, 2004; Ono, Ownsworth, & Walters, 2011); family members of TBI patients (Keow, Ng, & Ti, 2008; Springer, Farmer, & Bouman, 1997); elementary and secondary special education teachers, administrators, physicians and residents, nurses, nursing students, occupational therapists, speech-language therapists, recreational therapists, psychologists, and social workers (Ernst, Trice, Gilbert, & Potts, 2009; Farmer & Johnson-Gerard, 1997; Redpath et al., 2010); school psychologists (Hooper, 2006a); ethnic minorities (Pappadis, Sander, Struchen, Leung, & Smith, 2011); and school-based speech-language pathologists (Hux, Walker, & Sanger, 1996). Myths and misconceptions commonly pertain to unconsciousness, amnesia, rehabilitation, and recovery. Common false perceptions or beliefs include:

- people in a coma are aware of what is happening around them;
- constantly talking to a person in a coma will help the person come out of the coma faster;
- as soon as a person in a coma opens his/her eyes, he/she will immediately recognize and speak to others;
- people can recover from a severe TBI if they want to recover badly enough;
- people can fully recover from a severe TBI;
- having one TBI does not place a person at risk to sustain a second TBI;
- the harder you work at recovery or rehabilitation, the faster you recover;
- a person with TBI may not remember who they are or recognize other people, but he/she will be normal in every other way;
- a person with TBI won't be able to remember things in the past, but will have no problems remembering things in the present;
- if a person is irritable or has problems with anger control after TBI, it has nothing to do with the TBI;
- a lack of insight and self-awareness following a TBI is not related to the TBI;
- a second blow to the head will make people remember things they have forgotten;
- TBI can be prevented if a person is careful enough;
- it is okay to have a little brain damage because a person only uses part of their brain;
- it is easy to tell if a person has had a TBI because they look different;
- TBI won't result in changes in memory, cognition, behavior, emotion, or personality;
- most people who are knocked unconscious wake up quickly, with no lasting effects;
- once a person with TBI recovers the ability to walk, that person's brain is almost fully recovered;
- a headache caused by TBI will go away after two weeks;
- it is best to remain completely inactive after TBI;
- the main goal of TBI rehabilitation is to help with physical problems like walking;
- the best way to get the most accurate information about how well a person is recovering from TBI is to ask that person;
- a person with TBI-related impairments will have a good understanding of those impairments because they deal with them every day;
- people with TBI do not have trouble learning new things;
- once a person with TBI recognizes where they are after their injury, they will always know where they are;
- once a person with TBI feels back to normal, they have recovered;
- even though a person with TBI has severe memory problems, things can return to normal;
- TBI won't affect speech, coordination, or walking;
- in order to have TBI, you have to lose consciousness;
- people with TBI become upset and yell for no reason;
- having an x-ray is the only way to tell if someone has had a TBI;
- most people who have a severe TBI will eventually return to work; and
- TBI will affect the brains of men and women differently.

Misattribution of Causality

Myths and misconceptions about TBI, recovery, and rehabilitation occur because of ignorance, but they can also occur as a result of misattribution. *Misattribution* is when people mistakenly, or unintentionally, attribute the cause of an observable action to something that did not cause it (McClure, 2011). In the case of TBI misattribution, the TBI is discounted as an explanation (cause) for the TBI-related behavior(s) and some other cause is offered up to explain the behavior(s). An example of TBI misattribution is a parent attributing the cause of TBI-induced depression in their 15-year-old daughter to "normal adolescent moodiness." Another example is attributing a TBI-induced lack of motivation to "just being lazy." Misattribution of causality (and the subsequent myths and misconceptions about TBI) minimize the consequences of TBI, normalize observed behavior(s), lead to discriminatory behavior from others, often result in an unwillingness from others to help, make the individual with TBI (and caregivers) feel TBI-related behaviors are misunderstood, and cause others to have unrealistic hopes and strategies for recovery (McClure, 2011). Misattribution can happen as a result of peer group comparison (McClure, 2011). That is, it is a natural tendency to compare the behavior of one person to the most noticeable aspects of "normality" in others. Peer group comparison allows for this to occur.

Some Final Words About Recovery

One of the greatest difficulties in accurately recognizing the behavioral and neurocognitive effects of TBI is the typical absence of any outward manifestation of the injury, even in moderate-to-severe TBI. Neurosurgeons refer to this as the difference between the "eloquent" and "non-eloquent" regions of the brain. That is, neurosurgeons generally place all catheters, shunts and surgical probes in "non-eloquent" regions of the brain for the very reason that no major, easily discernible (meaning the child has a "normal" neurological examination) deficit results when these brain areas are used and damaged in the process. If one plots out the eloquent areas, they are less than 20% of the entire cortical surface but the only areas that truly cause immediate noticeable deficits are language and motor impairment areas and less than 7% of the brain surface is involved directly in those functions. Therefore, a child can have massive damage and appear outwardly normal with no physical stigmata of injury. As a result, many times parents and teachers will fail to see the "silent" or "invisible" injury that occurs with TBI and therefore they do not make the link, because outwardly and physically the child looks normal. Pediatricians often can make the same mistake. Therefore, if a student with TBI does not "look like he/she has been injured," that is, he/she doesn't have physical impairments that are observable to others (e.g., paralysis, scarring, or missing limbs), then the logic of Tweedledum and Tweedledee takes over and the student "must not be injured." There are also times, unfortunately, as illustrated in the case of Josiah (Case Study 6.1—Josiah; Moderate TBI; chapter 6), when parents do not keep records or even recall physician names. Further, there are also times when hospital professionals fail to properly assist in the transition process or unintentionally communicate to parents that everything will be "OK" or that "kids grow out of these things."

Further complicating the perception of recovery is that subtle or imperceptible phenomena can occur with TBI that go largely unappreciated by caregivers, through no fault of their own. Since parents live with the child with TBI, they sometimes aren't as perceptive to deficits as those who see the child less frequently—because they adapt and reset their internal reference as to the child's behavior. It is like one day seeing your son look you in the eye at 6 feet 1 inch and asking yourself "when did that happen?"—because these subtle, miniscule growth changes were imperceptible. The same phenomenon applies with behavior associated with TBI and parents do not always see it until the child experiences problems at school.

Related to this phenomenon, in the case of moderate and severe TBI, when parents bring their child home from the hospital, they are often overwhelmed, experiencing high levels of stress, and grateful their child has survived their injury. This can lead to inadvertently giving their child some leeway or slack regarding TBI-related deficits. That is, although the parents may be aware of negative changes or declines in their child's behavior, mood, or affect, they may not have the energy to address the changes, feel the child has already "suffered enough," and that addressing these behaviors would only cause the child more stress, and/or believe the changes are temporary and the child will improve as time goes on.

5 Neurological and Cognitive Consequences of TBI

Traumatic brain injury can result in neurological and/or cognitive difficulties ranging from the very subtle and difficult to observe, to the blatantly obvious and hard to overlook. In addition, such things as the nature, location, and severity of the injury; the age at the time the injury occurs; and the availability and quality of medical and rehabilitative interventions can all have an effect on how severe or debilitating these difficulties are for the individual and their families (Jantz & Coulter, 2007). When considering the onset of neurological and/or cognitive difficulties following a TBI, it is important to note that the onset may be delayed and not become apparent until a time far removed from, and apparently unrelated to, the original injury (Kiraly & Kiraly, 2007). Consequently, neurological and/or cognitive difficulties can easily be overlooked or misconstrued. With moderate and severe TBI the amount of cognitive functioning a person regains will vary and depend on the severity level and the impaired cognitive/neurological domain. However, there will be a noticeably accelerated rate of recovery during the first five months postinjury, followed by a period in which there are relatively fewer gains in cognitive functioning (Spitz, Ponsford, Rudzki, & Maller 2012).

Chapter Overview

Having a working knowledge of the nature and variability of possible neurological and cognitive consequences following TBI can help educational professionals conduct school-based assessments of students with a TBI more efficiently and better understand how these consequences can affect educational progress. It can also assist educational professionals as they develop school-based interventions. This chapter will provide a general overview of the most common neurological and cognitive consequences of TBI including:

- headaches;
- sleep-wake disturbances;
- sensory-motor difficulties;
- epileptic seizures and posttraumatic epilepsy;
- executive dysfunction and information-processing deficits;
- memory difficulties; and
- miscellaneous consequences.

Headaches

Regardless of injury severity, posttraumatic headache (PTH) is one of the most commonly reported persistent neurological symptoms following TBI. The onset of PTH usually occurs within days of the injury or shortly after awakening from coma; however, the onset can be delayed (Dikmen, Machamer, Fann, & Temkin, 2010; Formisano, Bivona, Catani, D'Ippolito, & Buzzi, 2009). Nearly three quarters of the individuals in a recent study were found to report headache symptoms during the first year following their injury and many continued to report symptoms beyond one year (Hoffman et al., 2011). If an individual continues to experience PTH more than three months after his/her injury, the headaches will fall into a category known as *chronic PTH* (Lew et al., 2006). Chronic PTH lasting more than six months following injury is generally a permanent condition and likely to become disabling to the individual. The frequency of PTH can vary and the individual may experience less than one PTH per month, one per week, several per week, or even daily (Lucas, Hoffman, Bell, Walker, & Dikmen, 2012). The frequency will also vary by type of headache (i.e., migraine, probable migraine, tension).

The *International Classification of Headache Disorders,* 2nd ed. (ICHD-2; 2004) identifies headache disorders as primary or secondary. *Primary headaches* are defined by subjective report of symptoms (e.g., type of pain, severity, duration) and are considered to have no known treatable cause. *Secondary headaches,* on the other hand, are defined by their relationship to a known cause (e.g., TBI) and consider the severity of the injury, the temporal relation of headache onset, and headache duration; however, they have no defining clinical features. PTH is typically considered to be a secondary headache; however, when a preexisting primary headache is exacerbated by TBI, it can be classified as either a primary or secondary headache. Although PTH has no defining clinical features, the primary headache criteria from the ICHD-2 can be used as a classification guide (Lucas et al., 2012). There are four major subtypes of primary headaches: *migraine; tension-type headache; cluster headache and other trigeminal autonomic cephalalgias;* and *other primary headaches.* Using ICHD-2 criteria, PTH most commonly resembles migraine or tension-type headaches (Formisano et al., 2009; Lucas et al., 2012). For specific descriptions of the primary headache criteria, the reader is directed to the International Headache Society's IDHD-2 headache classification website (http://ihs-classification.org/en/). Treatment for PTH can be pharmacological or nonpharmacological. Typical nonpharmacological treatments can include physical therapy and manipulation, anesthetic nerve blockade, biofeedback and relaxation, and behavior therapy (Lew et al., 2006).

Posttraumatic symptoms (PTS) including PTH (and others discussed below) are frequently discounted because they are established by self-report, cannot be independently verified, and often occur at higher rates when there is potential for secondary gain through litigation (Dikmen et al., 2010). This is especially true when there is a lack of obvious physical and/or neurological findings or other formal measures, as is often the case with mTBI. Regarding potential secondary gain and litigation, it is significant to note that of the estimated 1.7 million people arriving in hospital emergency departments each year with TBI (Faul et al., 2010), an exceptionally small number (approximately 400 a year) will ever reach formal litigation at the state or federal court level (Sweet & Westerveld, 2012).

Counter to intuition, PTH is not believed to be caused by direct damage to the brain itself; rather, it is believed to be due to the consequences related to injuries to the head and neck, vasculature, and meninges (Greenwood, 2002; Lucas et al., 2012). That is, PTH seems to result from such things as postinjury surgical interventions that address damage to the head, cranium, jaw, and/or neck that is sustained at the time of the injury; reactions to medication; disruptions to the vascular systems and meninges; or biochemical changes found in the brain (e.g., increased extracellular potassium). Given these combined factors, the exact etiology of PTH is unknown. PTH may be due to medical interventions, neurological issues, emotional reactions to injury-associated difficulties/circumstances, or exacerbation of preexisting conditions/dispositions (Dikmen et al., 2010). When it comes to secondary gain issues, the presence of many PTSs can be fabricated and the measures used to establish their presence (e.g., physical, neurological, and formal assessment measures) can be manipulated. Regardless of controversy or a lack of known cause, it is important to realize that PTH (and other PTSs) is frequently reported across all severity levels of TBI (even in the absence of litigation), and for many individuals PTH persists for long periods of time postinjury. Further, in the educational setting, PTH, even if it is being reported for the purpose of secondary gain, can have a detrimental effect on educational and social outcomes. PTH should not be taken lightly and should be treated as a social-emotional or psychoeducational issue.

Sleep-Wake Disturbances

The onset of new sleep-wake disturbances (SWD) is common following TBI (Baumann, Werth, Stocker, Ludwig, & Bassetti, 2007; Beaulieu-Bonneau & Morin, 2012; Mathias & Alvaro, 2012; Sundstrom et al., 2007). SWD have been found to occur in as many as one half to three quarters of individuals with TBI and include insomnia, hypersomnia (increased need for sleep within a 24-hour period), sleep apnea, excessive daytime sleepiness, and fatigue. In addition, SWD have the potential to become chronic (lasting for years) and significantly affect TBI rehabilitation, recovery, and outcome. The resulting loss of vitality that often accompanies SWD has been found to significantly affect quality of life and social functioning and may also cause, or exacerbate, a variety of coexisting conditions including depression, anxiety, irritability, fatigue, cognitive deficits, pain, and functional impairment. Excessive daytime sleepiness, fatigue, and hypersomnia are among the most commonly reported long-term SWD.

Fatigue can be reported several years after sustaining a TBI and is frequently cited as being one of the most distressing SWD due to its negative impact on quality of life. Although there are many definitions of fatigue, it can be defined as a "failure to initiate or sustain attentional tasks ('mental fatigue') and physical activities ('physical fatigue') requiring self-motivation" (Chaudhuri & Behan, 2000, as cited in Beaulieu-Bonneau & Morin, 2012, p. 598). Fatigue differs from sleepiness in that sleepiness refers to the inability to maintain a desired level of alertness or wakefulness during the daytime (American Academy of Sleep Medicine, 2005). Fatigue is common across all severity levels of TBI, is the most reported symptom one year postinjury, and is the second most reported symptom at one month postinjury (Beaulieu-Bonneau & Morin, 2012; Masson et al., 1996; van der Naalt, van Zomeren, Sluiter, & Minderhoud, 1999). Fatigue may be a direct manifestation of hypothalamic-pituitary damage arising from TBI (Zaben, El Ghoul, & Belli, 2013).

Sensory-Motor Difficulties

Unless sensory-motor difficulties (SMD) are visibly apparent (e.g., paralysis), they may go undetected at the time of discharge from the hospital. They may also go unevaluated in the educational setting, despite having a significant impact on a child's academic performance (Davis & Dean, 2010). SMD can include vision difficulties, motor difficulties, and difficulties with balance and dizziness. Common deficits that affect vision include, but are not limited to, cranial nerve injuries that result in diplopia (double vision); difficulty controlling the muscles that move the eyes when finding, identifying, and tracking things in the environment or on printed material, which may also be affected by upper brainstem injury (Heitger et al., 2009); difficulties controlling the muscles of the eyes used to focus the field of vision when changing from near vision to far vision and far vision to near vision; difficulty with peripheral vision; and sensitivity to light (Niemeier, 2010). Common motor difficulties include, but are not limited to, fine motor hand control (motor skills, speed, coordination); motor weakness; difficulties with gross motor speed, balance, strength, coordination, and gait; and partial or full paralysis (Jang, 2009; Kuhtz-Buschbeck et al., 2003). Difficulties with balance and dizziness are commonly reported and can range from lightheadedness to incapacitating vertigo, and include eye-head dyscoordination, and imbalance with stance and gait (Childs, 2010; Gottshall, 2011; Gottshall, Drake, Gray, McDonald, & Hoffer, 2003).

Epileptic Seizures and Posttraumatic Epilepsy

To understand TBI-related epileptic seizures and posttraumatic epilepsy, it is helpful to understand seizure nomenclature frequently used in TBI research on posttraumatic seizures. There is no agreed upon definition of what constitutes an epileptic seizure, immediate seizure, early seizure, late seizure, posttraumatic epilepsy, or epilepsy. For the purpose of this book these will be defined as follows: an *epileptic seizure* is a sudden, transient behavioral change brought on by abnormal, excessive electrical discharge in the brain. It is caused by a temporary synchronization of neuronal activity, which occurs for unknown reasons (Lezak et al., 2012). An *immediate seizure* is an epileptic seizure that occurs within the first 24 hours following injury (Lowenstein, 2009). An *early seizure* is a seizure that occurs within the first week after TBI and a *late seizure* (LS) is a seizure that occurs one or more weeks after TBI (Hesdorffer, Benn, Cascino, & Hauser, 2009; Lowenstein, 2009). *Epilepsy* is a condition wherein an individual has an enduring predisposition for recurrent epileptic seizures (Christensen, 2012) and *posttraumatic epilepsy* is an enduring predisposition for recurrent epileptic seizures that can occur at any time postinjury (Chen, Ruff, Eavey, & Wasterlain, 2009).

Immediate and early epileptic seizures most frequently occur following a severe TBI; however, they also are known to occur following mild or moderate TBI (Vespa et al., 2010). In addition, the more severe the TBI, the more likely epileptic seizures will develop into posttraumatic epilepsy (Kharatishvili & Pitkanen, 2010). It is important to note, however, that even with mTBI, there appears to be a continued long-term risk for the development of posttraumatic epilepsy beyond 10 years postinjury (Christensen, 2012). Further, there appears to be an elevated risk for the development of epileptic seizures in children who were 16 or older at the time of their injury (Christensen, 2012). Depressed skull fractures, intracerebral hematomas, and subdural hematomas are considered to be risk factors for immediate and early seizures, which are in turn risk factors for the later development of epilepsy, and the risk of recurrent late seizures appears to increase with injury severity (Christensen, 2012).

Executive Dysfunction and Information-Processing Deficits

Humans are naturally ambulatory, forward-moving beings. As a result, many TBIs involve striking the front of the head; therefore, injuries to the frontal lobes are common. Because the frontal lobes are involved with executive functioning (EF), TBI-related injuries to the frontal lobes frequently result in disruption of EF. Although there are many different definitions of EF, it can be defined as an individual's "ability to reason, problem-solve, set goals, prioritize, self-monitor, self-correct, self-regulate, initiate or inhibit response behavior, organize and plan, and effectively execute purposeful behavior" (Jantz & Coulter, 2007, p. 88). Relatedly, EF requires information processing by way of selective attention to stimuli and cognitive flexibility; both of these involve the frontal lobes.

Complicating the effects of damage to the frontal lobes, and the subsequent effects on EF, is the issue of normal brain development ("maturation"). In neurological terms, there are periods of time during which there are changes in the gray matter and periods in which there are changes in the white matter (Blakemore & Choudhury, 2006). Periods of gray matter change involve a proliferation in the production of synapses, called *synaptogenesis,* followed by periods of pruning and reabsorption. During the several months following birth, the brain overproduces vast numbers of synapses in the sensory regions of the brain that allows for the development of new connections between neurons in the gray matter of the brain. This period is followed by a pruning away and reabsorption of those neurons that are not frequently utilized (stimulated). At the onset of puberty there is another synaptogenesis, this time occurring in the prefrontal cortex (PFC). Gradual pruning and reorganization of synaptic connections next begins shortly after puberty and continues into adolescence. The purpose of synaptic pruning is to fine-tune functional networks of brain tissue regions which make the remaining connections more efficient. In addition to the synaptogenesis and pruning processes, there is change in the white matter of the brain (Figure 5.1). This consists of increased myelination of the neuron axons which results in an increased efficiency in the communication speed of neurons. A steady increase of myelination in the frontal (and parietal) lobes occurs during adolescence. When the neurons and axons in a brain region have completed the synaptogenesis/pruning and myelination processes, the region is said to have "matured." Different brain regions mature at different times, and the last brain region to mature is the PFC, which does not fully mature until early adulthood (Bunge & Zelazo, 2006; Gogtay et al., 2004). The PFC, which is located directly behind the forehead, is known, among other things, to play a role in the retrieval of rules that govern contextual behavior.

The cognitive skills involved in EF are correlated with normal brain development and are on a developmental continuum (Catroppa, Anderson, & Muscara, 2009). The development of EF skills can be divided into three sequential stages beginning in early childhood and ending in mid-adolescence or early adulthood: "emerging (early stage of acquisition and not yet functional), developing (capacity is partially acquired but

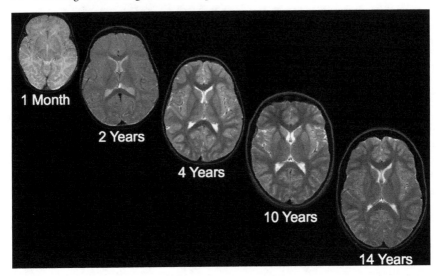

Figure 5.1 Magnetic resonance images of five young, healthy individuals, age 1 month to
14 years. Notable changes in morphology include enlargement of intracranial and ventricular
volume and change in conspicuity of tissue types on proton density images. For example,
before age 1 year, white matter is generally unmyelinated and appears brighter than gray matter
because of the higher water content in unmyelinated white matter compared with myelinated
white matter or gray matter. After 1 year of age, myelination proceeds, causing myelinated white
matter, with its high lipid content, to appear darker than gray matter, which has higher water
concentration than myelinated white matter.

With kind permission from Springer Science+Business Media: Sullivan, E.V. (2010). Development of brain
structures, connections, and functions. *Neuropsychology Review, 20,* 325–326, Figure 1. Images were produced
courtesy of Adolf Pfefferbaum, M.D., Director of the Neuroscience Program, SRI International and Professor
Emeritus, Stanford University School of Medicine.

not fully functional), and established (ability fully mature)" (Anderson, 2002, p. 76). It
is important to remember that TBI-induced EF dysfunction and related delays in the
ability to quickly and efficiently process information, attend to stimuli, and engage in
cognitive flexibility will be significantly related to age, stage of brain maturation, and
stage of EF skill development at the time of the TBI. In addition, although some EF dysfunction and frontal lobe information-processing deficits may be noticeable in the early
stages of recovery, they may not be apparent until much later when increased demands
on EF occur.

Memory Difficulties

As explained in chapter 2, the manner in which the temporal and frontal lobes are situated within the cranial vault, and the rough surface of the anterior and middle cranial
fossae, place the temporal and frontal lobes at high risk for significant injury during TBI,
especially with high-speed impact injuries (Bigler, 2007). Because various temporal and
frontal lobe structures are involved in memory, a TBI involving damage to the temporal
and/or frontal lobes frequently results in memory deficits. Memory deficits typically
recover slower than other cognitive deficits; slowly improving over the course of the

first one or two years postinjury. However, they can still persist up to 10 years postinjury (Vakil, 2005).

The complexities of memory, and how memory works, are beyond the intent and purpose of this book and the reader is directed to Lezak et al. (2012), for an in-depth discussion. Regarding TBI, however, it is important to understand that from a clinical perspective there are two types of memory that may be affected by TBI: declarative and nondeclarative. *Declarative (or explicit) memory* is what most people are referring to when they think of "memory" (Lezak et al., 2012), and it involves the conscious and effortful recall of facts and events. It also involves the processes related to the acquisition, storage, and retrieval of immediate and distant facts and events (Kern, Hartzell, Izaguirre, & Hamilton, 2010). These processes include remote, working, and semantic memory and learning and retention of verbal information. *Nondeclarative (or implicit) memory* is conveyed through the performance of a task rather than through conscious recollection, and it happens in the comparative absence of directed attention (Kern et al., 2010). An example of an implicit memory task is speaking a language. That is, an individual is able to speak a language without consciously having to remember the rules of sentence structure in order to do so (Ettlinger, Margulis, & Wong, 2011). Implicit memory develops very quickly from birth to approximately age 5 with little or no change during late childhood. Explicit memory quickly develops from approximately age 6 through 12; maturing in adolescence (Lah, Epps, Levick, & Parry, 2011). Given the developmental nature of implicit and explicit memory, it is likely that sustaining a TBI during these developmental periods will negatively affect memory systems. For example, a child who sustains a TBI (that does not affect motor areas of the brain) at age 9 may experience no difficulties with tasks requiring the writing of letters (implicit memory), but may experience ongoing difficulties retaining information that is to be written about (explicit memory). That is, TBI-induced dysfunction in the systems involved in working memory may prevent the child from being able to retain and later recall presented facts. On the other hand, a child who sustains a TBI at age 4 may have difficulty developing appropriate conversational speech prosody (failing to unconsciously recall the patterns of stress and intonation governing speech—an implicit memory task) due to TBI-induced disruptions in brain systems related to implicit memory functioning.

Miscellaneous Consequences

There are a number of other TBI-induced neurological and cognitive symptoms that have been reported as much as one year postinjury, at all levels of TBI severity, with the majority of reports involving multiple symptom reporting (Dikmen et al., 2010). These symptoms include difficulties with light (photophobia) and sound sensitivity (hyperacusis), concentration, irritability, temper control, dizziness, and blurred vision. Students who have sustained a TBI often have an impaired awareness of their neurological or cognitive deficits (anosognosia), especially when they have sustained a moderate or severe TBI (Evans, Sherer, Nick, Nakase-Richardson, & Yablon, 2005). Although the exact reason for anosognosia is poorly understood, it has been linked to the amount of damaged brain tissue rather than the specific location of the damage. Anosognosia improves over time, especially in the behavioral and affective domains, although it appears that a student who has sustained a TBI will typically continue to perceive his/her level of functioning to be much higher than do others.

6 Emotional, Behavioral, and Social Consequences of TBI

Emotional, behavioral, and social difficulties following TBI are common, especially with moderate and severe TBI (Gouick & Gentleman, 2004; Gould, Ponsford, Johnston, & Schonberger, 2011; Max et al., 2012; Rapoport, 2012; Williams & Wood, 2010). Often times these difficulties are interrelated. For example, neurologically-based damage to neurons of the brain structures involved in cognitive executive functioning can result in a student having a heightened tendency toward emotional outbursts (a behavioral difficulty). This, in turn, can lead to avoidance by peers (a social interaction difficulty) and depression in the student (an emotional difficulty). TBI-induced emotional and/or behavioral difficulties can be new to the individual, as is the case when a student with no past history of clinically significant depression experiences a major depressive episode after sustaining a TBI, or they can exacerbate preexisting difficulties, as is the case when a student with preexisting impulse control difficulties becomes significantly more impulsive following damage to the frontal lobes. Although emotional and behavioral difficulties following TBI are neurologically and/or cognitively based, in order to show how they can influence each other, as well as influence social interaction, they are being discussed in this chapter, rather than in chapter 4.

As noted in chapter 2, the temporal and frontal lobes are particularly susceptible to damage during inertial force—acceleration/deceleration injuries. Contained within the temporal lobe are the amygdala and hippocampal formation, parts of the limbic system, which also includes the hypothalamus, the cingulate gyrus, and other brain structures. Along with the frontal lobes, the limbic structures are involved in the monitoring and regulation of emotion and the physiological, behavioral, and psychological responses that accompany emotion. In addition, the frontal lobes are also involved in reasoning, planning, parts of speech, disinhibition, and problem solving, all of which have a direct effect on emotions. Damage to the temporal or frontal lobes, or their interconnecting pathways, can result in inefficient processing or interpretation of information, which in turn can lead to new emotional difficulties or the exacerbation of existing difficulties.

Chapter Overview

Understanding TBI-induced emotional and behavioral changes and their relationship to social difficulties can be helpful when developing appropriate academic interventions. This chapter will discuss:

- emotional consequences;
- behavioral consequences;
- social consequences;
- educational assessment and intervention; and
- general considerations.

Emotional Consequences

Emotional difficulties following a TBI can appear early on as a result of direct primary damage or their onset can be delayed—the result of secondary damage (e.g., apoptosis). Common emotional difficulties include, but are not limited to, the following:

Depression

It is well known that in non-TBI populations, as a student's age increases, so does the risk that he/she will experience clinically significant levels of depression. The same relationship has been found with depression onset after TBI (Max et al., 2012). That is, the older the student is at the time of the TBI, the higher the risk the student will develop clinically significant levels of depression. Risk for the onset of major depression does not appear to be related to the initial severity level of the TBI; however, it does appear to be associated with injury location (e.g., left temporal pole lesions). In addition, there appears to be a relationship between the onset of depression and family discord, the amount of available social support, the lack of adequate rehabilitation treatment, and socioeconomic status (Rapoport, 2012). That is, not only can depression be directly related to physical damage to the brain, it can also be the result of ecological changes that may result from TBI (e.g., changes in friendships, family relationships, career goals, participation on sports teams). Depression is the most common psychiatric complaint following TBI, and post-TBI depression can be influenced by previous psychiatric disorders, may negatively impact rehabilitation efforts, and may persist for many years. TBI-induced depression symptoms are the same as non-TBI-induced depression and can include depressed mood; sadness; irritability; angry outbursts; loss of interest in otherwise pleasurable activities; change in diet and accompanying weight gain/loss; sleep disturbance; psychomotor agitation/retardation; withdrawal; fatigue; loss of energy; difficulties with concentration/attention; feelings of worthlessness; feelings of inappropriate guilt; memory disturbances; difficulties with decision-making and/or thoughts of death or suicidal ideation. If there is a significant delay in the onset of depression, it can easily be misattributed to other causes instead of the TBI.

Anger/Irritability

Difficulty with anger and/or irritability is common following all severity levels of TBI and can worsen over time. In addition, there are many things that can cause difficulty with anger and/or irritability following TBI, including but not limited to, preexisting or new mental health issues, new levels of dependency on others, and damage to the areas of the brain involved in executive functioning (Hart, Vaccaro, Hays, & Maiuro, 2012).

If anger and/or irritability is the result of executive functioning deficits, a student will likely have difficulty controlling his/her temper or managing frustration. In addition, because deficits in executive function may lead to deficits in self-awareness, a student may not be aware that he/she is experiencing difficulties with anger and/or irritability. Or, conversely, he/she may be very aware of difficulties with anger and/or irritability, but will be unable to deescalate, recognize cause and effect relationships, or understand the consequences of their outbursts.

Apathy

The onset of apathy following TBI is generally associated with damage to the frontal lobes and/or limbic system (Lane-Brown & Tate, 2011). As a result, apathy can present as any of the following: indifference, decreased intensity of emotional expression, a reduction in speech output, a decrease in self-initiated behavior, a lack of persistence, decrease in strength or vigor, cognitive rigidity, a decrease in productivity, slowed thinking, or reduced physical movement. A student with TBI-induced apathy may be unconcerned about his/her own apathy.

Posttraumatic Stress Disorder (PTSD)

While there is little research on the relationship between PTSD symptoms and children and adolescents with TBI, the most current research suggests that children and adolescents are capable of experiencing symptoms of PTSD (reexperiencing symptoms, avoidance symptoms, or hyperarousal symptoms) for up to a year after the injury, despite having amnesia for the event and/or a loss of consciousness at the time of the TBI (Hajek et al., 2010). In addition, those children with a severe TBI report more PTSD symptoms than do those with moderate or mTBI. Although, children will rarely meet full diagnostic criteria for PTSD, it is believed by some that this is mainly due to developmental factors limiting children's verbal ability to describe experiences (Iselin, Le Brocque, Kenardy, Anderson, & McKinlay, 2010). Complicating the diagnosis when applied to TBI is the difficulty of differentiating TBI-related organic memory loss from dissociative amnesia.

Anxiety Disorders

Anxiety disorder symptoms in children have been reported following all severity levels of TBI and include obsessive-compulsive behavior, separation anxiety, and simple phobias (Karver et al., 2012; Max et al., 2011). In addition, the onset of new anxiety symptoms following TBI has been associated with the age at the time of injury, concurrent affective dysregulation, and injury location. That is, all of the following contribute to increase the risk of new onset anxiety: the younger the age at the time of injury; the presence of separation anxiety, simple phobia, adjustment disorder with anxious mood, generalized anxiety disorder, social phobia, or panic disorder; the new onset of depression or the presence of personality change due to TBI; and damage to the superior frontal gyrus or frontal white matter (Max et al., 2011).

Behavioral Consequences

Behavioral difficulties are common following TBI and can persist for years (Karver et al., 2012). In addition, age at the time of injury and TBI severity can influence the duration and nature of behavioral difficulties (Benedictus, Spikman, & van der Naalt, 2010). In general, it appears that the younger the age at time of injury and the more severe the TBI, the worse the behavioral difficulties will be and the longer they will persist. Behavioral difficulties can be related to damage to brain structures (e.g., frontal lobes) or they can be associated with TBI-induced emotional difficulties (e.g., impatience with others due to the effects of depression). Common behavioral difficulties include, but are not limited to, the following:

Executive Functioning Difficulties

Executive functions are a set of higher order skills that enable a person to engage in goal-directed behavior based on the ability to regulate attention, disinhibit impulses, set goals, plan future behavior, problem solve, engage in abstract reasoning, and engage in mental flexibility (Ganesalingam et al., 2011). Although there is ongoing debate as to the exact role of the frontal and prefrontal cortex in the regulation of executive functioning, what is not debated is that they are involved (Alvarez & Emory, 2006) and they are highly susceptible to injury. If TBI causes damage to the areas of the frontal/prefrontal cortex, to underlying connected areas (e.g., head of the caudate nucleus, nucleus accumbens, ventromedial caudate nucleus), or to white matter connective tracts, disruptions in executive function can occur, resulting in a variety of behavioral difficulties. Age-related effects are likely related to the degree of brain maturation (i.e., the frontal lobes do not mature until late adolescence), differing stages of development (e.g., fewer established skills), and a greater vulnerability of a younger brain to diffuse brain injury (Blakemore & Choudhury, 2006; Ganesalingam et al., 2011). Executive function difficulties can result in, but not be limited to, inconsistent behaviors (e.g., impulsive acts/responses), incongruent emotional outbursts (e.g., laughing when someone gets hurt), difficulties with completing complex or multistep tasks (e.g., completing an independent classroom work assignment, putting it into a folder, putting your name and the date on the folder, placing the folder into a works sample portfolio, and placing a checkmark in the "completed" box next to the assignment on a list of assignments), poor planning (e.g., not leaving enough time to complete a task), poor follow-through (e.g., partial task completion), poor problem solving (e.g., conflict with others), rigid thinking (e.g., failing to see other viewpoints), and impaired communication.

Limbic System Difficulties

The limbic system, as was noted earlier, includes the cingulate gyrus located just above the corpus callosum. The cingulate gyrus has extensive white matter connectivity with the prefrontal cortex and the rest of the limbic structures and is involved in many facets of cognition and emotion, including processing information, detecting cognitive conflict, and increasing attentional resources needed to resolve cognitive conflict (Wilde et al., 2010). Because the limbic system structures are involved in motivation, emotions, memory, and biological drives, and because they are interconnected with the frontal lobes, damage to any of these structures can result in dysfunctional or inappropriate behavior related to these areas. Some examples are: acting impulsively in response to emotions/urges (e.g., inappropriate sexual contact, inappropriate responses/comments); sexual promiscuity; unprovoked aggressive behavior; use of drugs or alcohol; reckless or dangerous behavior; withdrawal or isolation; noncompliance; over- or under-reaction to situations; engaging in behaviors without consideration for cause and effect relationships (e.g., picking a fight with dangerous others); and conflict with authority.

Pragmatic Skills Deficits

Further complicating behavioral difficulties is the fact that impaired communication skills are common following TBI, including difficulty with motor speech, difficulty with verbal fluency (e.g., word-finding difficulties), impaired attention, poor response inhibition, excessive distractibility, rigid thinking, impaired memory, and impaired pragmatic skills (Douglas, 2010). Pragmatic skills have to do with those skills that allow an individual to effectively communicate with others by using conversational context as a guide. Pragmatic skills deficits can occur as a result of damage to parts of the brain that are responsible for executive functioning. Possible TBI-related pragmatic impairments include: difficulty providing requested information to listeners; difficulty retaining logical structure and coherence in conversation; difficulty picking up on implied meanings in conversations; choosing inappropriate conversational topics/content; introducing new topics at the wrong time; engaging in tangentiality; and diminished content quality in conversation (Douglas, 2010).

Emotion Recognition Difficulties

Difficulty with spontaneously recognizing facial affect is often reported following a moderate TBI (Babbage et al., 2011). If a student with TBI is not able to spontaneously recognize the facial affect of others, it is likely that they will not respond appropriately. For example, if a student with TBI were unable to recognize from the facial cues of a peer that her comment offended the peer, she would not engage in the socially appropriate convention of apologizing to the student. Another example would be if a student with TBI were unable to recognize from the facial cues of a peer that the peer was angry and had the intention of engaging in a fist fight, he would not then be able to preemptively remove himself from harm's way or otherwise defend himself effectively.

Social Consequences

Like any student with emotional and behavioral difficulties, students with TBI-induced emotional and behavioral difficulties frequently encounter problems with social interaction. For example, if peers have difficulty following and making sense out of what a student with TBI is saying, they may make fun of the student, avoid the student, or ignore the student. On the other hand if a student with TBI is unable to pick up subtleties or implied meanings during conversations with his/her peer group, he/she may appear disinterested in the conversation of others or avoid further social interactions with others.

Often, the failure to associate emotional and behavioral difficulties with TBI can result in differential social treatment from peers, family members, and educational professionals (e.g., teasing, enabling of deficit behaviors, inappropriate educational disciplinary actions). While sustaining a TBI does not absolve a student from the consequences of his/her actions, it does provide context for the application of appropriate consequences and interventions. For example, recognizing that a 10th-grade student's emotional overreaction to incidental contact in the hallway during a class change (i.e., being bumped and punching the student who bumped him) is the result of TBI does not excuse the student from disciplinary consequences. It does, however, remind those involved in the disciplinary consequences that the student's behavior cannot be attributed to "normal adolescent moodiness" and that there is a need to implement an intervention program designed to help the student work on controlling his emotions, following/remembering school rules, and learning to read the intent of others (i.e., theory of mind).

The emotional and behavioral difficulties of students with TBI can be socially challenging because often they are ongoing and extreme. Perhaps the greatest challenge, however, occurs when there is no outward physical sign(s) that the student has sustained a TBI. In the absence of physical reminders, it becomes easy to disassociate the emotional or behavioral difficulties from their cause. When this happens, it is an easy next step to assume, or believe, the difficulties are within the control of the student. If this happens, it becomes difficult not to personalize negative interactions and act accordingly. That is, attempt to "stamp out" bad behavior (punish), rather than "stamp in the good" behavior (help improve/assist), or to avoid the problem altogether by withdrawing social interactions and supports.

Educational Assessment and Intervention

The assessment of emotional, behavioral, and/or social difficulties of a student with TBI in the educational setting are best addressed across multiple settings using multiple methods and multiple sources (see chapter 10 for a school-based problem-solving framework). When assessing the emotional, behavioral, and social functioning of a student with TBI it is important to consider the following:

Seek Information From Nontraditional Informants

Many times, students with TBI will respond differently to environmental stimuli, which in turn may exacerbate or ease emotional, behavioral, or social difficulties. For example, in a less structured, more chaotic environment (e.g., hallways, playground, lunchroom) a student with TBI may not be able to tolerate the increase in noise and activity levels. On the other hand, the open space of the playground may provide him or her with much sought after relief from the cognitive demands of the classroom environment. Often times, due to their constant presence and typically nonauthoritative demeanor, adults working within a school setting can become "invisible" to students. That is, students forget they are nearby and tend to act more like themselves. When this happens these individuals can become a valuable source of information about a student's functioning outside of the constraints of the classroom and their input should be obtained as part of the overall assessment process. These individuals include, but are not limited to, adult hall monitors, custodial staff, paraprofessionals, lunchroom workers, playground supervisors, and attendance secretaries.

Assess the Difficulties as Being Secondary to the TBI

Regardless of whether or not the observed emotional, behavioral, or social difficulties are new difficulties or exacerbated ones, it is important to keep the assessment focus on the TBI. By doing so, the individuals involved in the assessment process will avoid "blaming the student" or mislabeling the student as being "significantly emotionally disturbed" (a handicapping condition under the IDEIA 04). It will also help keep the assessment process focused on how the TBI has changed the student's behavior and what level of control the student has over the difficulties.

Use Strengths-Based Assessment

It is helpful for assessment teams to focus their assessment on determining what a student's emotional, behavioral, and social strengths are, and how these can be utilized to help compensate for any deficits the student might be experiencing. For example, a student's strength in written language could be used to overcome verbal word-finding deficits. Focusing on strengths provides valuable diagnostic information on what is successful, which can be used to help with what is not working well.

Seek Parental Input

When the focus of TBI assessment is on the educational manifestation of emotional, behavioral, or social difficulties, parents are unfortunately often overlooked as a source of information. Not only can parents provide assessment information on past school-based functioning, they can also provide information on how atypical the student's educational difficulties are from past functioning under similar circumstances.

Incorporate Medical Input

Medical (e.g., neurologists, physicians) and mental health professionals (e.g., neuropsychologists, psychologists) can provide school-based assessment teams with information on the nature of, and extent to which, a student's TBI is contributing to his/her difficulties in the educational setting. Discharge summaries and radiologist's neuroimaging reports can also be of value in the assessment process.

Educational Interventions

Educational interventions for the emotional, behavioral, and social difficulties of students with TBI are based on the same evidence-based practice approaches as for any other child with similar difficulties. However, these interventions are best developed within the context of the limitations and influences of the student's TBI. More information on school-based social, emotional, and behavioral interventions can be found in chapter 12.

General Considerations

The manifestation of interrelated emotional, behavioral, and social difficulties following TBI should always be considered within the context of development and the severity of the injury. For example, consider the following case of Josiah:

Case Study 6.1—Josiah; Moderate TBI

While traveling with his parents to visit relatives who lived outside his home state, two-year-old Josiah fell from the top of a playground slide to the ground below during a lunch stop in a park. As he fell, he struck his head just above the left ear on the edge of a concrete retaining wall. He was knocked unconscious at the scene and remained unconscious at the hospital emergency department for an additional three hours. He was discharged from the hospital four days later and the family continued to their destination. Because of his young age, posttraumatic amnesia could not be evaluated. Abnormalities on neuroimaging included damage in a region known as Wernicke's area and a small linear fracture. Although his physical functioning and language skills were diminished immediately after the injury, Josiah's parents were thrilled at his improvement over the next few months and within a year his doctors had declared that he was "fully recovered" from his injury.

When Josiah was 6-years-old, the family moved to another state and enrolled him in the first grade. That year, he exhibited significant behavior problems in the classroom (i.e., difficulty transitioning to new activities, frustration with himself and his classmates). He had learned his ABC's with ease as a preschooler, but now his emerging reading skills were stalled; he had difficulty with phonemic awareness and remembering sight words (neurological processes known to be associated with Wernicke's area).

Josiah was referred to the school's special education multidisciplinary team because of his significant behavior problems and to assess for the presence of a learning disability. Up to this point, the parents had not been asked about a history of head injury, and because Josiah appeared to have fully recovered from his TBI his parents never thought to mention his fall at age 2. During the special education evaluation, the school psychologist reviewed Josiah's school enrollment health file and noticed his parents had endorsed the item "Has a history of head injury." In consequence, the school psychologist asked the parents for a release of information in order to obtain a copy of Josiah's medical records. Unfortunately, his parents had not retained a copy of Josiah's medical records and they could not recall the name of the physicians who treated him or the hospital where he received his immediate care.

Josiah is a first-grade student who sustained a moderate TBI at age 2 affecting Wernicke's area. While he was able to successfully learn the alphabet in preschool, he is now stalled in acquiring reading skills as a result of difficulty with phonemic awareness and remembering sight words. Even if Josiah's brain is able to "rewire" by recruiting other brain networks to aid in the acquisition of the deficit skills, he will always struggle with reading because of the irreparable damage to Wernicke's area. Furthermore, in later years when educational demands begin to require the involvement of the "recruited" brain areas, it is very likely that these areas will not have the required resources available, and those skills will be performed less efficiently. In addition, as Josiah continues to experience educational difficulties, he will begin to fall behind his peers and be at increased risk for emotional and social difficulties.

Many times, as noted in chapter 4, students with TBI can appear to "look" normal, despite significant underlying damage. When this happens it is easy for parents, educators, and peers to assume that TBI-related emotional, behavioral, or social difficulties are either volitional or developmentally related. That is, moodiness can be misattributed to "going through a normal adolescence stage," socially inappropriate comments can be attributed to "just being an immature jerk," and educational failure can be attributed to being "lazy" or having a "learning disability."

When TBI occurs at an early age, especially in the case of moderate and severe TBI, it is not unusual for parents and teachers to "grow into" the student's behavioral, emotional, or social difficulties. That is, as the child recovers and the immediate difficulties are noted to improve or stabilize, delayed onset difficulties (e.g., depression) are less likely to be connected to the TBI and more likely to go unnoticed, because they have developed slowly over time.

7   Academic Consequences of TBI

TBI-caused neurological, cognitive, emotional, behavioral, and social consequences have the potential to significantly affect a student's academic performance in a negative way, regardless of the TBI severity level. While short-term consequences of concussion may only temporarily affect educational performance, more enduring consequences from a more severe mTBI and moderate or severe TBI can lead to significant academic difficulties. Regardless of the severity level, students with TBI are often unable to keep up with the rigorous demands of the academic environment as they adapt to, compensate for, and/or struggle with short-term and/or long-term TBI consequences. However, for a period of time following a moderate or severe TBI, some students may be able to perform reasonably well by relying on, or utilizing, knowledge and skills acquired before the TBI. When this happens, these students can appear to make adequate educational progress, when in fact they are learning at a significantly impaired rate. In these cases, the delay in the acquisition of new material may not become evident until long after the TBI, and the connection between injury and performance can be lost.

Compared to the majority of their peers, students returning to the school setting following TBI are often at a significant and immediate disadvantage due to the consequences of their TBI. For example, some students with moderate or severe TBI will only attend school on a part-time basis, or require special support upon their return to school. Depending on the nature of their TBI, academic consequences for students with TBI can include, but not be limited to, difficulties with the acquisition of new information; retrieval of previously learned information; integration of new information with previously learned information; short- and long-term memory; speed of information processing; attention; psychomotor skills; and/or executive functions. Academic consequences can also include difficulties with receptive and expressive language, reading accuracy, reading comprehension, spelling, and arithmetic. In other words, the consequences of a student's TBI can affect all subject areas and every component and neurological process involved in learning.

Chapter Overview

This chapter will discuss the possible academic consequences of TBI within the context of

- demands of the academic setting;
- interpersonal relationships;

- brain development;
- pre-injury knowledge and skills;
- concussion;
- pre-injury learning disabilities;
- age at injury; and
- recovery.

Demands of the Academic Setting

Daily life in a public school typically follows a consistent, often regimented, pattern of activities. Prior to the start of the official school day, students engage in a variety of interpersonal interactions with peers, usually outdoors or in common areas inside the building (e.g., hallways). Often these interactions are supervised, thereby providing opportunity for students to engage in interpersonal interactions with adult authority figures (e.g., teachers, principals, staff members). Once the school bell signals the start of the day, students transition from casual play and socialization to organized instructional activities and more formal social interaction. As they enter school buildings, the rules, norms, and social standards of the educational environment begin to place conformity demands on students—rules must be followed, authority must be respected, and individual behavior must be controlled and managed. In elementary schools, students are expected to hang outdoor clothing on assigned wall hooks; make their way to assigned seats; and sit quietly, awaiting the start of class. In secondary schools, students are expected to deposit outdoor clothing in lockers; gather together the day's educational materials; part ways with peers; arrive in classrooms within a specified few minutes' time; sit in assigned seats; and begin organizing themselves for the day's first educational activities. As class begins, at both the elementary and secondary level, a universal sequence of pedagogy ensues: review previously learned information, introduce new knowledge/concepts/skills, and provide opportunity for student practice under the ongoing supervision of the classroom teacher.

Academic success in this dynamic school environment requires that a student have a variety of intact, well-functioning, cognitive, communicative, neurological, and psychosocial skills and abilities. As noted in previous chapters, neurological consequences, cognitive difficulties, and/or emotional, behavioral, and social problems are common following TBI. Students with TBI who are unable to integrate, retain, and/or retrieve presented and learned information; pay attention to instruction, focus, and/or concentrate in class; or plan, organize, and follow through on academic tasks and homework assignments (all cognitive abilities) will, over time, begin to experience significant academic declines. Students with TBI who are experiencing receptive and expressive language difficulties (communicative abilities), visual-spatial difficulties, visual-motor difficulties, and/or fine-motor coordination difficulties (neurological abilities) will not be able to ask for clarification, readily receive and/or understand new information, demonstrate accurate levels of competency, or proficiently utilize educational manipulatives. Those students with TBI who have difficulty engaging in ongoing multiple interactions with principals, teachers, and peers—all of whom will demand adequate and appropriate emotional and behavioral self-control (psychosocial abilities)—will experience interpersonal difficulties that may ultimately interfere with their academic success.

Interpersonal Relationships

In part, academic success is related to the quality of a student's interpersonal relationships with peers/peer groups, teachers, and other important individuals (e.g., bus drivers, playground supervisors, hall monitors). Positive, wholesome interpersonal relationships not only have a direct effect on a student's motivation to learn, but they also help to create an all-around atmosphere conducive to learning. For example, if a student's relationship with others is positive, he/she will likely be eager to attend school, engage in group learning activities, approach teachers and others for help, and view the educational setting and process as a rewarding experience. The student will also be able to devote appropriate levels of attention, concentration, and focus to classroom learning tasks. If, on the other hand, a student's interactions with others are negative, strained, or filled with conflict, the student can easily become preoccupied with thinking about the damaged relationships—rather than thinking about what is being presented in the classroom. The student may also fail to seek help from those involved, or in the worst case scenario, avoid attending school.

Research has shown that TBI can cause significant impairments in emotion recognition, understanding the intentions of others, and cognitive flexibility up to one year postinjury (Dennis et al., 2013; Milders, Ietswaart, Crawford, & Currie, 2008). If students with TBI are experiencing any of these difficulties there can be significant ramifications as they interact with peers, teachers, and administrators; navigate crowded hallways; and/or engage in social problem solving. In addition, TBI-induced emotional consequences (e.g., poor emotional regulation, angry outbursts/irritability, mood lability, depression, anxiety, apathy) and behavioral consequences (e.g., inappropriate behavior, impulsivity, substance/drug use) can also impair/affect interpersonal relationships.

Brain Development

Complicating academic progress following TBI are issues surrounding brain development. As noted in chapter 5, from birth through early adulthood, the brain goes through a tremendous amount of growth and development—including increases and decreases in gray and white matter. The maturation of gray and white matter is experience-dependent (Stiles & Jernigan, 2010; Wilde, Hunter, & Bigler, 2012a), and those neurons that are most frequently used are strengthened and retained while those that are infrequently used are eliminated. In addition, at the same time the number of synaptic connections are being strengthened and reduced, white matter is becoming more efficient through the myelination process—increasing communication. These periods of over-production and elimination are ongoing and can last from months to years.

As noted in chapter 2, neurons connect with each other to form regionally located information-processing cortical hubs that are interconnected via white matter tracts with other regional cortical hubs throughout the brain, forming highly complex interactive neural networks. Like other developmental aspects of the brain, maturational changes occur in the development of brain networks. For example, as the brain matures, there is a reduction in short-range white matter connectivity and a strengthening in long-range white matter connectivity—suggesting greater functional integration at the whole-brain level (Supekar, Musen, & Menon, 2009). Any disruption of cortical hubs, or the interconnecting white matter pathways, has a deleterious effect on all other networks that are related to, or dependent upon, the affected hub or pathway (Menon, 2011).

Learning is a complex neurological process—the intricacies of which are beyond the scope of this book. However, in the broader sense, learning involves: developing new synapses, strengthening existing synapses, and improving the efficiency of interconnecting white matter tracts. That is, as different areas of the brain "come online" during the learning process, the synaptic connections within those areas and the white matter connections between those areas and other related areas (or networks) become developed and strengthened. From this perspective it is easy to see how learning is intricately linked to brain maturation.

If TBI occurs during critical timeframes of brain maturation or network development, there is a potential to significantly disrupt subsequent development or affect the ability to return to pre-injury developmental levels (Wilde et al., 2012a). This may be why, compared to older students who have sustained a TBI, students who sustained a TBI between the ages of 2 and 7 years were found to be more susceptible to deficits in expressive language, attention, executive function skills, and academic achievement (Wade et al., 2011). If TBI occurs after a brain area has matured, or a network has developed, the area or network will operate less efficiently, or not at all—which will affect all other interconnected networks/areas/pathways. Therefore, when it comes to the learning process, sustaining a TBI can significantly impair a student's ability to acquire new knowledge/skills or access old knowledge/skills.

Sometimes TBI can result in a similarly structured brain network taking over for the damaged network. When this happens, the new interconnecting pathways require significantly more synaptic interaction, which usually results in slower processing and less efficiency (Wilde et al., 2012a). This can result in less efficient or slower rates of learning and/or retrieval of previously learned information.

Pre-injury Knowledge and Skills

There are times when the effect of a student's TBI on academic progress will be immediately obvious, as may happen when a TBI involving an area on the left side of the brain—called Wernicke's area—results in a student being unable to comprehend spoken language (receptive aphasia). Conversely, at other times, determining the immediate effect of TBI on academic progress will not be easy or straightforward. This can happen, for example, when a student with TBI has difficulty acquiring new knowledge or skills, but is still able to access previously learned/acquired knowledge or skills. Much as a moving racecar's momentum can carry it forward at the same speed for a period of time after it runs out of gas, a student's pre-TBI "academic momentum" (i.e., existing knowledge or skill base) can allow the student to "coast" for a period of time. That is, although no new information is being acquired and stored in long-term memory, formerly acquired knowledge is being accessed and applied—allowing the student to keep up academically with peers. In addition, similar to a racecar that has run out of gas while moving, the reduction in forward progress is gradual and it may be some time "further down the road" before there is a noticeable difference between the performance of the student with TBI and that of other students. This is especially true if the student was "at the front of the pack" before the TBI (i.e., a high-achieving student).

This phenomenon also applies to normative academic testing, which is often used in the determination of academic progress. That is, normative academic testing does not measure a student's rate of knowledge acquisition, total knowledge base, or amount of newly acquired knowledge; rather, it samples what is presumed to have been learned by a particular point in time, or what the majority of same-sample peers have demonstrated should have been learned. Therefore, if a student with TBI was "ahead of the normative curve" before his/her TBI, it may take some time (possibly years) before an academic measure accurately reflects that a student with TBI is not acquiring new information.

Concussion

Each year in the United States, just over half a million children and adolescents between the ages of 8 and 19 will arrive in a hospital emergency department with a concussion (Bakhos, Lockhart, Myers, & Linakis, 2010). Of these, 50% will be sports-related concussions (e.g., snow skiing, skateboarding, bicycling) and 38% of these will be the result of an organized team sport (e.g., football, basketball, soccer, baseball, hockey). Research has shown that student athletes often believe "tough" athletes continue to play regardless of injury, and concussion is part of normal game play (Putukian, 2011). In addition, it has been shown that when student athletes are aware that they have sustained a concussion, many will not report their injury or they will go to great lengths to downplay the seriousness of their concussive symptoms when questioned—others will not realize their symptoms should be reported.

The vast majority of concussions in children and adolescents resolve spontaneously within 7–14 days (Davis & Purcell, 2013) with no lasting effects, so it is easy for educators to assume a concussion produces no educational consequences worth noting. In addition, when concussion symptoms are present, they can be viewed as being minor inconveniences, especially when compared to moderate or severe TBI consequences. Common symptoms following a concussion can include: difficulty thinking clearly; difficulty concentrating; difficulty remembering new information; feeling slowed down (cognitive difficulties); headaches; fuzzy/blurry vision; nausea/vomiting; dizziness; sensitivity to noise/light; balance problems; lack of energy; feeling tired (physical difficulties); irritability; sadness; emotional lability; nervousness/anxiety (emotional/mood difficulties); and sleep disturbances CDC, 2013a). All of these symptoms have the potential to interfere with a student's ability to focus and concentrate on academic tasks. If a student with a concussion is experiencing any of these symptoms after he/she returns to the educational setting, it is likely that the acquisition of new knowledge will be affected to some degree. It is also likely that a student's performance on any academic tests/measures during that time will be affected. If key educational concepts are presented during the time that a student with a concussion is experiencing any of these symptoms, it is very possible that he/she may not learn them. Should this occur, the necessary foundation for future learning may be disrupted, weakened, or missing altogether—resulting in future academic difficulties. In addition, the connection between cognitive functioning and mental effort requires metabolic energy. At rest the uninjured brain has high energy requirements and at full tilt, even only weighing in at 3 pounds, it may use up to 20% of the entire body's energy budget (Herculano-Houzel, 2011). In the postconcussive state, neuronal mitochondria are less efficient, and disruption to metabolites have been recorded up to 22 days postinjury, returning to normal levels by 30 days (Vagnozzi et al., 2010). This means a student who has sustained a concussion may be lacking the metabolic energy required to engage in meaningful learning.

Students with concussion are very aware of their postconcussion consequences, often to the point of minimizing them in an attempt to avoid unwanted outcomes (e.g., an athlete's failure to return to the game). See Case Study 7.1—Emalia; Concussion/mTBI.

Case Study 7.1—Emalia; Concussion/mTBI

During a weekend soccer game, 17-year-old team captain Emalia collided midair with a member of the opposing team. During the collision, the front of Emalia's head struck the other athlete's head and Emalia fell, hitting the ground with the top of the left side of her head. Both impacts caused displacement of her brain, in particular the frontal and temporal lobes moved unnaturally and compressed against boney surfaces within her skull. Although she did not lose consciousness, Emalia felt nauseous, disoriented, and confused for approximately 15 minutes following the incident. Eager to secure a soccer scholarship and worried that an injury would keep her out of the game, Emalia did not inform her coach about her symptoms. However, an observant teammate noticed Emalia's answers to her questions did not make sense and reported the signs to the coach. The coach took Emalia out of the game and called her parents. Concerned, Emalia's mother took her to the local hospital emergency department. While waiting to be seen, Emalia admitted that she had a severe headache, nausea, and blurred vision. The hospital lights and noise bothered her, so she wore sunglasses and sat in a quiet part of the waiting room. An x-ray of Emalia's head was unremarkable and she was diagnosed by the attending physician as having sustained a "concussion"— likely caused by the deformation and stretching of brain tissue during Emalia's collision with the opposing teammate. Emalia's mother was instructed that she should monitor Emalia for the next 24 hours, and if her headache did not subside or she was unable to wake Emalia from sleep, she was to immediately return her to the hospital emergency department. The next morning Emalia awoke with no headache but continued to rest at home. Two days postinjury Emalia returned to school. Prior to her concussion Emalia was taking two advanced placement honors courses, maintained a 4.0 grade point average, and was an active member of the debate team. She was very anxious that poor attendance and grades related to her concussion—along with being pulled from practices and games while managing concussion symptoms—would ruin her ability to be admitted to the college of her choice. Upon returning to school, she went "full-force" to catch up on missed work. Four days postinjury, Emalia began experiencing intermittent severe headaches lasting for one to two hours, difficulties with concentration and focus, and difficulty remembering information that was just covered in class. Emalia's school nurse brought the case to the attention of the school psychologist. The school psychologist immediately convened a meeting with Emalia's parents, coach, teachers, and principal. Foremost, she stressed that concussion research (Moser & Schatz, 2012) recommended the immediate need for cognitive and physical rest for the next week that included complete time off from school—with absolutely no homework; visually stimulating activities (e.g., reading, computers, video games, texting, cell phones, drawing, and no/limited TV); exercise, athletics, or chores that result in perspiration or exertion; trips/social visits to or from others; or driving, with plenty of opportunity for sleep and rest. She also stressed that research also recommended upon her return to school, that Emalia be given a modified schedule that would continue to limit her cognitive and physical activity—that is, a partial-day schedule; no note-taking, homework, tests, or computers; no athletics or physical education; and opportunities for periods of rest during the day until such time that her symptoms completely subsided. By receiving a community of caring and support Emalia now felt secure in accurately reporting symptoms. She was symptom-free and back at play within two weeks.

For a bright student, ongoing problems at school with intermittent headaches and difficulties with concentration and focus can quickly become a source of frustration, especially as they begin to interfere with academic progress and participation in the classroom.

Pre-injury Learning Disabilities

If a student has a known learning disability prior to sustaining a TBI, he/she will invariably be excluded from participating in research on the educational effects of TBI. This is because his/her premorbid functioning will act as a confounding factor when trying to isolate the effects of the TBI (Farmer et al., 2002). Therefore, it is not known specifically how TBI will affect the academic performance of a student with a previously diagnosed learning disability. The limited research that includes this population suggests that students with a previously diagnosed learning disability who sustain a moderate to severe TBI have significant declines in intellectual functioning and consistent ongoing impaired academic functioning (Donders & Strom, 1997), and students with mild, moderate, or severe TBI have worse overall memory difficulties following TBI (Farmer et al., 2002). Upon their return to the educational setting, it is possible that a student with a moderate or severe TBI who was previously receiving services under a special education classification (e.g., Specific Learning Disability, Significant Emotional Disturbance) may continue to receive special education and related services under their existing classification. If the student's TBI did not result in any significant TBI-related negative consequences, this is not problematic. However, if the student returns with known TBI-related negative consequences, or later develops any, and is not reclassified as a special education student with a Traumatic Brain Injury, there are possible educational ramifications. These can include inappropriately attributing the new difficulties to the preexisting disability, reclassifying the student under a new, but incorrect, classification (e.g., Significant Emotional Disturbance), or unintentionally minimizing the effect of the TBI. Should any of these occur, there is a risk that the student may not receive appropriate academic interventions designed specifically for the TBI consequences.

Age at Injury

Related to the brain development issues noted previously in this chapter, the age at which a child sustains a TBI has academic consequences. As with a student at any age, the more severe the TBI, the worse the educational outcome will be; however, the younger the age at the time of injury, the worse the potential becomes for later academic difficulties (Fulton et al., 2012). Specifically, academic learning involves many neurocognitive skills, and the younger a student is when he/she sustains a TBI, the less the number of consolidated skills have come online. Therefore, TBI at a younger age places a student at greater risk for neurocognitive difficulties later on in life. This is not only due to the loss of any previously acquired skills, but also to the failure of new skills to develop. Further, the failure to obtain early foundational academic skills can place the student at risk for future academic failure. If a TBI is severe enough and occurs during preschool age, it can easily result in a failure to obtain school readiness skills (Taylor et al., 2008). Deficits in memory and executive functioning that result from a moderate or severe preschool TBI have a significant potential to affect a student's later academic skills acquisition (Fulton et al., 2012).

Recovery

Research has supported the notion that, as a group, students will show distinct stages of change/recovery in academic domains over time (Fay et al., 2009). In general, students with moderate to severe TBI will show a period of significant improvement in neuropsychological functioning during the first year postinjury. This will then be followed by a plateauing with negligible rates of change for the next two years. There are, however, exceptions, with some students continuing to show neuropsychological improvements beyond the first year. In addition, as noted previously in this chapter/book, the change/recovery postinjury for children and adolescents occurs within the context of a developing brain, so it is possible that new deficits or impairments will also emerge as time goes on. Although academic deficits that result from a moderate TBI can resolve over time, those arising from a severe TBI may initially improve during the first year, but then persist without resolving, or even worsen over time (Fay et al., 2009). The long-term effects of concussion (single or multiple) are currently unknown (Davis & Purcell, 2013).

In general, neurological/cognitive consequences (e.g., difficulties with integration, retention, and/or retrieval of presented and learned information; attention, focus, and/or concentration difficulties; planning, organization, and follow-through difficulties), will be specific to the area(s) of the brain that are damaged and on a continuum ranging from mild to severe. Furthermore, each of these will have the potential to significantly influence the acquisition of, or retrieval of, new academic knowledge/skills differently. However, neurological/cognitive deficits can also manifest in many different ways. For example, difficulty with planning and organization can appear as an inability to follow multistep directions in a chemistry experiment, difficulty outlining an essay, not leaving enough time to walk to school, erratic performance on tests, etc. In addition, as a student becomes frustrated with planning and organization, he/she may cease to put forth effort, which can be misattributed to laziness or disinterest.

8 Transitions Following TBI

A student with TBI faces numerous transitions: from hospital or rehabilitation back to school; from one task to the next; from class to class; from one grade to the next; from one school to another; and from adolescence to adulthood. For a student with TBI, attending to these transitions in advance can minimize problems and maximize adjustment to changes in environment, routine, and expectation.

Chapter Overview

This chapter will address the importance of communicating and coordinating collaborative efforts between medical, mental health, educational communities, and parents. It will include discussion on

- transition challenges;
- improving transitions;
- confidentiality considerations;
- returning to school following mTBI;
- returning to play for student athletes;
- returning to school following moderate to severe TBI;
- identifying the unreported student;
- transitioning from preschool to school age;
- transitioning from elementary to secondary school; and
- transitioning to postsecondary options.

Transition Challenges

Returning to the educational setting following TBI can be challenging and problems can snowball if not addressed appropriately from the start. Far too often, students with TBI who need ongoing supportive educational services (e.g., special education, progress monitoring, emotional support) return to school settings in which these services are not provided. One reason this happens is because there is a breakdown in communication between educational professionals and medical professionals, neurological professionals, rehabilitation specialists, and/or parents. Ongoing communication and collaboration between school-based and non-school-based professionals and parents is vital. It helps maximize efforts of all involved parties and facilitates the return of students with

TBI to the educational environment. It also provides valuable bidirectional information exchange regarding the range of available educational services and assistance that can be provided at school; any changes in the student's medical progress; and changes in ongoing rehabilitation efforts. Appropriate assessment for, and development of, supportive school-based services requires ongoing communication and collaboration between school-based professionals, non-school-based professionals, and parents. It is important to note that involving parents in the collaborative communication process at every stage helps ensure they are directly involved in the educational planning of their child. The following are common transition challenges.

Problems with Communication and Collaboration

TBI happens suddenly and coordinating timely communication among all of the individuals involved can be difficult. Often parents are overwhelmed and have difficulty serving in a leadership role when it comes to advocating for their child's needs. In addition, children who sustain a TBI often experience the majority of their recovery at home, in school, and in the community, beyond medical surveillance; therefore, supportive doctors who were attentive and involved during the hospital-based recovery period may find themselves unintentionally removed from the collaborative process.

Complicating communication and collaboration efforts is the mutual lack of understanding about appropriate roles, professional guidelines, and legal processes in the medical and educational communities. At times this lack of understanding can lead to tension between collaborators. Therefore discussing these early on will help prevent tension from arising.

Lack of Knowledge and Skills

Another challenge to an effective transition can be a school professional's lack of adequate training in assessment and intervention for students with TBI. Because TBI is still perceived as a low-incidence disability, school-based professionals (e.g., psychologists, counselors, nurses, teachers) typically lack adequate training in how to best determine these students' needs (Glang, Dise-Lewis, Tyler, & Denslow, 2006; Jantz & Coulter, 2007). Further, they often lack knowledge about the consequences of TBI on school performance (Davies, 2013; Frank, Redmond, Ruediger, & Scott, 1997; Funk, Bryde, Doelling, & Hough, 1996). As a result, TBI policy makers have ranked teacher training as a critical childhood TBI priority for this century (Marino, 2000).

Inadequate Support Services

Even if student needs are appropriately identified, there may be inadequate support services available in schools to meet those needs. Although districts are legally obligated to provide special education and related services (IDEIA 04), the quality and extent of these services in some schools may pose challenges for students with TBI. That is, some schools may lack sufficient financial resources to provide innovative teaching methods, adaptive technology, school-based mental health resources, and/or personnel (e.g., nurses, speech and language pathologists, occupational therapists, physical therapists).

Improving Transitions

Critical to the successful transition from hospital or rehabilitation back to school is the early initiation of services. This allows the school time to prepare to meet the changing needs of a student with TBI. Therefore, early and ongoing communication and collaboration with hospital/community agencies and families is essential and should be initiated as soon as possible. The following will help to ensure that the transition process is successful.

School-Based Case Managers

An effective model for improving transitions from hospital or rehabilitation facilities back to school is to identify a specific school district-based case manager (e.g., school psychologist or school nurse with training in TBI) who can act as a consistent contact person, coordinate services, and facilitate transition. This case manager can coordinate meetings, ensure distribution of educational plans, assist teachers with progress monitoring, and communicate effectively with the parents, doctors, and outside service providers. He/she can also manage referrals for educational services if a "*Section 504 Plan*" or an *Individualized Education Plan* (IEP) is needed (see below). That is, he/she can ensure (a) a comprehensive assessment of student needs, (b) the design of an appropriate intervention plan, (c) the implementation of a simple way to monitor the efficacy of that plan, and (d) adjustments to the plan as appropriate (McAvoy, 2012). It is best if parents provide the school with a signed release to allow this facilitator to communicate seamlessly with health care providers.

Education for All School Staff

The school-based case manager can also ensure all school staff members are educated about such things as TBI prevalence rates, causes, signs, symptoms, and instructional strategies. This should occur at the beginning of a school year to prepare faculty members for working with any students who sustain a TBI throughout the year. It should also reoccur after TBI, when teachers and staff will need reminders of how to best serve the student. All adults who interact with a student with TBI throughout the day, including teachers, school-based mental health providers (psychologists, counselors, social workers), administrators, coaches, athletic trainers, and ancillary staff members (e.g., bus drivers, lunchroom workers, custodians) have a need for training in order to best assist the student. For example, a bus driver needs to know when a student has sustained a TBI so he/she can create a safe environment if the family chooses to continue bus services.

Needs-Based Services

With the help of the school-based case manager (who can synthesize information from different professionals), school team members can do an ecological assessment of potential student needs upon the return to school. Some needs-based questions to answer are:

What are the physical needs of the student?

- Are class changes necessary?
- What is the student's stamina and is there a need for a shortened school day or rest spot in the school building?
- Should there be a decrease in independent work upon return to school?
- Is there a need for specific behavioral programming to address functional issues? If so, who will be responsible for carrying out a full functional analysis so both the behavior and underlying problems are addressed?

Once the needs are identified, appropriate adjustments and interventions can be selected using the TBI-SNNAP process discussed in chapter 10.

Family Involvement

It is important, as stated previously, to involve the family in the transition process. For example, following a TBI, it is not unusual for parents to become overprotective and restrict previously enjoyed freedoms (e.g., driving to school, bike riding, climbing on playground equipment). This is often extended to siblings, even if they were not directly involved in the original situation. When this happens, it may cause siblings to experience issues of resentment, frustration, anger, jealousy, fear, and/or grief and affect their progress at school. If the family is not already addressing these issues in community-based counseling, school-based mental health providers can make referrals to appropriate service providers and provide school-based support services for siblings. In addition, it is important for families to communicate changes in a student's TBI-related behavior or level of functioning at home to the school case manager. Along the same lines, school professionals can let families know if there has been a change in functioning within the academic or social environments of school.

Confidentiality Considerations

U.S. federal laws protect the disclosure of student educational and medical information. The Family Educational Rights and Privacy Act (FERPA) of 1974 protects the privacy of student education records; it applies to all schools that receive funds from the U.S. Department of Education. Part of this act requires that schools obtain written permission from the parent (or students themselves if they are 18 or older) in order to release information from a student's educational record. The Health Insurance Portability and Accountability Act (HIPAA) of 1996 requires health care providers to protect the privacy of patients' personal health information. This act has nine parts, including the Privacy Rule, which regulates the use and distribution of identifiable health information. It gives individuals rights to determine and restrict access to health information. Once school personnel identify a student with TBI, it is best therefore, if the case manager immediately obtains the required written permission for the release/exchange of relevant medical and educational information. In order to exchange information or consult with doctors or rehabilitation specialists (in person, by email, or on the phone), school personnel must obtain a release of information document that is signed by the parents. Professionals outside the school setting are also required to obtain a signed release of information document if they are the ones initiating contact with school personnel. Therefore, school personnel should ask for a copy of the signed document prior to discussing the student, siblings, and/or parent(s).

Returning to School Following mTBI

After mTBI, brain functioning typically becomes reregulated within one to three weeks (Collins, Lovell, Iverson, Ide, & Maroon, 2006). However, as noted in chapters 2 and 3, recovery from mTBI is variable. Although the majority of students who sustain an mTBI will be on the least-severe end of the mTBI continuum, a small number will fall along the more-severe end. For these students, symptoms and difficulties may persist for years (Lezak et al., 2012). While for some students symptoms may persist for more than a year, the majority of students who sustain mTBIs are generally expected to quickly recover functioning; therefore, a permanent change in educational services is not needed. Regardless of how quickly a student's mTBI symptoms resolve, in addition to physical rest, students who have sustained an mTBI require rest from cognitive and mental exertion. This is because if demands on the brain are not managed appropriately, symptoms will likely worsen and recovery may be prolonged. In addition, a student who sustained an mTBI may return to school when symptoms are still present, and school personnel must be ready to intervene if symptoms worsen. Thus, activity levels must be managed to facilitate effective recovery during the transition back to the educational setting.

While some students suffering from mTBI symptoms might eventually require a Section 504 plan (see chapter 1 and below), in general what is needed for this population are "adjustments" to expectations in school. Unfortunately, because these students often "look" fine, school administrators and teachers may resist allowing needed accommodations. That is, some school personnel may be resistant to implementing these adjustments for a student with mTBI, arguing that the student "seems fine" and the adjustments would not be "fair." For teachers who have concerns about accountability for the curriculum, permission to grant adjustments should be made explicit to teachers by administrators. If resistance continues, it might be helpful to compare a student with mTBI to a student with a sprained ankle. That is, allowing a student with a sprained ankle to sit out of physical education class, giving that student extra time to transition to class, or having someone carry books are reasonable recovery accommodations. In comparison, allowing a student who is recovering from mTBI to have a temporary reduction in his/her homework load or giving him or her extra time to hand in assignments is also a reasonable recovery accommodation. In addition, whereas doing jumping jacks in PE on a sprained ankle would prolong recovery, exposure to bright lights, loud noises, and long tests would prolong concussion recovery.

In order to help promote cognitive rest and recovery, students with mTBI may need to stay at home for a period. During this time, families should encourage their student to have complete physical and cognitive rest—meaning no television, computers, music, video games, cell phones, social networking, or texting. Lying in a quiet, dark room will minimize the student's exposure to bright lights and loud noises, which can exacerbate symptoms. Stimuli can gradually be reintroduced, beginning with short periods of light reading, soft music, or short periods of television watching.

In general, a student who has sustained an mTBI may gradually return to school for a shortened school day (perhaps only coming for half-days or for core courses) as long as symptoms do not worsen. If physical or mental exertion worsens symptoms, the level of activity should be decreased and the school-day length should be increased as tolerated. It should be noted that some students may attempt a return to school before it is advisable because they may be stressed about missing instruction. If this happens, they may try to take on too much in order to "catch up" with their classmates. Not only can this exacerbate physical symptoms (headache, fatigue), but it can also elicit emotional symptoms, such as depression, anxiety, or frustration.

In order to prevent difficulties, clear policies and procedures for returning a student with mTBI to school should be established in advance and reviewed annually (before the school year starts) so the school can best respond to any student who sustains an mTBI.

Although concussion is generally considered to fall along the milder end of the mTBI continuum, it warrants additional comment because until recently, concussion and its effects have been considered to be insignificant. Even after symptoms are no longer reported, students who have sustained concussions may still demonstrate cognitive impairment on neuropsychological testing and/or ongoing metabolic abnormalities (Sady, Vaughan, & Gioia, 2011). While most students report relief from symptoms and reach normal levels of neurocognitive functioning within 7 to 10 days, some experience symptoms and impairment well beyond that period. In addition, the period of recovery from concussion may be impacted by premorbid conditions (e.g., a learning or behavior problem, history of headaches, previous concussions); therefore, information about these contextual variables can be important for families to share with school teams. Sady and colleagues (2011) recommend that cognitive exertion be viewed on a continuum from no activity (full rest) to full activity (no rest). Therefore, concussion recovery requires finding the appropriate level of cognitive exertion that does not exacerbate symptoms; in other words, the student should engage in cognitive activity that is below his/her symptom threshold. Thus, it is important to not only observe postconcussion restrictions on physical activity, but also on cognitive activity.

Returning to Play for Student Athletes

Essential to sound return-to-play decision-making is requiring a health care professional's clearance for a student to return to play after sustaining a concussion. This professional needs to have expertise in concussion evaluation and management. Returning to play before being cleared by medical professionals can increase the risk of subtle neuroinflammation, which may become chronic, and repeated injury may affect the immune environment of the brain (Anthony, Couch, Losey, & Evans, 2012; Kumar & Loane, 2012). Thus, it is important that an athlete not return to play until a concussion has healed 100%. However, the process and timeline for a student's return-to-play may be different from the same student's return to school ("return to learn"). Each child is different, and these differences must be taken into account in the team's decision-making.

The Third International Conference on Concussion in Sport held in Zurich in 2008 resulted in a Consensus Statement on Concussion in Sport (McCrory et al., 2009). The panel of professionals recommend that a student athlete proceed through the following steps to return to play. The athlete proceeds to the next level if asymptomatic at the current level for at least 24 hours.

- No activity, complete physical and cognitive rest
- Light aerobic activity
- Sport-specific activities and training
- Noncontact drills
- Full-contact practice training after medical clearance
- Game play

Education about concussion signs and concussion management is important for athletes, coaches, athletic trainers, and families in advance of play. Chapter 15 discusses effective prevention programs and describes legislation that is being enacted in many states in response to poorly managed safety protocols.

Establishment and distribution of policy is also critical for concussion-related return-to-play decisions for student athletes. McAvoy (2012) recommends that parents follow these guidelines for returning their child who sustained a concussion to school:

- If 10 minutes of concentration on a mental activity worsens symptoms, rest is required. Do not return to school. No television, video games, texting, reading, homework, or driving. Consult a health care professional if this state lasts more than a few days.
- If the student can concentrate on mental activity for up to 20 minutes, consider keeping the child at home, but total bed rest may no longer be necessary. Between periods of rest, attempt light mental activity, such as reading or watching television, as long as symptoms do not flare.
- If the student can tolerate 30 minutes of light mental activity, consider returning the child to school. Communicate with the school-based facilitator and sign a release for that person to communicate with your health care provider.
- Together with the school team, determine the level of academic adjustment needed.

Returning to School Following Moderate to Severe TBI

While most students who sustain an mTBI experience a resolution of most symptoms in less than a month, those with moderate to severe TBI may have more persistent deficits, which may be life-long. Thus, the return-to-school plan for these students may look quite different than that of the mTBI group. The Individuals with Disabilities in Education Act (IDEA, 1990), which became IDEIA with the 2004 revision (Individuals with Disabilities in Education Improvement Act) and the Americans with Disabilities Act (ADA, 1990) offer some protections to students with TBI.

Individuals with Disabilities Education Act (IDEA)

As noted in chapter 1, *Traumatic Brain Injury* was added as a special education category under IDEA in 1990, and codified in the Federal Registry in 1992. Students with moderate or severe TBI have a higher likelihood of qualifying for special education services.

Eligible students receive an *Individualized Education Plan* (IEP), which details academic and social/behavioral annual goals based on student needs; it describes specially designed instruction to meet those goals. Related services, such as speech and language therapy, occupational therapy, and physical therapy may also be included on the IEP. The IEP must include transition services/plans for the child not later than age 16. A transition plan describes a plan to facilitate postsecondary transition to work, independent living, and/or postsecondary education. In some states, this transition plan is written earlier (e.g., at age 14).

Section 504 of the Rehabilitation Act of 1973 (Section 504)

Although a student may have documented deficits after TBI, that in-and-of-itself does not automatically qualify the student for special education services under IDEIA 04. However, if the student is continuing to perform at pre-injury levels academically and does not require specially-designed instruction, but requires accommodations to the school environment in order to attain a free and appropriate education (FAPE), he/she may be eligible for a "*Section 504 plan.*" As noted in chapter 1, Section 504 is intended to remove barriers to a FAPE, gives no additional funding to schools, and has a broader definition of a disability than does IDEIA 04. If a student qualifies under Section 504, the *Section 504 Accommodation Plan* documents reasonable accommodations that can help the student access the curriculum, such as a modified schedule, physical accommodations, or the use of assistive technology. For a student with TBI, Section 504 accommodations can help compensate for persisting disabilities and provide access to a FAPE.

Identifying the Unreported Student

If a TBI was recent and clearly documented in medical records, school teams may not have difficulty linking a student's change in performance or behavior to the brain injury. However, as noted in chapters 1–3, the effects of TBI are not always immediately obvious and it may be years before problems manifest. In these cases, the school team may have difficulty securing medical documentation of the TBI. The inability to obtain medical documentation for students can lead to the misidentification or under-identification of students with TBI in the school setting and can be problematic in securing special education services under IDEIA 04 (or Section 504). Therefore it is best practice to obtain medical documentation from hospital records or from a doctor with knowledge of TBI, but this may not always be possible. In addition, states—and districts—vary in terms of the type of medical documentation required to pursue an identification of TBI under IDEIA 04. If state eligibility criteria do not include a statement related to obtaining medical documentation, clarification from the state's department of special education may indicate they expect school teams to include medical records and the injury criteria used by the team in the evaluation team qualification report.

Some entities recognize that a TBI may have occurred so long ago that medical documentation is no longer available. The Colorado Department of Education (CDE), for example, permits school-based evaluations teams to determine a "credible history" of TBI (see http://cokidswithbraininjury.com/ckwbi/wp-content/uploads/2009/11/Cred -hx.pdf for a description of this process). In contrast, other states may not only require medical documentation, but may require that a physician be part of the evaluation team. This parallels the difficulty of schools making an educational identification of autism in the absence of a medical diagnosis of autism in order to qualify students for special education services under IDEA. To minimize difficulties, it is important for school-based professionals to clarify whether they can make an educational identification of TBI without medical records if they follow the process of establishing a credible history. It should be noted that while medical documentation confirms the presence of TBI, it does not establish the effect of the TBI on the child's cognitive, academic, social, or emotional functioning. Thus, it is only one part of a comprehensive school-based evaluation of educational impact.

Josiah's case (Case Study 6.1—Josiah; Moderate TBI; chapter 6) illustrates the difficulty school teams face when there is no clear medical documentation of TBI. This is compounded by the delayed manifestation of symptoms.

Transitioning From Preschool to School Age

Preschoolers who sustain a TBI—whether as infants or shortly before transitioning to kindergarten—require special considerations when transitioning to school-age services. This is because oftentimes a preschooler who did not qualify for an Individualized Family Service Plan (age < 3) or an IEP (age 3–5) will begin to show emerging deficits as cognitive demands increase. It should be noted, however, that there can also continue to be rapid improvement and growth of skills that indicate many services are no longer warranted. School-based professionals must establish baseline levels of functioning for all domains and plan progress monitoring of the expected skills and behaviors. This can be accomplished using the TBI-SNNAP assessment process described in chapter 10. In addition, setting an expectation of regular meetings to review progress can help teachers understand that their students with TBI may have more erratic progress and need more frequent changes to goals, schedules, and plans than those students without TBI. The preschool teacher should be particularly mindful of the possibility of fatigue; rest periods may still be required.

Transitioning From Elementary to Secondary School

All transitions for students with TBI require planning. As a child moves from elementary school to secondary school, it is important that school professionals (and professionals outside the school that are involved in the student's care) convene and discuss issues that might arise. Keep in mind that this transition between schools may mean there will be a new school-based case manager. Either way, the school-based case manager will need to continue to coordinate school and community services. At this meeting, the case manager can facilitate a discussion in which the student, parents, and former teachers convey effective strategies (e.g., for home-school communication, organization, and behavior management) to new teachers. There can also be an open discussion of differences between curriculum, teacher expectations, and school rules. During this meeting, school professionals can determine the best way to provide ongoing assessment and progress monitoring and—depending on the circumstances—this initial face-to-face meeting may be the best time to schedule follow-up meetings. This ensures that the student is on everyone's radar (and calendar!) and lets all involved personnel know that changes can be made to the program as necessary. In transitioning from one school to the next, it may be helpful for the student to visit the new school in advance, walk the schedule of classes while the hallways are empty, and meet teachers.

Regardless of whether or not the student is receiving special education services and has an IEP in place, it is helpful to provide written educational information to new teachers and administrators on TBI. Parents can share ongoing medical or rehabilitation information if services are being provided outside of the school setting and medical and mental health professionals can provide information directly as well. At follow-up meetings, it is important to give parents and medical/mental health professionals information about how the student is adjusting to the new setting and allow for them to provide the school with related information as well. At this point, the student should be actively involved in transition planning and encouraged to provide information on perceived strengths, needs, goals, and concerns. The student may also need to be actively taught self-advocacy skills and given opportunities to practice them in middle school and high school so he/she can use them effectively in postsecondary settings.

Transitioning to Postsecondary Options

The transition from high school to "the real world" is a difficult adjustment for almost everyone. The effects of TBI can make it particularly challenging. The older adolescent with TBI faces a new set of challenges. These might include:

- Should the student graduate with same-age peers or continue school-based services until age 21?
- What vocational training options might be a good match for the student's skills and abilities?
- Is independent living or a group home a good option for the student? Is it best to continue living at home? In an apartment with roommates?
- Should the student go to college now, later, or not at all?
- What supports and services were previously given to the student at school and should they continue?
- What skills are needed by the student? Cooking and housekeeping? Managing appointments and health care needs? Managing money, budgets, and bills? Safe use of public transportation or driving a vehicle?
- How will the student manage adult relationships? Are friendships and romantic relationships loving and safe?

As stated previously, IDEA (1997, 2004) requires a transition plan for students in special education be in place no later than age 16. These plans are written by all members of the IEP team, including parents and any medical/mental health professionals involved in the student's care, and include specific steps that help prepare the student for life after high school. Team members must ensure that transition plans and programs optimally prepare the student for adulthood and address the concerns listed above. Postsecondary options considered may include college, vocational training, employment, adult services, independent living, and participation within the community. However, once the child leaves the public schools (i.e., graduates or drops out), he/she is no longer entitled to the services afforded under IDEA. Further, many older adolescents who sustained a TBI but did not require special education services may have relied upon the help of parents and school staff in order to be successful. These adults may have helped the student organize materials, get up on time, complete assignments successfully, and navigate social systems. Therefore, even if a child was not on an IEP, it can be beneficial to have a team meeting (e.g., student, parents, teachers, school psychologist) for future planning and preemptive problem solving.

Both Section 504 of the Rehabilitation Act of 1973 and the Americans with Disabilities Act (1990) offer some protections for individuals with TBI in the workplace and at college. Section 504 ensures individuals with disabilities are not denied access to federally-funded programs or activities based solely on their disability. ADA extends this to all programs, activities, and services made available by state and local governments, regardless of whether they receive federal funding. Under these laws, any accommodations must be reasonable and timely; they might include modifications or adjustments like allowing an employee to wear a headset or earplugs to filter distractions and noise, or adjusting the settings on a computer screen to accommodate someone who has impairment in his/her visual field. It is important to note that these laws do not mean that a student with TBI would be automatically admitted to any university regardless of disability; the student must meet academic criteria for admission to the college.

College Services

Despite Section 504 and ADA, university personnel who do not understand the nature of TBI may not readily provide the support required for these students to be successful. Students who sustain a TBI before college have significantly lower college graduation rates than peers (Wagner, Newman, Cameto, & Levine, 2005). College planning for students with TBI should therefore include:

- Researching the resources and supports that will be available. Is there a tutoring center? Academic counselors? Writing assistance centers? Academic accommodations? Accessible housing?
- Teaching young adults with TBI how to take initiative to develop supports in college.
- Gathering required documentation of the disability.

High school IEPs and transition teams are critically important to successful college entry (Glang et al., 2008). Studies have shown that college students with TBI require more effort in study, need to use study strategies, and have decreased grade point averages and extracurricular activity participation, and changes in relationships with peers (Stewart-Scott & Douglas, 1998). Further, they have more difficulties with concentration, memory, and problem solving than do students with learning disabilities (Beers, Goldstein, & Katz, 1994).

Half of the students who sustained TBIs as children who went on to college were not linked to campus disability services (Todis & Glang, 2008). There are also many instances of students sustaining a TBI during college. Many of these students also fail to access campus disability services; they may end up dropping out, take longer to graduate, or go to great lengths to hide their newly acquired impairments. Therefore it is important that campus disability services be aware of a student who has sustained a TBI. When utilized properly, campus disability services can maintain medical and psychological documentation; help determine if a condition is a disability; ensure rights of individuals with disabilities; assist with identifying and implementing reasonable accommodations; assist the university in meeting it obligations to students with disabilities; and promote physical and programmatic access to students. However, it is important that students and their parents take the initiative and provide appropriate documentation to the college services office, participate fully in the process of identifying and implementing accommodations, and inform the office when accommodations are not effective.

One desirable service to add to campus disability services is a "coach" who can serve as a liaison between the student, the university, and medical personnel. This person can help decrease dependence on parents and increase independence by prompting or cuing the student to utilize available services, follow through with accommodation plans, identify additional programs of support, help the student identify long-term goals, and use documentation (e.g., medical and neuropsychological reports) to help guide recommendations. The coach can help individualize an approach that meets the student's needs, eliminate strategies that are unproductive, identify technology that might be useful, and include social goals (i.e., meeting new friends, attending campus activities, joining an organization). This person might serve many of the roles of the school-based case manager described earlier.

Regardless of when a TBI occurs, there are clear benefits to ongoing communication and collaboration between the medical community, the educational community, and the parents of students with TBI during transition back to school and between educational settings.

9 Understanding Community-Based Assessment Findings

After sustaining a TBI, if a student is treated in the hospital emergency department (HED), hospital inpatient setting, and/or a rehabilitation facility, he/she will likely have received a variety of assessments in each of these settings. In addition, assessment may occur in the home setting (e.g., the family system's emotional readiness of the student to return to school). Successful return to school following TBI involves review and consideration of assessment data from all of these settings.

For children who go to an HED following a TBI, injury assessment can range from a brief medical examination (possibly including an x-ray) and a brief neurological screening interview (perhaps administered by an attending physician) to a more in-depth medical examination that includes advanced neuroimaging (e.g., magnetic resonance imaging—MRI) and a full neurological examination (performed by a neurologist or neurosurgeon). If the TBI is significant enough, the child is admitted to the hospital and if he/she is referred to the inpatient neurorehabilitation unit, a neuropsychological assessment will be completed. Results of neurological examinations, neuropsychological assessment, and neuroimaging are typically transcribed into reports and discharge summaries. These reports/summaries contain information that can be useful to educational professionals involved in the planning of school-based educational assessments and interventions. These data may also come from a variety of community-based professionals, including medical doctors, neuroradiologists, neurologists, neuropsychologists, nurse practitioners, speech pathologists, occupational therapists, licensed social workers, licensed professional counselors, or clinical psychologists. A basic familiarity with neuroimaging techniques, common report formats, terminology, and recommendations help educational professionals better understand a student's strengths, weaknesses, and limitations following TBI.

Chapter Overview

The focus of this chapter will be brief descriptions of the types of possible TBI-related medical, neurological, and neuropsychological assessments a student may receive prior to returning to the educational setting, the content of typical assessment reports/summaries, and how assessment results are helpful to educational professionals. Sample reports are provided on the webpage accompanying this book. The chapter will discuss

- TBI severity classification systems;
- neurological examinations;

- neuroimaging techniques;
- neuropsychological tests;
- school-based implications of community-based assessments;
- content of community-based assessments; and
- translating community-based assessment results into school-based service plans.

TBI Severity Classification Systems

As noted in chapter 3, injury severity is established according to alterations in the level of consciousness, amnesia, and anatomical damage to the head or brain. Common assessment systems used to establish severity level in hospital emergency centers include: Glasgow Coma Scale (GCS; Teasdale & Jennett, 1974), Rancho Los Amigos Level of Cognitive Functioning (RLCF; Hagen, Malkmus, & Durham, 1972), and various concussion grading scales. Following is a brief description of each:

Glasgow Coma Scale (GCS)

As discussed in chapter 3, the GCS results in a total score between 3 and 15, which is based on the sum of the highest score obtained in each measured dimension. The child norms score a child's best responses in Eye Response, Verbal Response, and Motor Response (Peiniger et al., 2012). As shown in Table 9.1, TBI severity is often determined by a combination of the GCS score, length of loss of consciousness (LOC), and length of posttraumatic amnesia (PTA). For children under the age of five, a pediatric GCS rating system is available. This scale is useful for young children who may not be able to respond to verbal commands in the same way as adults and older children.

Rancho Los Amigos Level of Cognitive Functioning (RLCF)

The "Rancho" is primarily used by clinicians in rehabilitation facilities to identify patterns of recovery. Developed by Hagen, Malkmus, and Durham in 1972, the Rancho evaluates an individual's current cognitive and behavioral functioning by placing the individual in one of eight categories (e.g., Level 1, No Response: Total Assistance; Level 8, Purposeful and Appropriate). The Rancho is often used to assist teams in tracking improvement, evaluating potential, and designing appropriate treatment programs (Lezak et al., 2012).

Table 9.1 TBI severity classification

Mild TBI		Moderate TBI		Severe TBI	
GCS score:	13–15	GCS score:	9–12	GCS score:	3–8
LOC	0 to 30 min.	LOC	30 min. to < 24 hrs.	LOC	> 24 hrs.
PTA	< 1 hr.	PTA	1 to 24 hours	PTA	24 hrs. to > 1 week

Galveston Orientation and Amnesia Test (GOAT)

The GOAT (Levin et al., 1979) is a mental status exam commonly used for assessing posttraumatic amnesia and confusion (Lezak et al., 2012). It was designed to be re-administered and is often used multiple times a day and can be used for weeks if necessary. This scale measures orientation to person, place, and time, as well as memory for events preceding and following the injury. Patients are asked to recall and describe the last event before the injury and the first event following their injury.

Concussion Grading Scales

There are numerous published grading systems for describing concussion severity that generally rely on LOC and presence/absence of symptoms. However, in 2008, because delineations in published grading systems tended to be arbitrary and not meaningful for treatment, the International Consensus Statement on Concussion in Sport recommended abandoning concussion grading scales in favor of a symptom-based approach for determining return-to-play (McCrory et al., 2009).

Neurological Examinations

A neurological examination is an evaluation of the physical functioning of the nervous system. A neurological examination can be conducted in a medical office or hospital, at an accident scene, or on the sidelines of an athletic event. This evaluation may involve an individual being checked for memory and concentration, vision, hearing, strength and sensation, balance, coordination, and/or reflexes. The typical evaluation in a medical facility (e.g., office, HED) immediately postinjury will involve a medical history, head and neck examination, and neurological examination. The neurological examination generally involves a mental status exam and evaluation of the cranial nerves, motor functioning, coordination and balance, reflexes, and sensory functioning (Allen, Hulac, & D'Amato, 2005). If a structural brain abnormality is a concern, neuroimaging may be ordered. A neurological examination may also be used to plan for rehabilitation. Much of the neurological examination information for moderate and severe TBIs will come from emergency medical technicians who respond to the incident, as well as from a parent(s), who can include details about the nature of the injury (i.e., how it happened, how long an LOC lasted, pre-injury status, drug/alcohol involvement).

mTBI

Sport-related concussions, including organized team sports (e.g., football, hockey), are common occurrences. Concussions sustained during organized team sport activities are generally evaluated on-site. Because concussion may involve periods of posttraumatic amnesia (Halstead, Walter, & The Council on Sports Medicine and Fitness, 2010) standard postconcussion reporting methods are now being more commonly used by Level 1 trauma centers and sports trainers to track a student's degree of posttraumatic amnesia. Unfortunately, this is not always the case in smaller hospitals, HEDs, and family practice facilities.

Nonsport mTBI/concussions—particularly those on the more severe end (e.g., when there is a depressed skull fracture)—are typically evaluated in the emergency department where medical needs, such as bleeding, are addressed first. If there is a loss of consciousness, amnesia, or severe headaches, then neuroimaging is usually ordered to rule out a more severe TBI. A few specific neuroimaging techniques are discussed later in this chapter. Following are descriptions of commonly used on-field sideline neurological evaluations:

Maddocks questions. This brief set of questions developed by Maddocks, Dicker, and Saling (1995) evaluates orientation and short- and long-term memory related to the current game and sport (e.g., "What team did you play last week?"). More information can be found at http://cogstate.com/go/sport/concussion-management/sideline-assessment.

Standardized Assessment of Concussion (SAC). The SAC takes approximately five minutes to administer and includes measures of orientation (month, date, day of week, year, time), immediate memory, neurologic screening, loss of consciousness, amnesia, strength, sensation, coordination, concentration, exertional maneuvers, and delayed recall (McCrea, Kelly, Kluge, Ackley, & Randolph, 1997). The SAC is not validated for elementary school-aged athletes. (More information can be found at http://www .momsteam.com/health-safety/standardized-assessment-of-concussion-a-valuable -tool-for-sideline-evaluation.)

Balance Error Scoring System (BESS). Postural stability assessment, performed on site includes the majority of accepted sideline assessments (including the ones described above) in a comprehensive evaluation (Halstead et al., 2010; McCrory et al., 2009; Riemann, Guskiewicz, & Shields, 1999. See http://www.sportsconcussion.com/pdf/management/ BESSProtocolNATA09.pdf for more information.)

Moderate and Severe TBI

As discussed in chapter 4, after immediate medical needs are addressed (e.g., maintaining an airway, controlling bleeding), there is generally a rapid, focused evaluation of TBI severity (e.g., GCS), and as the patient begins to stabilize, the neurological examination continues. As the patient moves from the emergency department to intensive care units, to a regular hospital room, and home, ongoing neurological examination will likely occur, including monitoring of retrograde/anterograde amnesia. These acute and postacute evaluations are generally included in the various reports (neurologist's report, surgeon's report, discharge summaries, etc.).

Neuroimaging Techniques

While neurological examinations look for symptoms, neuroimaging techniques look for the physical causes of symptoms (Allen et al., 2005). They are also used to help determine injury severity and drive medical interventions (e.g., surgery). Neuroimaging techniques (e.g., CT, MRI) provide visual images that allow doctors/neurologists to see inside the brain of a living individual and help determine the extent of damage from TBI. As noted in chapter 3, when the brain is damaged, a wide variety of consequences may happen. For example, the brain may swell, resulting in decreased blood flow, decreased oxygen, and pressure on brain tissue; there may be chemical reactions affecting the flow of neurotransmitters. Neuroimaging can reveal these TBI consequences, as well as other consequences such as contusions (bruises) and white matter changes—damage that can occur from the stretching of axon filament or from the ripping/shearing effect on axons. Different neuroimaging sequences can be used to reveal different types of injuries and repeated scans can track changes. Various structural and functional imaging techniques are described below.

Structural Imaging Techniques

When assessing TBI in the HED, x-ray and CT are the most commonly used neuroimaging techniques. Although MRI can show much more detailed information than an x-ray or CT, a lesser number of students will likely have had an MRI. This is because MRI is very expensive and cannot be done if the child is on any type of life support that requires equipment with magnetic properties. In addition, braces and other metallic dental devices may generate major artifacts that distort images of the brain. Further, MRI may require sedation so the patient will not move. Therefore, many students returning to school after TBI will have only had an x-ray and CT.

X-ray. X-rays are relatively inexpensive and x-ray machines are readily accessible in the HED. However, because x-ray exposes the patient to radiation, its use will be limited to those cases where a skull fracture or foreign objects (e.g., pieces of bone or metal) are suspected. Beyond this, however, x-rays are not particularly useful in detecting subtle traumas to the brain.

Computed tomography (CT). Because CT scans (a form of x-ray) are inexpensive to administer and quick (some done in merely seconds), they are now routine in the assessment of TBI and are typically administered on the day of injury, pre- and postsurgery, and/or at follow-up evaluations. However, like x-ray, in order to minimize exposure to radiation, they are only used when clinically indicated (Davis, 2007). Because CT uses x-ray, it is very good at distinguishing denser material (e.g., the skull) from less dense material (e.g. brain tissue, blood, water). Therefore, CT is very good at detecting skull fractures, internal hemorrhaging, and brain swelling; however, compared to MRI it does not do a very good job of distinguishing between white and gray matter (Wilde, Hunter, & Bigler, 2012b). The majority of mTBI will result in normal CT scans (Wilde et al., 2012b). On a CT scan, bone will appear white, cerebral spinal fluid (CSF) will appear dark gray, white matter will be medium gray, and gray matter will appear light gray (Figure 9.1).

Magnetic resonance imaging (MRI). MRI machines use a magnetic field and radio frequency waves to manipulate hydrogen protons found in CSF and brain tissue. Depending on the density of hydrogen protons, and the magnetic environment of the tissue, this manipulation creates radio waves that are then processed into detailed images

CT   **T1**   **T2**

FLAIR   **GRE**   **PD**

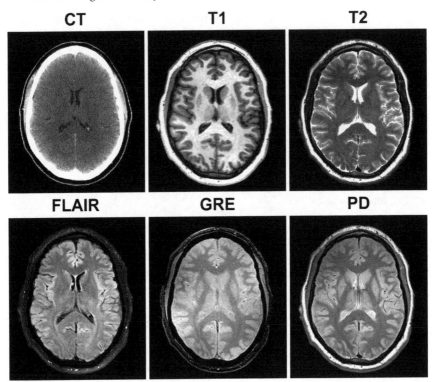

Figure 9.1 Comparison of computed tomography (CT) and magnetic resonance imaging (T1, T2, FLAIR, GRE, PD) scans showing the anatomical clarity produced by the various MRI images compared to the CT image. Note how different tissues appear brighter or darker depending on the MRI acquisition method used, and how CSF will also vary in signal intensity. All images were obtained in the axial plane, at the same level, from the same brain.

of the brain (Wilde et al., 2012b). The strength of magnetic field used, the turning on and off of radio waves at different intervals, and the manner of signal acquisition will result in different types of images. MRI types include, but are not limited to, T1-weighted, T2-weighted, T2*-(pronounced "T-two-star") weighted, proton density (PD; which combine T1 and T2 scans), fluid attenuated inversion recovery (FLAIR), and gradient recalled echo (GRE), susceptibility-weighted imaging (SWI), and diffusion tensor imaging (DTI). On MRI images, different tissues appear brighter or darker depending on the MRI type used, and CSF will also vary in signal intensity (Figure 9.1). This makes the various MRI types useful in showing different parts of the brain and different types of TBI abnormalities. Similar to CT scans, MRI results will typically appear unremarkable in students who sustained mTBIs. Based on these two sources, Figure 9.1 illustrates the utility of the following MRI types: CT, T1-weighted, T2-weighted, FLAIR, GRE, SWI, and DTI.

The science behind the different types of MRI presented here is beyond the purpose of this book and the reader is directed to Hunter, Wilde, Tong, and Holshouser, 2012, and Lezak et al., 2012, for reviews. If neuroimaging was conducted, school-based evaluation teams should always obtain a copy and integrate these results into the school-based evaluation of a student with TBI as it has been shown to contribute significantly to the understanding of TBI consequences (Jantz & Bigler, 2013).

Neuropsychological Tests

A neuropsychological assessment focuses on functional brain-behavior systems; it generally provides quantitative data that is a valued piece of a comprehensive evaluation. The overall purpose of a TBI neuropsychological assessment is to determine behavioral, cognitive, and/or emotional status and predict later levels of function. Typically a neuropsychological assessment yields conclusions and recommendations to guide treatment and is developed by integrating information from tests, observations, interviews, and records. A neuropsychological assessment for a student with TBI is an ongoing process from injury to return-to-school; different tests are used at different stages to determine different things. In general, atypical findings on a neuropsychological assessment is described in terms of

- *Deficits.* Deficiency in quality or quantity, impairment in functional capacity, and/ or decrease in function (e.g., cognitive, memory, processing speed);
- *Delays.* Failure to reach developmental milestones when expected;
- *Dissociations.* Difference between developmental rates in two areas of development; and
- *Deviance.* Unevenness in development; appearance of an atypical developmental indicator.

Neuropsychological tests that are used as part of a complete neuropsychological assessment can assess function in a variety of areas, including: sensory-motor function, attention, visual-spatial function, language, memory and learning, executive function, cognitive speed and efficiency, and overall cognitive function. The following is a description of several neuropsychological tests frequently used for students with a known or suspected TBI.

Neurocognitive Tests for Concussion

Computerized neurocognitive tests allow for comparison of functioning at baseline and following a concussion. These are often administered to student athletes preseason. Then, if the athlete sustains a concussion during practice or play, these multicomponent tests can be re-administered to compare postinjury results to baseline. When used in conjunction with other measures, these tests can help determine if the athlete needs further medical supervision.

One example of computerized neurocognitive testing is Immediate Post-Concussion Assessment and Cognitive Testing (ImPACT; http://impacttest.com/). ImPACT can be administered by an athletic trainer, school nurse, athletic director, team doctor, or psychologist who is trained in administration of the test. The test typically takes about 20 minutes to complete; it measures attention span, working memory, sustained and selective attention, response variability, nonverbal problem solving, and reaction time. Other popular computerized neuropsychological tests for concussion include: Automated

Neuropsychological Assessment Metrics (ANAM; Cernich, Reeves, Sun, & Bleiberg, 2007), CogState (Falleti, Maruff, Collie, & Darby, 2006), and HeadMinder (Barth et al., 1989).

Neuropsychological Assessment Batteries in Rehabilitation Settings

Several neuropsychological assessment batteries are commonly used in the inpatient setting. The NEPSY (Korkman, Kirk, & Kemp, 1998) and Dean-Woodcock Neuropsychological Battery (Dean & Woodcock, 2003) are contemporary measures; the Halstead-Reitan Neuropsychological Test Battery (HRNB; Reitan & Wolfson, 1993) and the Luria-Nebraska Neuropsychological Battery (LNNB; Golden, Hammeke, & Purisch, 1978) are older tests, but are still used by neuropsychologists with a fair degree of frequency, especially select components of these batteries. These normative assessments help neuropsychologists determine how behavior and functioning differ from that of typical same-age peers. The tests provide quantitative information related to learning, reasoning, attention, memory, and language. The contemporary measures lend themselves to facilitating a practical approach to assessment for intervention (Davis & D'Amato, 2005). Familiarity with the basic structure and use of these tests can help school-based professionals better understand reports containing data from these instruments.

NEPSY: A developmental neuropsychological assessment. The NEPSY takes a process approach to identifying underlying processes of academic skills; it was based on the work of Russian neuropsychologist Alexander Luria (1979). A goal of the test is to provide a description of a comprehensive pattern of neuropsychological strengths and weaknesses. Subtests were specifically designed for children ages 3 to 12. The test includes 27 subtests that explore functioning in five domains: attention/executive functions; language; visual-spatial processing; sensorimotor; and memory and language.

Dean-Woodcock Neuropsychological Battery (DWNB). The DWNB is a standardized neuropsychological test battery that can be administered along with the Woodcock-Johnson Tests of Cognitive Abilities (WJ-COG; Woodcock, McGrew, & Mather, 2001b) and Woodcock-Johnson Tests of Achievement (WJ-ACH; Woodcock, McGrew, & Mather, 2001a). The DWNB offers a sensorimotor battery of 18 subtests (DWSMB); they measure auditory, visual, and tactile stimulation. It also includes the Dean-Woodcock Emotional Status Examination and the Dean-Woodcock Structured Neuropsychological Interview. Combined with the WJ-COG and WJ-ACH, the DWNB creates the Dean-Woodcock Neuropsychological Assessment System (DWNAS). For a thorough discussion of the NEPSY and the DWNAS, the reader is directed to Davis and D'Amato (2005).

Halstead-Reitan Neuropsychological Test Battery (HRNB). The HRNB has versions for adults, children and adolescents, and younger children. The battery includes classic neuropsychological tasks, some used since 1947: Finger Tapping, Grip Strength, and Sensory-Perceptual Examination. The Halstead-Reitan is widely used, even though it lacks a comprehensive normative sample, well-organized protocols, portability, and thorough standardized instructions. Further, the test can be difficult to interpret without extensive training.

Luria-Nebraska Neuropsychological Battery (LNNB). The LNNB was first published in 1978, and is based on the work of Luria. The LNNB was designed to obtain qualitative evaluation data of one's neurological status, and the goal of the instrument was to standardize Luria's test procedures by providing an objective scoring system. Although the LNNB has received mixed reviews and a body of research indicates relatively poor psychometric properties and limited links to intervention (Davis, Johnson, & D'Amato, 2005), it is still used. In 1987, a children's version (LNNB-C; Golden, 1987) was released for examinees ranging from 5 to 12 years. Scales on the original battery include motor, rhythm, tactile, visual, receptive speech, expressive speech, writing, reading, arithmetic, memory, intellectual processes, and intermediate memory.

School-Based Implications of Community-Based Assessments

Community-based assessment findings, including medical and neuropsychological reports, discharge summaries, findings, and recommendations, can be helpful in informing school-based assessment and intervention planning. In consultation with relevant community-based personnel, school professionals (e.g., psychologists, nurses, speech therapists) can examine these records as part of their evaluation of students who have sustained a TBI; and as part of the TBI-SNNAP (chapter 10). When appropriate, school-based evaluators can utilize data from community practitioners as a way of recognizing and documenting the recovery period. Becoming familiar with assessments administered by other professionals, including format and terminology, can help school-based professionals gain a more complete picture of a child's functioning that can, in turn, affect learning (see webpage for a sample psychological report).

Content of Community-Based Assessments

The content of reports, discharge summaries, and findings from community-based professionals vary based upon injury severity. An mTBI treated in the emergency room may only lead to a brief discharge summary. Severe TBI that warranted a lengthy stay in a hospital and rehabilitation setting may involve multiple reports from a number of community-based professionals including medical doctors, neuroradiologists, neurologists, neuropsychologists, pediatricians, nurse practitioners, speech pathologists, occupational therapists, licensed social workers, licensed professional counselors, and clinical psychologists. Consultation with the original report author is always recommended when school personnel obtain and read reports, discharge summaries, and findings. In addition to helping school professionals better understand the contents, consultation also helps establish a collaborative working relationship.

Translating Community-Based Assessment Results Into School-Based Service Plans

TBI medical and neuropsychological reports are often complex and filled with difficult terminology, which makes it difficult for school teams to translate the findings into school-based service plans, IEPs and 504 plans, and/or interventions for students with TBI. While the focus of a TBI neuropsychological evaluation is to identify neurological deficits in functioning (e.g., executive functions, memory, cognition) caused by altered brain functioning, the school-based evaluation generally focuses more on how these affect academic achievement and skills needed for success in school. Rather than focusing exclusively on within-child strengths and weaknesses, the school-based evaluation also provides information that is context-specific, including an ecological assessment of classroom variables. For example, school-based professionals can observe students across settings and within a mix of individuals. This makes them uniquely positioned to collect data that might be seen as the "next phase" of evaluation; that is, after a child has been discharged from a medical or rehabilitation facility. Such data might include information on gross motor skills (on the playground, in physical education class, in the hallways); fine motor skills (handwriting, art skills); and speech and language skills. Once collected, educational plans can then use data from both community-based and school-based assessments to: (a) build on strengths that were identified in the evaluations, (b) build on developing compensatory strategies for identified areas of weakness, (c) modify the environment when appropriate, (d) teach the tools to help the student learn and generalize new behaviors, and (e) specify the vehicles to reach the objectives. In addition to providing information for educational planning, this information can be shared with noneducational professionals.

10 School-Based Assessment
A Problem-Solving Framework

Many students with TBI return to school needing educational services ranging from direct interventions (e.g., contingency management procedures, positive behavior supports) to indirect interventions (e.g., training and support for teachers; Ylvisaker et al., 2001). Although medical, neurological, and neuropsychological professionals are experts in their respective fields, few consider themselves experts in meeting the psychoeducational needs of students with TBI. In this chapter, *psychoeducational needs* are defined as: educational needs of students as they relate to child development, learning, academics, behavior, social interaction, and overall mental health. Within the school setting, many professionals (e.g., school psychologists, special education teachers) are trained to be experts in psychoeducational assessment and intervention. Unfortunately, when it comes to the psychoeducational assessment of students with TBI, and the subsequent development of educational interventions, educational professionals have typically received little, if any, training in these areas.

The *TBI School-Based Neuroeducational Needs Assessment Process* (TBI-SNNAP) provides educational professionals with an effective means to assess the psychoeducational needs of students with TBI and develop effective education-focused interventions. The TBI-SNNAP also provides educational professionals with a convenient framework for integrating relevant medical, neurological, and neuropsychological assessment results into their school-based assessment and intervention processes; operationally define an assessment plan for a student with TBI; make informed decisions about developing effective academic/psychoeducational interventions; tailor interventions to fit the unique needs of the individual student with TBI; gather useful school-based data on a referred student's cognitive, academic, behavioral, emotional, and social functioning in the educational setting; maintain ongoing communication with parents; initiate and maintain ongoing communication with community, agency, and allied health providers involved in the aftercare of a student with TBI; and utilize functional behavior assessment in the school-based assessment of children with TBI.

Chapter Overview

This chapter will discuss

- the TBI School-Based Neuroeducational Needs Assessment Process (TBI-SNNAP);
- collaboration and the TBI-SNNAP;

- IDEAL and the TBI-SNNAP;
- ICEL/RIOT and the TBI-SNNAP;
- Functional Behavior Assessment.

The TBI School-Based Neuroeducational Needs Assessment Process (TBI-SNNAP)

The TBI-SNNAP is a multimethod, multisource, solution-oriented, problem-solving assessment process that incorporates adaptations of two models: the IDEAL Problem Solver (Bransford & Stein, 1993) and ICEL/RIOT (Heartland Area Education Agency, 2005). It includes two interactive components: an overarching five-step decision-making process (IDEAL) and an integrated eight-part multisource, multimethod assessment matrix (ICEL/RIOT) that helps school-based teams make informed decisions regarding educational interventions for students with TBI. Central to the TBI-SNNAP is the belief that informed decision-making is the key to effective assessment and intervention. *Informed decision-making* can be defined as the process by which a single course of action is selected from among alternative courses of action, after relevant information (obtained from multiple sources) has been critically examined and considered. Within the TBI-SNNAP, informed decisions are made at each step of the IDEAL and ICEL/RIOT processes (explained below). Integral to the TBI-SNNAP is ongoing, two-way consultation, dialogue, and the exchange of relevant student information between school-based professionals, parents, medical professionals, and mental health professionals. The focus of the TBI-SNNAP is on the integration of existing relevant noneducationally based neurological and medical assessment data with new or existing educationally based assessment data. Therefore, collaboration between educational professionals, noneducational professionals, and parents is critical to the success of the TBI-SNNAP. The goal of the TBI-SNNAP is twofold:

- provide educational multidisciplinary teams with a comprehensive systematic process that results in the development of appropriate school-based interventions designed to help a student with TBI become more successful in the educational setting; and
- provide information that can be shared with other noneducational professionals working with the student and his/her family outside of the educational setting.

Collaboration and the TBI-SNNAP

A key element of the TBI-SNNAP is open, ongoing educational collaboration between school-based professionals, parents, and individuals/agencies outside of the school setting. *Educational collaboration* within the TBI-SNNAP is defined as: a process in which equal partners work together to reach common educational goals for a student with TBI, which cannot be achieved by a single individual/institution working in isolation. Therefore, it involves the active participation of school-based professionals, medical professionals, mental health professionals, parents/guardians, and if appropriate, the student with TBI. The TBI-SNNAP educational collaboration procedure requires that these individuals jointly develop and agree upon a set of common goals while sharing relevant information with each other. It also necessitates that all individuals involved in the collaboration process use their expertise, individual perspectives, and available resources to work together toward helping achieve the previously agreed upon goals. In order to set appropriate educational goals for a student with TBI, however, school-based professionals must first assess the educational functioning of a student with TBI. Within the TBI-SNNAP, the educational collaboration procedure provides a means by which medical, neuropsychological, and psychological data can be obtained and integrated when assessing the educational functioning of a student with TBI.

Educational collaboration within the TBI-SNNAP requires the understanding that collaborative relationships take time to establish and require a period of trust-building. They also require the understanding that issues surrounding "turf" must often be overcome before true, productive educational collaboration can occur. Although the responsibility of all members involved in the collaborative relationship is considered to be equal, the importance of school-professionals being the first to initiate communication with other professionals cannot be overlooked. It is also important that school-based professionals not assume that medical and mental health professionals "automatically" know who to contact within the educational community when they are ready to refer a student with TBI to a school. Further, it is helpful for educational professionals to remember that parents and professionals outside the educational setting are not always familiar with state and federal protections afforded to students with TBI or with the intricacies of the referral and assessment process.

As defined above, the main goal of educational collaboration within the TBI-SNNAP is working together to reach common educational goals for a student with TBI. This is accomplished, in part, by the exchange of relevant information. For example, medical, neuropsychological, and psychological professionals can provide test results and summary reports to school-based professionals, who can in turn provide information on special education *Traumatic Brain Injury* classification requirements to other professionals. An additional example is the mutual exchange of relevant test results between educational, psychological, and medical professionals.

Educational professionals typically do not have the training or expertise to understand medical, neuropsychological, and psychological data. Therefore, inherent in the educational consultation process is the presumption that when educational professionals obtain, consider, and integrate relevant medical, neuropsychological, and psychological test results into their assessment of the educational functioning of a student with TBI, they are engaging in regular ongoing communication with the medical and mental health professionals who provide that information.

IDEAL and the TBI-SNNAP

Within the context of the TBI-SNNAP, an adaptation of the IDEAL problem-solving model (Bransford & Stein, 1993) provides a sequential, five-step guiding framework

Table 10.1 Application of the TBI-SNNAP to the IDEAL Problem Solver Model

Identify . . . the reason for referral	➤ Goal: Correctly identify the underlying reason for the referral. ➤ Consider data from multiple sources that will "triangulate" or "dial-in" the referral concern. ➤ Use ICEL/RIOT to make informed decisions.
Define . . . the expected student outcome in measurable terms and gather relevant test data	➤ Goal: Describe the student outcome in specific terms so that effective interventions can be implemented successfully. Answer the questions: Once we complete the entire assessment process, what *specifically* do we (the team) want the outcome of this assessment to be for this student? How will we know when that outcome happens? ➤ Use ICEL/RIOT to make informed decisions.
Explore . . . general intervention strategies that will address the defined student outcome and choose the best intervention strategy	➤ Goal: Develop the top 3–5 "best" general intervention strategies designed to attain the defined student outcome. ➤ Use multidisciplinary team's wealth of specialized knowledge to conceptualize the student outcome in a new and previously unappreciated way. ➤ Choose the best intervention strategy. ➤ Use ICEL/RIOT to make informed decisions.
Act . . . on the chosen intervention strategy and monitor the results	➤ Goal: Implement a single chosen strategy and track the progress. ➤ Gather intervention-specific data on a regular basis across a pre-established period of time to assist with informed decision-making. ➤ Determine student's response to the intervention strategy.
Look . . . at intervention data and evaluate intervention effectiveness.	➤ Goal: Maintain interventions that are effective in addressing the defined student outcome. Answer these questions: Does the data indicate that sufficient progress has been made toward attaining the defined student outcome? Does the student need the continued support of the intervention strategy to continue to be successful in meeting the defined student outcome?

(described below). When used in the TBI-SNNAP, the IDEAL acronym stands for *identify* the reason for referral; *define* the expected student outcome in measurable terms and gather relevant test data; *explore* general intervention strategies that will address the defined student outcome and choose the best intervention strategy; *act* on the chosen intervention strategy and monitor the results; and *look* at intervention data and evaluate intervention effectiveness (Table 10.1).

Step One: Identify the Reason for Referral

A student with TBI typically will be referred to a school's multidisciplinary team for assessment consideration by a school-based source (e.g., teacher, school psychologist, counselor, administrator), a community-based source (e.g., parent, medical provider, juvenile justice agency, mental health professional), or occasionally a student will self-refer. Regardless of the referral source, a student with TBI will be referred when his/her behavior, emotional state, or academic progress differs significantly from that of other same-age students in similar circumstances.

The reason why a student is referred to a school's multidisciplinary team for assessment consideration is the starting point for all subsequent assessment and intervention decisions in the TBI-SNNAP. The reason why a student is referred is contained within the initial referral statement, which can be given verbally or in writing. Unfortunately, many times the initial referral statement for a student with TBI is of little diagnostic use to the multidisciplinary team because it is stated too vaguely. For example, the referral statement "Neilia has trouble paying attention" provides the team with very little useful information other than at some time, in some location, for some length of time, under some circumstances, and for some reason, Neilia is not attending to some person, task, and/or conversation that the referent feels she should be attending to. Even when the referral statement appears to provide more specific information, it can remain significantly uninformative. For example, while the referral statement "Neilia is talking in math class when she should be completing her daily seatwork" may provide a degree of detail, it does not provide enough useful information. What does the referent mean by "talking"? Is Neilia initiating conversation or acting in response to conversation from others? To whom is she talking? Is she talking to herself? Is she talking on her cellular phone? Is she talking loudly or softly? What does the referent mean by "daily seatwork"? Is it a reading assignment or a writing assignment? Does it involve working in a group or individually? Does it occur at the beginning, middle, or end of the class period? Is it before or after class instruction? Does it involve new or previously learned material? Why should Neilia be "completing" her daily seatwork? Is she behind on completing previous assignments? Was she asked to do so by her teacher? Is there a spoken or unspoken rule or expectation that Neilia complete her seatwork prior to talking?

If the referral statement is worded in a vague or inaccurate manner, the result is wasted team time and effort or the development of incorrect or ineffective interventions. Therefore, the first step in any successful decision-making process involving a student with TBI is to accurately identify, in a clear and informative manner, the specific reason why the student is being referred to the school's multidisciplinary team for assessment consideration. However, this can be difficult at times, due in part to the range of possible consequences that result from TBI—including subtle manifestations that can be often overlooked or misinterpreted. Therefore, it is important to understand that the stated referral concern for a student with TBI may not be the student's primary underlying difficulty; rather, it is only the concern that "got the student noticed." For example, a teacher might refer a student with TBI for arguing and noncompliance with teacher requests (the behavior that triggers the referral); however, the student's primary underlying difficulty is that he/she is experiencing the side effects of a prescribed medication as illustrated in the case of Raylan (Case Study 10.1):

Case Study 10.1 — Raylan; Severe TBI

In early summer, prior to his 10th-grade year, 15-year-old Raylan's mother was in the process of making a left-hand turn from the street into the parking lot of a grocery store. At the time, Raylan was seated in the passenger side of the family car, wearing his seat belt. Midway through the turn, while still in the oncoming traffic lane, the car in which Raylan and his mother were riding was struck on Raylan's side by an oncoming pickup truck. A small concrete brick in the back of the pickup truck was ejected upon impact and traveled through Raylan's open window; striking him in the upper right portion of the forehead (dorsolateral prefrontal cortex). Raylan was knocked unconscious by the blow and remained unconscious for six hours following the accident. Raylan underwent surgery at the hospital the following day to repair a severely depressed skull fracture, received two weeks of rehabilitative therapy, and was discharged from the hospital after six weeks. Discharge summary information from the hospital indicated Raylan suffered a "very severe TBI with primary neurological damage to the dorsolateral prefrontal cortex and the orbitofrontal cortex."

Three months after the accident, Raylan began to suffer unexplained bouts of severe depression. As a result, his neurologist prescribed an antidepressant medication to relieve his symptoms of depression and informed his parents that a common side effect of the medication was dryness of the mouth (dry mouth). Shortly after Raylan began taking this medication he began experiencing dry mouth. This resulted in Raylan making multiple requests every day to be allowed to "get a drink of water" during his 55-minute 10th-grade math class. Raylan's classroom teacher initially responded to his requests by allowing him to get a drink of water. However, as the semester progressed and the drink requests became more frequent, his teacher started denying Raylan's repeated requests. This resulted in Raylan responding to each denial by arguing with the teacher. If Raylan was standing at the teacher's desk making the request, he would argue with the teacher and refuse to return to his seat until the teacher threatened to send him to the principal's office. If Raylan was seated at his desk at the time of the request, Raylan would argue until the teacher resumed teaching or ignored him.

In addition to arguing with the teacher, Raylan exhibited difficulty maintaining attention and concentration during class lectures, assigned seatwork time, and quizzes. He experienced difficulty with distractibility, transitioning to new activities, planning and following through on assigned tasks, and blurting out answers during class lectures. Raylan's math teacher eventually became concerned enough about Raylan's behavior that she referred him to the school psychologist. The stated reason for the referral was: "Raylan is frequently argumentative, noncompliant with teacher's requests, and is off-task."

Collecting data from multiple sources and utilizing multiple methods (see ICEL/RIOT below) helps ensure that the multidisciplinary team makes informed decisions that lead to accurately identifying the underlying reason why a student with TBI is being referred. It also helps the team and the referent write a clear referral statement.

Step Two: Define the Expected Student Outcome in Measurable
Terms and Gather Relevant Test Data

Once the school's multidisciplinary team has accurately identified the underlying reason why a student with TBI is being referred for assessment—and helped the referent to write a clear referral statement—the next step is to define the expected student outcome in measurable terms and gather relevant test data. This step in the TBI-SNNAP is crucial because it drives the remaining three steps in the problem-solving process.

When defining the student outcome and deciding what relevant test data to gather, the multidisciplinary team should answer these two questions:

- Once we complete the entire assessment process, what *specifically* do we (the team) want the outcome of this assessment to be for this student; and
- How will we know when that outcome happens?

Consider the case of Georgina (Case Study 10.2).

Case Study 10.2—Georgina; mTBI

Georgina (8-years-old) and her cousin, Elbert (15-years-old), were playing croquet in the backyard when Elbert hit the croquet ball with a baseball bat instead of the croquet mallet. Georgina was struck a glancing blow just above the left temple by the wooden croquet ball and she was briefly knocked unconscious. She was taken by her parents to the hospital emergency department where a GCS of 13 was obtained. CT revealed intracranial abnormality (edema), and a small depressed skull fracture over the lower portion of the left frontal lobe (Broca's Area) which did not require neurosurgical intervention. A diagnosis of mTBI was made. Because of the skull fracture and cerebral edema, and out of an abundance of caution due to persisting symptoms of severe dizziness and headache, she was monitored in the hospital for several days. Upon her return to school, Georgina was noted to "not be the same chatterbox she was before the accident" and when she did speak, her speech often appeared abrupt, halting, and broken. For example she would say "hungry . . . lunch" instead of completing a full sentence like "I'm hungry and I want to go to lunch," or "bathroom . . . hallway . . ." instead of "Can I go to the bathroom?"

In the case of Georgina, the multidisciplinary team might define the expected evaluation outcome in the following measurable way: "Georgina will increase her verbal fluency from the prereferral level as evidenced by her use of sentences that contain pronouns, articles, and conjunctions." Using the ICEL/RIOT multisource, multimethod assessment matrix (see below) is helpful in providing a systematic approach to deciding what relevant test data to gather. Once the team has clearly defined the expected student outcome and decided what data to collect, the next step is to choose the appropriate test instruments, administer those instruments, and gather baseline performance data that will be used by the multidisciplinary team to make informed decisions regarding intervention strategies. When choosing the appropriate test instruments, the team should avoid the temptation to resort to the use of a "cookie cutter" assessment approach, such as automatically using a "favorite" battery of tests (e.g., intelligence measure, academic measure). To help avoid this approach, the multidisciplinary team should ask the following questions:

- What specific information will this test provide that we do not already have, and is that information relevant to the expected student outcome decision-making process; and
- Is this the most appropriate test for gathering relevant information on this student or is it the one the team is most familiar with?

Step Three: Explore General Intervention Strategies That Will Address the Defined Student Outcome and Choose the Best Intervention Strategy

After the student outcome has been defined in measurable terms and the multidisciplinary team members have collected baseline performance data, the next step is for the team to use the referral definition and performance data to explore three to five intervention strategies that will lead to the attainment of the defined student outcome. During this step of the TBI-SNNAP, the individual expertise of all multidisciplinary team members is utilized to conceptualize the defined student outcome in a new and previously unappreciated way. That is, individual team members use their respective specialized knowledge to help other team members understand when, how, and why to apply specific steps for each of the intervention strategies. Although ultimately the multidisciplinary team will choose only one strategy, and its respective specific steps to implement, by developing three to five intervention strategies the team will

- minimize the chances of prematurely choosing a "knee-jerk solution," that is, choosing a solution based on having addressed a similar referral problem (and student outcome) in the past; and
- have alternative interventions available for their consideration should the chosen strategy prove to be ineffective in significantly improving the defined student outcome.

Once the multidisciplinary team has developed three to five intervention strategies that include specific steps for each, they must then reach a consensus on which strategy will most likely lead to the attainment of the defined student outcome. This is done by reviewing all available data and information collected to this point and making an informed decision regarding the best strategy. After the multidisciplinary team has reached a consensus, a single intervention strategy is chosen and they are ready to implement and monitor that strategy.

Step Four: Act on the Chosen Intervention Strategy and Monitor Results

Once the multidisciplinary team has reached consensus and chosen a single intervention strategy, which they consider to be most likely to help the student with TBI attain the desired outcome, the team must implement that intervention strategy and monitor the results. During this step, decisions are made on:

- who will be responsible for implementing the strategy's specific intervention steps;
- who will be responsible for making sure the intervention strategy steps are implemented with integrity; and
- who will be responsible for monitoring the outcome progress of the intervention strategy.

In order to reduce the risk of losing objectivity when monitoring strategy implementation integrity and outcome progress, the multidisciplinary team should consider assigning a nonimplementation team member to monitor the implementation integrity and outcome progress. If this is not feasible, the team should reconvene on a regular basis to discuss implementation integrity and outcome progress. Gathering intervention-specific data on a regular basis across a preestablished period of time will also be helpful, as it helps establish implementation accountability. The multidisciplinary team should not limit data collection to the intervention strategy only (i.e., the defined student outcome as it applies to the referent's setting), but rather it should use the ICEL/RIOT multisource, multimethod assessment matrix (see below) to gather data across multiple settings. Using the ICEL/RIOT multisource, multimethod assessment matrix will help establish how effective the intervention strategy is in other settings (compared to data previously collected in those settings during Steps One and Two above) and whether or not the defined student outcome is being generalized to other settings.

Step Five: Look at Intervention Data and Evaluate Intervention Effectiveness

The final step in the sequential five-step guiding framework of the TBI-SNNAP problem-solving model involves looking critically at the actual effect of the intervention strategy and making an informed decision about whether the intervention should continue. Before this can be done, however, the multidisciplinary team must confirm that the specific steps of the intervention strategy have been implemented with integrity and that sufficient data on the implementation strategy results have been collected across multiple settings and over time. Once this has been confirmed by the team, the final step is to review the data within the context of the defined student outcome. If it is determined that the intervention strategy was successful in meeting the defined student outcome, to an acceptable level, the multidisciplinary team must decide whether or not the strategy should be continued or discontinued. However, if it is determined that the specific steps of the intervention strategy have not been implemented with integrity, and/or that sufficient data across multiple settings have not been collected on the implementation strategy results, and/or that data have not been sufficiently collected over time, these issues must be addressed before the decision can be made to continue or discontinue the intervention strategy.

In determining whether or not to continue or discontinue an intervention strategy, the multidisciplinary team may find it helpful to answer the following questions:

- Does the data indicate that sufficient progress has been made toward attaining the defined student outcome; and
- Does the student need the continued support of the intervention strategy to continue to be successful in meeting the defined student outcome?

If the multidisciplinary team decides that the chosen intervention strategy will be discontinued because collected data indicate insufficient progress was made toward attaining the defined student outcome, the team should return to Step One (identify the reason for referral) and Step Two (define the expected student outcome in measurable terms and gather relevant test data) for an in-depth review. If the in-depth review of all data from Step One and Step Two indicate the team has correctly identified the reason for referral (Step One) and has correctly defined the expected student outcome (Step Two), the team should move to Step Three (explore intervention strat-egies that will address the defined student outcome and choose the best intervention strategy) and select the next best intervention strategy for implementation. Once the team has chosen a replacement intervention strategy, they should proceed to Steps Four and Five.

ICEL/RIOT and the TBI-SNNAP

Within the context of the TBI-SNNAP, the ICEL/RIOT multisource and multimethod assessment matrix (Heartland Area Education Agency, 2005) is a useful evaluation tool. It is comprised of two interrelated processes in which the acronym ICEL stands for *instruction* variables (e.g., instruction delivery style, type of materials used in instruction, grouping of students, opportunities for students to respond), *curriculum* variables (e.g., subject content, scope, and sequence), *environmental* variables (e.g., distractions, lighting, noise levels), and *learner* variables (e.g., hearing/vision, social skills, motivation). The acronym RIOT stands for *review* all available data (e.g., school files, medical/neurological records, assessment data, observational data), *interview* all knowledgeable sources (e.g., student, parents, teachers, administrators, neuropsychologists, physicians), *observe* the student within the context of the school environment (e.g., all ICEL variables, various educational settings, classroom systems), and *test/assess* (e.g., functional behavioral assessment, assessment instruments, strengths, limitations). The ICEL/RIOT multisource and multimethod assessment matrix is best used in Steps One, Two, and Four of the TBI-SNNAP IDEAL problem-solving process. Table 10.2 shows how the ICEL/RIOT matrix may be compiled within the context of the TBI-SNNAP model.

For reproducible blank ICEL/RIOT worksheets and completed ICEL/RIOT worksheets based on Case Study 10.1—Raylan; Severe TBI, see the accompanying website.

Table 10.2 Application of the TBI-SNNAP to the ICEL/RIOT Matrix

	Review	Interview	Observe	Test
Instruction	*Review* all relevant past/present records of instruction including but not limited to: student grades, state/ local assessments, tests, quizzes, work samples, special education Individualized Education Program goals, etc. *Review* all information about instructional practices, variables, and strategies including but not limited to: instruction delivery sources, instruction delivery format, type of material(s) used in instruction, instruction strategies, and administrative evaluations of instruction.	*Interview* possible informants (e.g., student, parents/guardian, teacher, paraprofessionals, principal) about instructional delivery style, type of materials used during instruction, how students are grouped during work sessions, opportunities provided for student to respond, opportunities to solicit help, expected ratio of frustration to success in work assignments, discipline and rules, etc.	*Observe* classroom instruction by teacher, paraprofessional, and/or parent; student response to classroom instruction; use of technology during instruction by teacher, paraprofessional, and student; use of instructional materials; student participation in instruction (passive, active); peer interaction during instruction; etc.	*Assess* effectiveness of instructional delivery style, type of materials used in instruction, how students are grouped during work sessions, opportunities provided for student to respond, opportunities to solicit help, expected ratio of frustration to success in work assignments, discipline and rules, student progress, achievement, success, etc.
Curriculum	*Review* all relevant materials such as textbooks, workbooks, worksheets, etc., used in teaching curriculum. Explain how materials are used in teaching curriculum.	*Interview* possible informants (e.g., student, parents/guardian, teacher, paraprofessionals, principal) about subject content, scope and sequence, etc.	*Observe* student response to curriculum content and sequence, etc.	*Assess* the effectiveness of subject content, scope and sequence, etc., on student progress, achievement, and success.
Environment	*Review* the school environments the student visits regularly (e.g., classroom, hallway, playground, lunchroom, etc.). Discuss relevant environmental variables (e.g., possible distractions, lighting, student seating arrangement, etc.).	*Interview* possible informants (e.g., student, parents/guardian, teacher, paraprofessionals, principal) about distractions (e.g., lighting, noise levels, seating arrangement, room temperature, proximity of student to other students, doorways, etc.).	*Observe* environment for distractions (e.g., lighting, noise levels, doorways, windows, seating arrangement, room temperature, proximity of student to peers, etc.).	*Assess* the impact of distractions (e.g., lighting, noise levels, doorways, windows, seating arrangement, room temperature, proximity of student to other students) on student progress, achievement, and success.
Learner	*Review* relevant student school/ agency/psychological reports, school/ agency counseling records, parent interview data, student interview data, hospital/medical reports, psychiatric reports, disciplinary referral records, etc. Identify significant information related to referral.	*Interview* possible informants (e.g., student, parents/guardian, teacher, paraprofessionals, principal) about student's social skills, motivation level, learning strengths/ weaknesses, interests/dislikes, friends/peers, leisure activities, eating habits, sleep patterns, medical conditions, psychiatric conditions, hearing, vision, counseling/therapy, etc.	*Observe* interaction between student and environment, student response to environmental distractions, etc.	*Assess* the impact of student's social skills, motivation level, learning strengths, learning weaknesses, interests, dislikes, circle of friends/peers, leisure activities, eating habits, sleep patterns, medical conditions, psychiatric conditions, hearing, vision, counseling/therapy, etc, on student progress, achievement, and success, etc.

Adapted with permission from: Heartland Area Education Agency (2005). *Special Education Procedures Manual.* Johnston, IA: Heartland AEA 11.

Functional Behavior Assessment

An effective means of obtaining school-based assessment data on TBI-induced behavior is functional behavior assessment (FBA). FBA is a systematic, seven-step assessment process (described below) designed to help determine the function of a targeted, undesirable, or maladaptive behavior. FBA is used to generate a behavior support plan (BSP) designed to replace the target behavior with a new, more productive behavior. Therefore, FBA for a student with TBI involves examining, measuring, and treating specific TBI-related deficits (e.g., increased impulsiveness, inappropriate outbursts, inattention, aggression). The FBA process is intended to identify events/variables that predict and maintain problem/target behaviors. Consequently, setting events, ecological factors, antecedents of behaviors, consequences of behaviors, functions and efficiency of behaviors, current communication methods, competencies and skills, reinforcer effectiveness, and intervention history are all examined. Assessing these immediate and distant variables can assist a school-based assessment team in developing effective strategies. The FBA process includes a descriptive assessment based on observations, interviews, and manipulation of variables to determine the function of problematic behaviors. The function of behavior generally falls into one of three categories: positive reinforcement—access to something (attention/tangible items/etc.); negative reinforcement—escape/avoidance of something; and sensory stimulation—cognitively mediated events that may be both positive and negative.

For a student with TBI, it is easy for a school-based assessment team to overlook conducting an FBA because they "know" the reason for the change in behavior—"He is acting out because of the TBI." However, as with any behavior concern, an FBA can help school-based teams determine the function behind a student's behavior problems and then select the most appropriate intervention strategies for that problem. Available research involving the use of an FBA assessment for students with TBI supports its efficacy for treatment (Gardner, Bird, Maguire, Carreiro, & Abenaim, 2003; Ylvisaker et al., 2001). An FBA and the ensuing development of a behavior support plan (behavior intervention plan) can be conceptualized and conducted in several different ways, depending on the intensity of needs. For more information on completing a full FBA, the reader is directed to Crone and Horner's 2003 text *Building Positive Behavior Support Systems in Schools*. Following is a brief description and example of how a school-based assessment team can conduct an FBA for a student with TBI (Crone & Horner, 2003). These seven steps will be explained:

1. Define target behavior and goals.
2. Identify Antecedents, Behaviors, and Consequences (ABC).
3. Collect and analyze data.
4. Develop hypotheses.
5. Build a "competing behavior pathway."
6. Create the Behavior Intervention Plan (BIP).
7. Monitor and modify.

Define Target Behavior and Goals

Prior to selecting a target behavior, the school-based assessment team must first develop a list of prioritized concerns. Considerations include: Which areas most interfere with daily functioning? Which areas can be resolved quickly or compensated for easily? Which concerns have been identified by others? Are there new environmental demands that must be addressed? What does the behavior look like? What does the child say or do? Next, they should choose one or two targets from the list, define and describe the behavior problem, and determine the desired behavior. Strong goals will both eliminate the problem behavior and involve the demonstration of an appropriate replacement behavior. In other words, the goal is not just for the student to stop hugging everyone. The goal is for the student to start a conversation appropriately.

Identify Antecedents, Behaviors, and Consequences (ABC)

The second step involves having assessors record events, including setting events, that occur immediately before (antecedents) and after (consequences) the undesirable behavior. This helps establish the function of the target behavior. *Antecedents* are "quick" triggers of a behavior and *consequences* are the maintaining variables that happen immediately after a behavior that keeps it going (e.g., attention, tangible reinforcers, escape/avoidance, sensory input). *Setting events* are physical/medical events, environmental issues, instruction/curriculum variables, relationships/interactions, and/or other personal issues within the setting that might be precipitating factors contributing to the target behavior (e.g., pain or cognitive limitations).

Collect and Analyze Data

The third step involves collecting and analyzing information about the target behavior (e.g., when, where, and with whom it happens, rate and type of reinforcers). This helps a school-based assessment team select an appropriate replacement behavior and develop an effective behavior intervention plan. This information (obtained from a review of records, interviews, rating scales, analysis of intervention history, identification of relevant reinforcers, and/or direct observation) should be collected in many settings over time and analyzed according to the frequency (how many), intensity (severity), and duration (how long). This baseline data can take some time to collect, so it is important that a school-based assessment team be mindful of the fact that the absence of baseline data in the case of a student with TBI should not preclude the school team from implementing an intervention upon return to school. However, baseline data is helpful in intervention selection and design for a student who is already back in school and demonstrating behavior problems.

Develop Hypotheses

The fourth step involves developing hypotheses to help a school-based assessment team understand the purpose or reason behind the behavior. The development of appropriate hypothesis statements can help a school-based assessment team understand the function of the behavior, why the behavior is occurring, and therefore select the most appropriate interventions. One primary consideration is whether the behavior is a "can't do" or "won't do" situation. Often with TBI, it appears the student is being defiant or deliberately difficult ("won't do" what is expected) when in fact he/she may have lost the

capability or skill ("can't do"). Further, a single behavior can have more than one function and several behaviors can have the same function.

Build a "Competing Behavior Pathway"

The fifth step, the competing behavior pathway, is a way to create a link between the FBA
and BIP. Competing behaviors are mutually exclusive behaviors; for example, a student
cannot yell out in class and sit quietly at the same time or sit with folded hands and hit
a peer across the aisle at the same time. The competing behavior pathway emphasizes
the importance of building a BIP around hypotheses, identifies desirable alternatives to
the problem behavior, and highlights ways to make problem behaviors "ineffective, inefficient, or irrelevant through changes to the routine or environment" (Crone & Horner,
2003, p. 56). The function of the problematic behavior is not necessarily the issue—
for example, the function might be to receive attention—however, the way the student
achieves that function (e.g., calling out) is disruptive. The effective BIP teaches acceptable alternate behaviors that serve the same function as the problem behavior. For the
student with TBI who impulsively calls out to gain attention, this replacement behavior
may be quietly raising a hand or putting a red chip at the corner of her desk as a signal
to request attention from the teacher.

Create the Behavior Intervention Plan (BIP)

A Behavior Intervention Plan (BIP) is designed to promote appropriate behaviors conducive to learning. The goal of the BIP is to replace the target behavior with a new, more
productive behavior. The first part of a written BIP typically includes data collected in
the FBA, including the target behavior; medical history and medication; hypothesis for
why the behavior occurs; current level of functioning (frequency/intensity/duration of the
behavior); goals and objectives; and data collection method. A BIP then requires the school
team to select appropriate environmental modifications/positive behavior supports and
intervention strategies to teach new behaviors. Along with this, the team must determine
the required intervention intensity and specify how the intervention will be monitored
over time. A crucial step in implementing a BIP involves selecting strategies that help make
the target behavior become irrelevant, inefficient, and ineffective for the student. For example, changing the environment to reduce the antecedent triggers, using direct teaching of
appropriate behaviors, and changing consequences to allow the student to access what they
want or need in more appropriate ways are all examples of helpful intervention strategies.
The next step in implementing a BIP is to determine the intensity of intervention required.
In doing so, interventions for students with TBI are best approached using a variation of
the familiar three-tiered problem-solving model. The variation from how school-based
practitioners typically approach this model (e.g., in response-to-intervention, RTI) is that
rather than gradually increasing the intensity of a research-based intervention if there is
insufficient response, the team first implements intensive interventions upon return to
school—and then gradually reduces support as data indicates the student is responding.
This reverse approach is important for students with TBI because failure to provide supports in the early months following injury can result in significant failure and growing

disability (Ylvisaker & Feeney, 1998). The implementation of intensive interventions during this window of opportunity therefore is optimal.

It is important to know when to initiate the intervention, when during the school day it will occur, how long the intervention will last, and how the team will know whether the intervention should be stopped. A written intervention plan will help a school-based assessment team formalize these logistics of setting, time, resources, and personnel required for interventions.

Monitor and Modify

An important part of the BIP is the continual monitoring and modification of interventions over time. Because students with TBI can undergo significant changes during the healing process, it is important that a BIP be monitored frequently and adjusted accordingly (e.g., increasing/decreasing intensity, selecting a new intervention) based on collected data and observed progress. A variety of methods can help determine the efficacy of the BIP; however, one simple way is to use the same tools used to collect baseline data. The data can be collected by teachers, parents, and/or the student (self-monitoring). Collected data is then charted over time and analyzed. An essential part of data collection to determine intervention efficacy is to evaluate whether the intervention was implemented as intended and whether or not it was acceptable to those involved (e.g., student, parent, teachers).

In chapter 6, the reader was introduced to Josiah (Case Study 6.1—Josiah; Moderate TBI), who sustained a moderate TBI at age 2 and now, at age 6, is exhibiting moderate behavior problems in the classroom, including difficulty transitioning to new activities. He is also easily frustrated with himself and classmates. The website accompanying this book has a sample BIP and IEP (with social/emotional behavioral goals objective; see chapter 13 for academic goals) for Josiah. Note that different forms may be required by different states' departments of education; therefore, the sample BIP and IEP are general and can be adapted to meet the needs of different users.

11 School-Based Psychoeducational Reports

The results of school-based assessments of students with TBI typically lead to educationally-focused interventions and services. However, before educational professionals can develop and implement appropriate interventions, assessment results must be communicated to them in a clear and coherent manner. A psychoeducational report that summarizes the assessment results of various professionals provides a way for school personnel to communicate assessment results to parents and those involved in the education of students with TBI.

Chapter Overview

This chapter will discuss the rationale for, and the importance of, writing clear and concise reports. It will focus on how school-based assessment teams can best integrate and clarify the results from any existing medical, neuropsychological, and psychological data into the school-based TBI psychoeducational report. Because these reports are often the basis for orally communicating assessment results to parents, team members, and teachers, basic guidelines for providing such oral feedback is offered. The complete coverage of psychoeducational report writing is beyond the scope of this book; therefore, the focus of this chapter is on unique aspects of TBI that might affect how a report is written. The sections in this chapter include information on the following specific matters:

- special considerations for the TBI report;
- areas to address in the school-based TBI psychoeducational report;
- providing oral feedback on assessment reports; and
- incorporating assessment report information into educational plans.

Special Considerations for the TBI Report

As noted in previous chapters, TBI has an abrupt onset, and depending upon the severity level, it can include an acute, subacute, and chronic stage of improvement. In addition, the chronic stage of improvement is frequently accompanied by a wide range of dynamic changes in symptomology requiring ongoing close monitoring and follow-up assessment. Unique to TBI, especially in moderate and severe cases, is the involvement of medical professionals such as neurologists, neurosurgeons, emergency department physicians, radiologists, and rehabilitation specialists. As a result, a unique aspect of a school-based psychoeducational report on learning problems, as well as on the specific emotional/behavioral/social problems associated with the TBI, is the inclusion of information from these nonschool-based professionals. This can include pertinent medical and neuropsychological documentation and related rehabilitation documentation that discuss pre- and postinjury levels of performance and variability of results.

Incorporating Information From Nonschool-Based Professionals

Under IDEA, in order for a student to qualify for special education services under a TBI category, most states require medical documentation of the event that likely caused the TBI (Glang et al., 2008). Because medical documentation may be confusing and cumbersome to read, it is helpful to include at the beginning of the school-based psychoeducational report a summary of how and when the injury was sustained, followed by a summary of findings from medical personnel (including the doctor's name and the dates of evaluation) that is put into terms more readily grasped by nonmedical personnel (see report sample on website).

Whereas a neuropsychological evaluation describes cognitive and/or behavioral strengths and weaknesses resulting from altered brain functioning, a school-based psychoeducational report focuses on academic achievement and skills needed for success, including social, emotional, and behavioral skills. An evaluation planning meeting, therefore, will include a discussion on what information needs to be collected in addition to the information provided by medical or rehabilitation personnel using the ICEL/RIOT process discussed in chapter 10. After the school-based evaluation has been conducted, the school psychologist is generally responsible for writing the integrative school-based psychological report that summarizes assessment results from school- and nonschool-based professionals.

As discussed in chapter 8, a school-based assessment team should obtain data from neuropsychological and medical tests completed in an outpatient or rehabilitation setting. While all original reports should be attached to a school-based report (if a release has been signed and reports are provided to the school), it is important for the school-based assessment team to include a brief summary of results, rather than simply stating "see attached report." Such a summary should include the dates and names of tests administered, where the tests were administered, and by whom. It should then include an overview of the results and specific implications as noted in these reports. It is important to credit the original evaluator, summarize his/her results accurately, and include quotation marks when appropriate. It would be ideal if the original evaluator attended the school-based assessment team meeting, but whether or not this evaluator does, he or she should receive a copy of the school's psychoeducational assessment report. If a school professional, such as a school psychologist, summarizes a professional's findings in a report, it is also helpful to send that professional a copy of the summary in advance for review. All of the district-specific approvals for release of records, forms, and consents to communicate about the student should be completed in advance.

At times, parents may wonder why a community-based professional's findings seem "dismissed" or "ignored" by the school team. There are several reasons this may occur. For example, some physicians, neuropsychologists, or therapists may not understand how eligibility and provision of services in schools work or such a professional's recommendations may not be within the purview of the schools. By law, students are entitled to a free and appropriate public education (FAPE), but interpretation of the term appropriate can be subjective from state to state. Further, outside recommendations based on private evaluations may not be substantiated by the school-based evaluation. That is, they may no longer exist or they may not impact a student's ability to be successful within the educational setting to the degree that the student needs special education or accommodations. Put another way, a student may have exhibited a deficit in a clinical setting or at a past point in time that is no longer problematic within the school setting or that no longer exists because the student has recovered those previously deficit skills. If any of these cases apply, it is important that the school team preserve documentation of the previously-identified problem area and clearly present data on present levels of performance and note this in the school-based psychoeducational report. It is also important to note whether the deficit impacts the child's achievement to the extent that it requires specially-designed instruction. Finally, defensiveness/turf issues on both sides have the potential to block effective collaboration between school and community-based professionals, so it is important to communicate effectively throughout the assessment process. This is one of the reasons why the identification of a case manager, as described in chapter 8, is important.

Describing Pre- and Postinjury Levels of Performance

School-based evaluation team members often craft psychoeducational reports within a certain framework. A novel section for a school-based report on a student with TBI is one comparing pre-injury to postinjury levels of performance. This should be in narrative form and/or tables, charts, and graphs of cognitive ability describing specific academic skills, such as reading fluency, comprehension, math skills, communication skills, and social/emotional/ behavioral status. Teachers and parents frequently will have completed multiple checklists or rating forms to estimate pre- and postinjury skills in each area being evaluated. For example, a classroom teacher may have collected objective data, such as reading fluency with curriculum-based measures or a parent may have completed a behavioral rating scale. This data should be included in the school-based psychoeducational assessment report of a student with TBI as it provides valuable information about the dynamic changes (or lack thereof) a student makes as they improve over time.

Variability of Results

As noted throughout this book, improvement in a student with TBI can be variable and unpredictable. Consequently, a school team may spend time carefully crafting a detailed report, only to find that within weeks the results are no longer a valid representation of current levels of performance. This is to be expected, particularly during the first weeks and months following TBI. Nevertheless, this data provides the school, family, and community-based care providers with a good overview of levels of performance at given points in time. When this happens, any follow-up assessments are added to the report to help team members chart the recovery trajectory.

Areas to Address in the School-Based Psychoeducational Report

Different states will require different report formats, and many use standardized forms. Most school-based psychoeducational reports, however, will contain the same general structure and content such as:

Referral and Background Information

The school-based psychoeducational report generally opens with sections on referral information and a student's background, including medical, educational, and family history.

Medical history. Much information in this section will be based on hospital and rehabilitation discharge summaries and data from parent interviews. Information in this section should include the date of injury; how the injury happened; level of severity; whether the student was in a coma and if so, for how long (including GCS scores); whether other injuries were sustained; how long the student was hospitalized; and whether the student went to rehabilitation and if so, for how long. Medical history should also include data from medical interventions (e.g., neurosurgery) following the TBI and radiology reports indicating the visible extent of damage to the brain found in neuroimaging. It is equally important that this section of the report include whether the student has vision or hearing correction, whether he/she takes medication (type, dose, purpose, and how long he/she has been taking it), and any other health/developmental/physical problems.

Developmental history. Many school-based reports combine developmental history with the medical history; however, because TBI is a medical event and because that section of the report will be substantial, it is helpful to separate these sections. It is important that any developmental history in this section be viewed and reported through the perspective of the relationship between the TBI and any current direct effects, or potential future effects, on development/developmental stages. In other words, as noted in chapter 5, the human brain is not physiologically stagnant during school-age years; rather, it is a dynamically changing and growing organ. Therefore, depending on a student's age at the time of the injury, TBI can significantly affect the development of social, emotional, and behavioral skills. It can also significantly affect the acquisition of gross and fine motor skills.

Educational history. This section should include schools attended, previous retentions or special services, information about the student's progress in the general curriculum before and after the TBI (both classroom data and standardized test data, including universal screeners and statewide assessments), and data from previous interventions. In reports for disability issues other than TBI, the educational history section often precedes the medical information; however, TBI reports should put the medical information first in order to lay groundwork for the information that follows.

Family/Social history. TBI frequently affects the entire family, not just the student. That is, depending on the severity level, the special needs of the student with TBI can put emotional stressors on caregivers and siblings, create financial stresses that did not exist prior to the injury, or result in the dissolution of the family unit. Therefore, this part of the background section should describe family structure and social relationships, both before and after the injury. It should also include environmental factors that might affect performance in school. This might include information on whether other family members have sustained life-changing injuries as a result of the incident that injured the evaluated student. It would also include any other changes in the family unit related to the TBI that may affect the ability of the student with TBI to be successful within the educational setting.

Summary of assessment results. Although different states may vary how they title and structure this section of the report, it should contain information that will help the evaluation team determine whether a student meets TBI eligibility criteria. Each of the sections described below will generally open with a description of the evaluation method and of the strategies used to gather information about the student's performance (e.g., observations, interviews, review of records and relevant trend data, scientific research-based interventions, curriculum-based assessments, norm-referenced assessments, classroom-based assessments, or other methods). One important benefit of an educational evaluation is that the information is context-specific. For instance, an ecological assessment will focus on classroom variables that may impact outcomes beyond those variables usually considered to be within-child issues. For a student with TBI, such classroom variables could include a teacher who rapidly states lengthy instructions or a bright classroom full of visual stimuli. Such a teacher and classroom might positively stimulate other students; however, the student with TBI might become overwhelmed and overstimulated.

The summary section usually includes the name and date of all administered tests, name and title of the person conducting the assessment, and a summary of assessment results. The summary typically includes a description of the test, any professional observations about the student during testing, the test results (presented in both a table and narrative summary), and an error analysis of what the student did and did not do in each area. Data in tables and the narrative section generally present standard scores or T-scores; practitioners will differ in whether they choose to report percentiles, age equivalents, grade equivalents, confidence intervals, and/or qualitative descriptions (e.g., low average, average). It is particularly important that the school-based assessment team include a paragraph in each section that contrasts pre-injury levels of performance to postinjury performance, documenting specific skills with a summary stating areas impacted or not at grade level. A brief statement of educational needs as a result of each of the evaluation areas (e.g., cognitive, academic, social/emotional/behavioral) generally follows assessment results, and these are followed by implications for instruction and for progress monitoring.

Behavioral observations. A section on behavioral observations may precede the rest of the report to describe general notable behaviors (e.g., motor deficits). In the case of a student with TBI, behavioral observations should be included any time an assessment is given. This is because many times the performance of a student with TBI is affected by subtleties related to their injury (e.g., fatigue, headache) and close observation during testing can pick up on these contributing factors. In addition, it is helpful to know when a student with TBI is not experiencing behavioral difficulties during assessments.

Additional Sections

The following are additional sections that should be included in a school-based psycho-educational evaluation of a student with TBI:

Cognitive. The school psychologist usually completes any cognitive assessment and writes the cognitive section of the report. This section will typically involve the reporting of norm-referenced IQ tests and will describe overall cognitive ability and indexes or subareas, such as working memory, verbal ability, or processing speed (depending on the specific IQ test). If different IQ tests were administered by both a community-based practitioner and a school-based practitioner, the school-based assessment report should include scores from both tests, along with a statement regarding whether results were congruent with one another and regarding possible implications of any discrepancies. A statement regarding behavioral observations during subtest performance should be included.

Academic. This section often first presents data from the classroom teacher, curriculum-based measures, and/or standardized norm-referenced tests. Standardized test summaries generally begin by reporting overall performance, followed by broad scales and subtests. The academic section should also include any observational data of how a student reacted to a task or assignment; it is helpful to frame the information in terms that are as objective as possible (e.g., "he had difficulty remaining focused on double-digit addition" rather than "he struggled with math"). The evaluator should also add specific examples of what the child did and did not do, including as much objective data as possible.

Communication skills. A speech pathologist generally evaluates communication skills by observing the student in and out of the classroom; by talking with parents, teachers, and the student; by reviewing discharge data from the hospital; and by conducting norm-referenced assessments on articulation, receptive language, expressive language, and language memory. A summary of the results of this assessment are often given to the school psychologist or team member writing the report, to be incorporated into the school-based psychoeducational report.

Social/Emotional/Behavioral. This section should include observational data gathered at multiple points in time, in multiple settings, and by multiple observers. It might include anecdotal information, narrative summaries, on-task/off-task systematic observations, and/or functional behavior assessment data including the frequency, intensity, and duration of targeted behaviors. The report writer should also detail results of both teacher and parent rating scales and checklists (e.g., the Child Behavior Checklist [CBCL; Achenbach, 1991], Behavior Assessment Scale for Children, 2nd ed. [BASC-2; Reynolds & Kamphaus, 2004], or Behavior Evaluation Scale, 3rd ed. [BES-III; McCarney & Arthaud, 2005]).

Executive functioning. Any impairment of executive functioning may impact all of the previously mentioned areas. Thus the report for a student with TBI might contain a separate section on executive functioning, it might be combined with another section, or it may be infused throughout the report. Regardless of the structure, it is important to address executive functioning skills in the school-based TBI psychoeducational report. The results of executive functioning assessments (e.g., the Behavioral Rating Inventory of Executive Functioning [BRIEF; Gioia, Isquith, Guy, & Kenworthy, 2000] or Child Behavior Checklist [CBCL; Achenbach, 1991]) and so forth are summarized in this section. It is also helpful to link observational assessments and interview data with the standardized test data.

Adaptive behavior. This area of concern often falls to the school psychologist and is based on observations, interviews, and norm-referenced tests (e.g., Vineland Adaptive Behavior Scales-II [VABS-II; Sparrow, Cicchetti, & Balla, 2005] or the Scales of Independent Behavior-Revised [SIB-R; Bruininks, Woodcock, Weatherman, & Hill, 1996]). These scales evaluate self-care behaviors, such as daily living skills, functional communication, socialization skills, and maladaptive behaviors. Specific examples of what the child is reported to do/not do are helpful.

Fine and gross motor skills. The school psychologist may have parents and/or teachers complete screener checklists. If there are concerns prior to evaluation or as a result of the screeners, an occupational therapist (OT) will generally conduct a fine motor assessment, and a physical therapist (PT) will conduct the gross motor assessment. Fine motor assessment often includes fine manual control (precision and integration) and manual coordination (manual dexterity and upper-limb coordination). Gross motor assessment includes evaluation of mobility, running speed and agility, maintaining and changing positions, ability to go up/down stairs, bilateral coordination, strength, and balance. The OT and PT ideally will observe the student in contextual classroom situations and in the structured testing setting and will also collect interview information from the teachers, parents, and student about motor skills in and out of the classroom. The OT/PT may write a report or provide a summary of results to the report-writer (typically the school psychologist).

Health appraisal. This section should summarize medical/physical conditions (other than those related to the TBI), including relevant medical history (pre/postnatal complications, convulsions, fevers, head injuries), medications, and known handicapping conditions. This section of the report also includes results of vision and hearing abilities. The school nurse may complete this section of the report or provide results to the report-writer. Hospital discharge medical information may be found here, but for students with TBI this is generally best presented at the beginning of the report, in the medical history section.

Vocational/Transition. Reports for older students (depending on the state, this means students age 14 or up or students age 16 and up) will include evaluation data on vocational aptitude, interests, and skills.

Summary. The end of the report generally includes a summary or conclusions section in which all parts of the evaluation are synthesized. For the school-based and nonschool-based

TBI evaluation data, a separate paragraph should be dedicated to summarizing pre- and postinjury levels of performance, including the recovery trajectory to-date. The report will reiterate areas of deficit, compiled from all sources.

Description of needs and implications. This section of the report may also be titled "Impressions and Recommendations." Any needs are based on areas of deficit listed in the summary. Regardless of whether or not a student qualifies for special education, the implications section of the report is arguably the most important part. The implications are essentially the team's justification for the level of support required for the student to be successful. The four main areas to address in describing implications include:

1. What is the impact on achievement in each area (e.g., academic achievement, social skills, independent living skills)?
2. What interventions are recommended?
3. What accommodations or modifications are recommended?
4. What data collection tools will be used to monitor progress and how often will this data be recorded?

A student may not qualify for special education under IDEA, but that does not mean he/she will not receive extra help at school. The student may qualify for a 504 plan, which considers whether a student has a substantial limitation in one or more major life activities, including learning, as a result of the TBI. If neither an IEP nor 504 plan is warranted, the school may still implement an intervention plan based on an FBA and the implications reported in this section.

Eligibility. This section provides a justification for any eligibility determination decision, describing how the student meets or does not meet eligibility criteria under IDEIA 04 and/or Section 504. This should include a statement of how the TBI affects the student's progress in the general education curriculum and in what areas. This is also where many states will have school districts identify related services for which the student qualifies, such as speech and language therapy, occupational therapy, or physical therapy. In order to be eligible for special education services, the school-based report must show documentation of adverse effects, such as the negative impact of the TBI on the student's ability to learn and participate in school. These might include things such as an inability to meet grade-level expectations, maintain social relations, function independently in the school setting, express needs and wants, or understand and follow directions. This negative impact must be substantial—to a degree that special education services are required. In order to qualify for special education under TBI, the student's deficits also must be such that specially-designed instruction is required. In other words, the student requires more support than classroom accommodations alone. This information is conveyed in this section of the report. Because a student who sustained a TBI may demonstrate variable performance across time and settings, it is important that documentation in the report clearly illustrate the need for specially-designed instruction.

Signatures. All members of the school-based assessment team should sign the report and include their highest level of educational attainment (e.g., MA, PhD). If any team member disagrees with the team's determination, he/she is typically required to attach a written statement of disagreement to the report.

Providing Oral Feedback on Assessment Reports

While some school-based evaluation teams spend hours conducting assessments and crafting written reports, they often give less consideration to how they will verbally communicate assessment results to families and teachers. It is important to understand that the parents of students with TBI have been through difficult times as the child they used to know becomes the child they now know. In addition, they often feel overwhelmed by the rush of information that they receive as the larger medical and educational systems evaluate and treat their child. Therefore, the tone and the content of such feedback meetings and just how the information is conveyed often set the stage for what follows and thus should get serious consideration. Depending on their interactions with school personnel, parents will see such communications as either supportive or as yet another source of stress and disappointment. School team members must consider the following questions: Do the parents feel included as important members of the team? Do evaluators take the time to clearly explain and often to repeat confusing information? Will the student be present at the meeting(s)? If so, how does that change how parts of the report will be communicated? Have team members truly listened to and considered the parents' fears and frustrations about their child's current and future status?

It is important that the person leading any meeting open with a friendly greeting and introductions. Although it may seem a natural prelude to a conversation, it is critical that parents do not encounter "clinically cold" team members who only speak of their child in terms of deficits and failures to achieve. In addition, they should be sensitive to the grieving process of the parents as they struggle with the loss of the child that "was" before the TBI. Therefore, the team spokesperson should set the stage for what follows by not only describing what will happen at the meeting and about how long it will last, but letting the parents know that it is all right to ask questions or ask for clarification. When each school-based evaluator shares his/her evaluation results, it is also important to pause to ask the parents if the skills or behaviors described are congruent with what parents continue to see at home. A note taker will ensure that updated information is recorded appropriately and integrated as an addendum to the report. It is also important that team members are mindful that this may be the parents' introduction to the world of special education; acronyms and jargon should be avoided.

Team members must be sensitive to the fact that an entire family is affected by a child's TBI. While the school may be focused on educational issues, parents may be grieving, coping with stress and anxiety, and dealing with other family members, including siblings. Parents who seem argumentative may simply be trying to be assertive and advocate for their child, they may be frustrated with their child's lack of progress, or they may be fearful that their child's needs may not get met. Parents may also be frustrated and angry without knowing why. They may be tired, stressed, and impatient. Some of this may be due to the red tape and time-consuming process of special education (Robinson, 2011). By listening, by validating parents' feelings, by avoiding defensiveness and blame, by recognizing fear and frustration for what it is, and by focusing on solutions, school personnel will more effectively work with parents who are emotionally overwhelmed.

Rather than arguing a point, school team members should see this as a positive point of advocacy and reinforce to parents that they, too, are advocates for the student—that the group will work together toward common goals.

Incorporating Assessment Report Information Into Educational Plans

If a student's school-based psychoeducational evaluation team report supports an eligibility determination, an Individualized Education Plan (IEP) is developed. The report should be so well written that results can be "poured" directly into the Present Levels of Performance (PLOP) section of the IEP. The PLOP is a statement of the child's present level of academic achievement and functional performance. Present levels must be written in observable, measurable terms, and the report should state both educational and social needs. These are the basis for IEP goals and objectives.

Educational plans (IEPs or other intervention plans) for students with TBI should be based on strengths that were identified in the neuropsychological and educational evaluations. Goals may include such things as modifying the environment (when appropriate), teaching compensatory strategies, and/or providing tools to help the student learn and generalize new skills and behaviors. Information on specific intervention strategies that modify the environment or provide student-directed strategies are provided in chapters 12 and 13. The IEP will also specify learning objectives and the vehicles for reaching the objectives, including who will provide services, service location (e.g., regular education classroom, special education classroom), and service frequency or intensity. A sample school-based assessment report is available on the website accompanying this book.

12 School-Based Interventions
Emotional, Behavioral, and Social Consequences

As noted in chapter 6, TBI often results in significant emotional, behavioral, and social difficulties that may affect a student's mental health and interpersonal relationships. When this happens, there can be a significant impact on educational performance. It is important, therefore, that school-based professionals have available a range of intervention strategies designed to minimize the negative consequences of TBI-induced (or exacerbated) emotional, behavioral, and social difficulties. School-based interventions should begin upon school entry/reentry and reinforced across all settings, including home and community. While interventions cannot be provided for every possible form of TBI consequence, they are provided for some of the most common issues.

Chapter Overview

Existent literature is sparse in terms of emotional, behavioral, and social interventions designed specifically for students with TBI. Therefore, this chapter will discuss evidence-based interventions that have been successful for students with related deficits (e.g., chronic illness, ADHD, executive functioning deficits). Intervention strategies will link to the multimethod, multisource, multidisciplinary TBI-SNNAP approach described in chapter 10. Sections will include information on

- environmental and curriculum modifications; and
- intervention approaches for emotional, behavioral, and social issues.

Environmental and Curriculum Modifications

In some cases, a student returning to school while still recovering from a TBI will have limited physical and mental endurance. In such cases, the school should allow the student to gradually attend school for longer periods of time or change class schedules to incorporate a less demanding load. Flexibility is important and should be based on changing needs. Other schedule adjustments, such as putting academic classes in the morning or allowing the student to have a study hall at the end of the day, may also be helpful.

Making up missed work can be especially stressful for a student with TBI (Bowen, 2005). Therefore, rather than requiring that students with TBI make up classes and assignments, they should be permitted to work at their current ability level and allowed additional time to relearn concepts and regain skills (Bowen, 2005). This may include entirely excusing students from some assignments, giving shortened assignments, or temporarily providing instruction in a separate classroom setting.

Students who exhibit attention problems, sensitivity to overstimulation, disinhibition, or emotional lability may benefit from a classroom that does not have unnecessary distractions, including noise. Placing these students near a teacher, having them use a study carrel, removing unnecessary materials from work desks, and using earplugs or a personal FM unit to reduce external noise may be helpful (Bowen, 2005). In addition, these students might be allowed to transition between classes before or after the rest of the group or eat lunch in a quiet room. It may also be helpful to provide an aide or peer to help with hallway transitions, particularly in the first weeks following return-to-school.

Returning to the demands of school can be stressful and frustrating for students with TBI—this can elicit or exacerbate a range of emotional, behavioral, and social problems. Therefore, some students may benefit from having a designated rest place, such as the nurse's office, where they can go for a break. A time-out within the classroom may also be effective. This may simply involve having a separate space in the classroom where the student can escape or decompress without entirely leaving the instructional environment. Rather than labeling the spot "time-out," the teacher might let the student name it (e.g., "my rest zone"). In addition, the student should be allowed to determine when he/she is ready to use the time-out area or rejoin the others.

It can give students a sense of empowerment when they are given choices rather than directives. This can be particularly true for a student with TBI who previously functioned with a higher level of independence and success. Thus, for a student who was once able to function independently, but whose TBI has resulted in damage to the part of the brain that disinhibits impulsive actions, rather than saying, "Lucy, keep your hands to yourself," the teacher might say, "Lucy, keep your hands to yourself or move to the other table." In addition, students with TBI may need to experiment with different approaches to educational material and school expectations. The best teacher for a student with TBI, therefore, is generally flexible, helps the student try and select the strategies that work best for his/her unique needs, and provides alternative choices.

Memory impairment and low frustration tolerance in students with moderate to severe TBI may be minimized by avoiding unnecessary changes in routine. A written schedule or visual chart may keep the student from being confused or repeatedly asking for clarification of expectations. Lists or picture schedules of task steps, simplified instructions, maps, or signs may all help the student with TBI become more successful and independent in the classroom environment. It may be helpful to review this schedule at the beginning of the day or class period and verbally review the steps. If there is going to be a change in routine or transition, the student with TBI should be given advance warning or cues so he/she can prepare both mentally and physically for the change. In order to be most effective, all of the student's teachers should apply the same strategies consistently throughout the school day (Bowen, 2005).

If specific social skills are an issue for a student with TBI, it may be helpful if teachers deliberately create an environment in which empathic or helpful behaviors toward the student with TBI are reinforced ("You helped Jenny calm down. Thanks for being a good friend."). Structured activities that allow for time with prosocial peers may allow students with TBI to see the positive consequences of appropriate social skills and behavior.

Intervention Approaches for Emotional, Behavioral, and Social Issues

There is no consistent set of observable emotional, behavioral, or social characteristics for individuals who have sustained a TBI; thus, students' unique characteristics need to be matched with evidence-based interventions for their unique presenting concerns. For example, some students with TBI are more withdrawn, others are more emotionally labile, and others are more belligerent. There are several types of interventions with empirical support for students with different types of emotional, behavioral, and social problems. Some of these include behavioral interventions, cognitive-behavioral remediation, direct skills training, and family-centered approaches. While there is limited research on these strategies specifically for students with TBI, they have been effective for students with similar presenting problems, as described below.

Behavioral Interventions

Behavioral intervention techniques that are effective for a variety of childhood disorders (e.g., attention deficit hyperactivity disorder, oppositional defiant disorder, intermittent explosive disorder) generally focus on modifying antecedents or consequences of behavior, stating the desired behavior in specific, operational terms, and emphasizing elicitation of observable changes, which can be measured and charted before, during, and after an intervention to help determine efficacy (Cooper, Heron, & Heward, 2007). Effective interventions for students with TBI might focus on promoting new or replacement behaviors/skills, increasing existing behaviors/skills, reducing interfering problem behaviors, and/or facilitating generalization. In addition, the strategy might involve administering a reward or pleasurable event following the exhibition of a desired behavior. As Bandura explained, if no positive incentives are offered when a new skill is being acquired, then one's potential is likely to remain undeveloped (1986). Therefore, when Lucy has difficulties with inappropriate touching, she might earn teacher praise for keeping her hands to herself in line.

It has been suggested that intensive positive reinforcement can create a rewarding environment and help successfully reintegrate students with TBI into school settings (Gardner et al., 2003). Therefore, such interventions may include a combination of primary and secondary reinforcers. For example, reinforcement might include token economies (e.g., points that can be turned in for desired reinforcers), privileges, edible reinforcers, social reinforcers (high five, thumbs up), or the opportunity to engage in a preferred activity. The intervention agent (who might be the teacher) may need to be instructed on how to use shaping to reinforce successive approximations of a desired behavior. If immediate, specific verbal praise is used, it should be given over reprimands in at least a 4:1 ratio.

Positive behavioral momentum. Positive behavioral momentum is a behavioral intervention that has demonstrated success for students with TBI (Feeney & Ylvisaker, 2003). Before introducing stressful or difficult tasks, the instructor makes sure the student has experienced success with less difficult or less stressful tasks. The student ideally will have experienced sufficient success with easier tasks so that difficult tasks begin with a reasonable level of confidence. The theory behind this intervention is related to the momentum of objects in motion; the establishment of a high rate of reinforcement for compliance increases momentum and carries over to less desirable tasks. For example, consider a student who prior to sustaining a TBI is able to easily complete multiplication and division problems. Now, as a consequence of his TBI, double-digit division problems have become difficult to complete and a source of frustration, but single-digit division skills remain intact. For this student, first completing simple single-digit division before attempting more difficult, and now aversive, double-digit division problems would provide this student with positive momentum that would carry over into the double-digit problems.

Overall, externally managed behavioral methods may be effective, but they also may prevent students from developing the skills needed to become more self-reliant (Cole & Bambara, 1992). Traditional behavioral methods are monitored by external agents, such as teachers, and thus minimize opportunities for students to learn how to manage their own behavior (Shapiro & Cole, 1994). The teacher may become a cue for appropriate actions because he/she is the administrator of the consequences for a behavior, thus making generalization to situations outside of school difficult. Further, when behavioral techniques are used alone, the underlying reason for a behavior may be masked. In such cases, once a reinforcer is removed, the negative behavior might return. Thus, combining behavioral techniques with cognitive strategies described below may help the student with TBI self-monitor more effectively and become more self-reliant.

Cognitive-behavioral remediation. Cognitive-behavioral theory (Schacter, Gilbert, & Wegner, 2010) emphasizes the role of thinking in how people feel and what they do. It explores the importance of cognitive workings and private thoughts as mediators of behavior change. Working within this model, one believes that when students understand how and why they are doing what they are doing, then they can begin to alter behavior. A fundamental assumption of cognitive-behavioral theory is that overt behavior, such as hitting or pushing a peer when teased, is mediated by cognitive events (e.g., thinking "I'm going to let him have it") and that individuals can influence cognitive events to change behavior. Such student-operated systems can allow students to generalize their newly learned behavior beyond teacher-operated systems that rely on external reward and punishment procedures (Harris & Pressley, 1991). Cognitive-behavioral strategies can help teachers remediate behavioral deficits and excesses by providing students with the tools necessary to control their own behavior. Some cognitive-behavioral techniques include verbal self-regulation, which is positive inner speech or "self-talk" to guide problem solving or behaviors. This idea of metacognition (sometimes referred to as "thinking about thinking") is supported in the literature as a way to improve mental health and behavior (Anderson, Nashon, & Thomas, 2009; Azevedo, 2009; Coutinho, 2008).

Self-management. Self-management, in which the goal is to teach the student to manage his/her own behavior, is one cognitive-behavioral strategy that may address the lack of self-awareness issue in students with TBI. To increase the effectiveness of such a strategy, it must be designed to promote the student's awareness of his/her own behaviors and ability to function independently (Nelson, Smith, Young, & Dodd, 1991). In addition, it should require the student to not only monitor his/her behavior, but also to evaluate and reinforce his/her performance (Barkley, 1989). Therefore, an effective cognitive-behavioral strategy utilizing self-management might be giving a student with TBI a small device that clips to his/her belt and emits a silent vibration at random intervals to cue the student to ask himself/herself "Am I paying attention?"

Damage to frontal lobes and associated areas is widely believed to impair cognitive functions (e.g., self-awareness and insight) and the degree of impairment is correlated with injury severity level (Flashman & McAllister, 2002; Sherer et al., 1998). As noted in chapter 3, the frontal lobes are highly susceptible to injury; thus, a significant number of students with damage to the frontal lobes have difficulty with self-awareness and insight. Typical deficits in self-awareness include being unaware of existing deficits, not recognizing emotional responses to existing deficits, an inability to comprehend the impact or consequences of a deficit on day-to-day life, and an inability to explain or account for a deficit. In addition to having a possible physiological basis, students who lack self-awareness of deficits after TBI may lack awareness because of emotionally-motivated denial (a coping mechanism), because insufficient information has been given to them, because they have a lower level of cognitive development, or because they had an unsophisticated knowledge base prior to their injury. This can make the teaching and implementation of cognitive-behavioral remediation strategies and self-monitoring interventions challenging.

Data Comparison

One way to assess awareness in a student with TBI is to compare self-report (via self-monitoring) to a more objective measure, such as ratings by families, rehabilitation staff, or teachers. Self-monitoring might involve instructing the student at random intervals to ask himself/herself "Am I listening?" and then have him/her mark a plus (+) or minus (−) on a tracking sheet, based on whether or not he/she was paying attention. A teacher might utilize a computer program like *Get 'Em on Task* (Althouse, Jenson, Likins, & Morgan, 1999), which gives audio prompts for students to record their behavior. Students with TBI can also self-manage by completing a checklist for assignment completion or rubric for self-evaluation of progress on a behavioral goal. For example, one effective self-monitoring intervention for students who sustained a TBI utilized twice-daily ratings on a five-point rubric. Student ratings were compared to teacher ratings, and students were reinforced for both accuracy and positive scores (Davies, Jones, & Rafoth, 2010). As expected, there were some idiosyncratic effects, but overall the intervention positively impacted students' classwork and behavior. Self-monitoring with student ratings compared to others' evaluation of the student could also be employed for a variety of social issues, such as initiating and maintaining conversations, playing cooperatively, or refraining from sexually inappropriate comments.

Direct Skills Training

It is certainly not only lack of self-awareness that causes inappropriate behavior, emotional responses, and social interactions in students with TBI. Recent research focusing on "theory of mind" deficits in students with TBI indicate that the inability to decipher social cues sufficiently impairs ability to effectively interact (Dennis et al., 2012).

This may be due in part to focal volumetric reductions in white matter within the brain regions involved in social information-processing (Yeates et al., 2013). Direct skills training may be one way to teach students with TBI to better read intention, emotion, and other type of indirect communication from others (theory of mind). This, in turn, can improve behavior, emotional well-being, and social skills. It can also teach them classroom routines and coping strategies for frustrating situations. For example, students with TBI who are aggressive towards others might be directly taught to verbally express their needs instead of hitting peers to get what they want.

Direct Instruction

DI is based on principles of applied behavior analysis and includes pacing, frequent opportunities to respond, feedback, and reinforcement to maintain engagement. Bowen (2005) summarized DI steps as follows:

1. Select a meaningful goal or skill the student will need to learn and present it at the level of the student.
2. Provide a simple rationale to help the student understand the relevance of the skill.
3. Give clearly stated task directions (limit the number of steps) and ask the student to repeat or paraphrase the directions to ensure understanding.
4. Break tasks into small steps and demonstrate each step.
5. Provide opportunities for student response and practice at an appropriate pace.
6. Provide immediate feedback and error correction when necessary—feedback should be positive and systematic.
7. Use verbal praise and encouragement frequently.

Using the case of Josiah (Case Study 6.1—Josiah; Moderate TBI, chapter 6), a DI sequence might look like this:

1. Josiah's teacher, Mr. Holden, wants Josiah to transition between activities promptly and without protests or commentary.
2. When no other students are in the room, Mr. Holden says to Josiah, "Josiah, it's important that you move from circle time back to your desk as soon as I give that direction. When you move to other places in the room or complain, it bothers the other students and distracts me from teaching. When you go straight to your desk, we can move on to the next activity faster."
3. *Mr. Holden:* "To follow this rule, you need to move straight to your desk as soon as I give that direction. No stopping and no talking. Please tell me what you need to do."
   Josiah: "I need to go to my desk."
   Mr. Holden: "Yes, you need to go straight to your desk as soon as I say circle time is over."
   Josiah: "Go to my desk as soon as you say circle time is over."
   Mr. Holden: "Yes."
4. *Mr. Holden:* "So first, we will be at circle time. Here, I'll pretend to be the student." (He sits at the carpet). "Then I'll tell everyone it's time to go back to

your desks, and you go straight there without stopping and without talking." (He gets up and goes straight to Josiah's desk and sits down.)

5. *Mr. Holden:* "Now you try." (Gives Josiah opportunity to practice without classmates around.)

6. When circle time occurs, Mr. Holden gives the class a cue to transition. When Josiah begins to wander toward the window, Mr. Holden gently redirects him, "Josiah, remember it's important to go straight to your desk."

7. Mr. Holden gives Josiah reinforcement when he transitions successfully: "Josiah, you went straight to your desk like I asked. Thank you. Now we can start our art project."

Skillstreaming

A skills training curriculum like *Skillstreaming* can use direct training to teach communication, coping, relaxation, pragmatic social skills, problem solving, study skills, and more to students with TBI (McGinnis, 2011). There are three books in the *Skillstreaming* series, one for early childhood, one for elementary students, and one for adolescents. The method uses modeling, role-playing, performance feedback, and generalization to teach essential prosocial skills to children and adolescents.

Functional Communication Training

Functional communication training is another example of a validated direct training approach that may reduce maladaptive behaviors in individuals with TBI (Ducharme, 1999). This involves using FBA to identify the communication function of the behavior (what is the student trying to say with his or her behavior?) and teaching a communication skill (e.g., through a picture exchange communication system [PECS] or American Sign Language [ASL]) that serves the same function. For example, if as a result of frontal and temporal lobe damage, a student with TBI does not know it is inappropriate to hit a peer in order to get their attention, functional communication can be used to teach the student to use words to gain peer attention in the place of hitting. If a student with TBI is unaware that she is shouting to let a teacher know she is finished with a task, functional communication can be used to teach her a nonverbal sign for "finished" so she can give the teacher a silent cue. Teachers then reinforce the student for using the functional communication method and provide ready access to a reinforcer or outcome previously gained by the problematic behavior.

If social skills and pragmatic communication are the primary areas of concern, students with TBI may benefit from a combination of self-monitoring, direct skill instruction, and functional communication training by videotaping practice of specific social situations and having the student rate performance on scoring sheets (Bowen, 2005). This allows the student to see himself/herself as the main character in a realistic situation rather than envisioning a hypothetical scenario.

Family-Centered Approaches

While school personnel may have minimal opportunities to directly work with families of students with TBI, it is important that they have an awareness of the student's family dynamics and be able to communicate effective strategies to parents. Depending on the severity level, parents of students with TBI may experience depression or conflict over how to manage their child. Family-centered strategies, which focus on changing the parent/child functioning, may be helpful when working with the families/parents of students with TBI. Studies have found evidence for organizing cognitive and physical supports for students with TBI around the everyday routines of their lives, with intensive support for their family (Braga, DaPaz, & Ylvisaker, 2005). While school personnel can provide families with resources on the positive impact of these techniques, education alone is not sufficient to create behavior change. The child and family need to develop skills and have the opportunity to practice the skills, preferably with support from a skilled clinician. Therefore, school personnel can direct families to clinicians who support family-centered approaches and offer to collaborate with other care providers to create a seamless home-school-community system of support.

Technology

Technology can be used to facilitate family-based intervention for students with TBI by allowing families access to self-guided web-based sessions and synchronous online videoconferences with a therapist. Online family problem-solving (OFPS) training, a family-centered skill-building intervention focused on improving postinjury family adaptation, has helped adolescents acquire and practice student-specific skills, including problem solving, organization, self-regulation, anger management, communicating needs effectively, social skills, and crisis management (Wade, Carey, & Wolfe, 2006). OFPS web-based sessions include video clips of adolescents with TBI discussing the effects of their injury and information about the skills being taught. They then model the skills they have learned. Interactive exercises help students and family members practice the skills in their own home and community.

13 School-Based Interventions

Academic

When consequences of TBI significantly affect a student's academic functioning, the school is responsible for providing support and services. However, specific evidence-based academic interventions for students with TBI are limited. This is due to a number of factors, including the range of possible TBI consequences, lack of educator training, and limited research resources. Thus, TBI interventions are often based on those designed for individuals with similar symptom patterns (McGrath, 2010). Whenever possible, school-based TBI accommodations and interventions should be linked to the TBI School-Based Neuroeducational Needs Assessment Process (TBI-SNNAP) discussed in chapter 10 and monitored over time.

The emotional, behavioral, and social interventions for students with TBI described in chapter 12 can improve academic performance if they help students feel calm, self-confident, and supported by classmates and teachers. At the same time, the academic strategies in this chapter may positively affect internalizing and externalizing behavior.

Chapter Overview

The TBI-SNNAP described in chapter 10 may be linked to academic intervention strategies that are categorized by TBI consequence. Sections in this chapter include information on the following:

- academic problems;
- specialized teaching strategies;
- interventions for students with specific cognitive issues;
- interventions for students with communication and academic problems; and
- guidelines for writing and implementing educational plans.

While academic strategies cannot be provided for every possible form of TBI consequence, they are provided for some of the most common consequences.

Academic Problems

As described in chapter 7, TBI can result in problems with cognition which often translates to difficulties with academic performance, especially if adaptive intelligence is affected. That is, if as a result of damage to the brain a student's ability to be adaptive (flexible) is compromised, he/she will have difficulty organizing, planning, initiating, understanding, or processing information—abilities essential to acquiring academic information and completing academic tasks. In consequence, in the classroom, students with adaptive difficulties will, among other things, find it difficult to follow what the teacher says, solve novel problems, or plan a long-term project. Academic problems may also occur as a result of other TBI-related consequences (e.g., short-term memory deficits, impaired visual fields, loss of fine motor control).

Regardless of the specific TBI-related cause of academic problems, for many students with TBI, a combination of modifications to the educational environment and specialized teaching strategies—implemented to varying degrees with ongoing progress monitoring—will be the most successful approach. While it is important to continue efforts to develop skills that were lost or diminished following TBI, interventions should also emphasize the development of compensatory strategies.

Specialized Teaching Strategies

Specialized teaching strategies may positively impact the academic performance of students with TBI. A few such strategies include direct instruction, self-monitoring, and differentiated instruction.

Direct Instruction

Direct instruction may also be referred to as systematic instruction. This strategy involves identifying instructional targets (what does a student need to learn?); breaking the skill, information, or strategy into components or steps (a task analysis); delivering instruction; and collecting progress-monitoring data to determine efficacy. Direct instruction also includes errorless learning (tell, don't ask), teaching to mastery, and systematic review (Ross & Frey, 2009).

When using direct instruction, it is important to use a range of examples for each instructional target (Table 13.1). For example, when using direct instruction for the

Table 13.1 Direct instruction examples for instructional targets

What is the instructional target? What does a student need to learn?	Example	Task analysis
Multistep skills	Entering assignments into a smartphone	· Get out phone · Turn phone on · Open notes application · Read assignment · Enter assignment on notes application · Set a reminder for the assignment · Click save · Close phone
Written expression	Writing a cohesive paragraph	· Brainstorm ideas · Use graphic organizer · Organize ideas · Create topic sentence · Create body, 3–5 sentences · Create conclusion sentence

multistep skill of entering assignments into a smartphone, the teacher would include a variety of assignments in terms of content, timeframe, and complexity to enhance generalizability. The instructions or models should be worded in a clear, concise manner; a script may keep instruction consistent across examples.

After designing such an instruction for a skill, the teacher then delivers the instruction by first modeling the skill one step at a time. In this errorless learning, the teacher maximizes the probability that the student will perform correctly on every trial. The teacher trains the student on each step until the student makes few or no mistakes. The steps are then linked together. The teacher's primary role in direct instruction is to facilitate the student's success, using the student's performance as the primary indicator of how many steps should be taught at a time and when or how to fade support. During the process of direct instruction, the student is provided ample opportunity to practice the new skill or strategy across time. Repetition is often particularly helpful for the learning and retention of information and skills in individuals with TBI (Kennedy, 2004), so teachers need to be patient at this phase of direct instruction. This repetition should be meaningful, temporally distributed practice—not rote repetition. The distributed practice involves deep learning that is tied to meaning for the student, recall practice—giving oneself tests or practice recalling the material from memory, and systematic presentation. It is especially important to pace instruction at a rate that is appropriate for the student's processing speed and current skill level. The teacher then provides immediate corrective feedback to errors and ample positive feedback to correct performance and progress (no matter how small). Corrective feedback is most helpful when it is clear, specific, contingent, and genuine (i.e., avoid the vague "Good job!" and the disingenuous "Wow! Amazing!" if the student is wary of unearned praise). Corrections should be specific and stated in a positive manner, telling the student what to do rather than only what not to do. For example, a student with TBI who has significant problems with visual attention to details and fine motor coordination may make numerous calculation errors on an assignment and the numbers may be difficult to read. In this case, the teacher might say, "You answered the first six problems correctly and your problems were lined up neatly. You had four mistakes in the next row of problems and the numbers are hard to read. Redo those four problems and make sure your rows are as straight as those you completed at the beginning. When you redo those four problems, make sure your numbers are written clearly." The teacher should use knowledge of the student's style to tailor such reinforcement so that it meets the learner's preferences, whenever possible.

Conducting this direct instruction within the school setting is particularly beneficial to students with TBI because of the importance of context during instruction. Teachers and/or other members of the school team should be sure to collect ongoing assessment data to determine effectiveness of the strategy. Goal Attainment Scaling (GAS) is a useful way to determine whether level of mastery is less than expected, indicating a need to modify design and delivery of instruction (see Hunley & McNamara, 2010; for more information on collecting GAS data).

Self-Monitoring

Because students with TBI often have difficulty with self-monitoring and remaining focused, especially if executive functioning is impaired, they frequently fail to complete tasks. For academic issues that involve task completion rather than learning new skills and information, students with TBI may be taught self-monitoring to mark whether specific elements of a task were complete. This technique encourages independence and a sense of control. During self-monitoring, students ask themselves whether a task is finished, what still needs to be done, and whether they were successful on the task. Self-monitoring can also be useful for issues such as staying on-task and reading comprehension. To this end, teachers should encourage students with TBI-related task completion deficits to stop and think about whether or not they are doing what they should be doing (or understanding what they are reading) and what might be done to get back on track if they find themselves getting lost. As discussed in chapter 12, self-monitoring can also include a teacher evaluation procedure in which student self-monitoring is compared to teacher monitoring to help increase student self-awareness and accuracy.

Differentiated Instruction

The concept of differentiated instruction began with the Individuals with Disabilities Education Act's mandate to provide the least restrictive environment for students with disabilities by including these students more regularly in classrooms (De Jesus, 2012). Differentiated instruction gives unique learning opportunities for each student based upon individualized needs (Pham, 2012). Differentiated instruction is the process of adapting instruction to a student's unique style of learning.

Interventions for Students with Cognitive Issues

The following strategies target cognitive and academic problems that may occur in students who have sustained a TBI, including attention difficulties, memory impairment, difficulty learning new material, slow processing speed, expressive and receptive language impairments, and problems in specific academic subject areas.

Attention/Concentration Difficulties

Due to symptom similarities between TBI and ADHD, particularly in executive functioning deficits, interventions for students with ADHD are often applied to students with TBI. For example, students with TBI often have difficulty sustaining attention and may benefit from accommodations that students with ADHD receive, such as being given preferential seating, taking tests in small groups or quiet settings, or having a note taker or scribe (McGrath, 2010). To improve students' sustained focus on work, teachers may provide an advance organizer, shorten assignments, provide a study carrel, or clear the student's desk. Color coding or underlining important text may help these students focus on the most salient details of the work. If teachers notice a student is off-task, redirection—verbal, visual, or physical—may be helpful. Finally, teachers might break down an assignment into more manageable parts, abbreviate requirements, or extend the deadline.

Self-awareness is an important skill for students with attention difficulties. As discussed earlier, self-monitoring can also be a valuable strategy for increasing attention to tasks. These attention interventions should also help students recognize and communicate when too much information has been presented at once. In these cases, students should be encouraged to ask the teacher to repeat instructions. If this would be disruptive in a classroom setting, having directions on the board or handout, or pre-teaching instructions to the student with TBI can help prevent him/her from being over-loaded with information.

Memory Impairment

Memory impairment following TBI can manifest as problems with short-term memory, long-term memory, declarative memory, working memory, or all of the above. Once the school team has determined which tasks pose difficulty, it should consider strategies from the following list:

- Use direct instruction to teach the student in the use of memory techniques and organizational aids.
- Provide the student with an organization notebook for assignments, schedules, maps, and a daily to-do list.
- Use auditory signals, such as beepers or cell phone applications, to remind the student of important events.
- Appoint a "study buddy" to help the student review key points.
- Shorten directions and break down larger tasks into smaller chunks.
- Use graphic organizers, flowcharts, or task checklists for academic information.
- Provide check-ins in the morning and again at the end of the day (more often if needed) with a resource room teacher or other support provider.
- Supply an extra set of books to keep at home.
- Reduce changes (e.g., locker location, schedule, assignment format).
- For tests, use a strategy that relies more on recognition than recall, such as true/false, matching, multiple choice, or fill in the blank with word banks provided.

Along the same lines, Pershelli (2007) described three general types of memory strategies specifically for students who sustained a TBI: lock-in memory strategies, recall memory strategies, and ease of burden memory strategies. Lock-in memory strategies help students with data retention. These strategies include:

- Rehearsal: meaningful, temporally distributed. Note that the positive effect of rehearsal on memory is more effective when distributed over time. Example: A student is trying to remember her multiplication tables. She repeats them out loud five times a day, every day for a month.
- Grouping: dividing information into groups, pairs, or categories; helpful when students are trying to remember lists. Example: A student is trying to remember foreign language vocabulary by grouping words into categories like household items or occupations.
- Association: words are matched with objects or pictures, helpful for developing meaning and context when reading or thinking. Example: A student is having trouble remembering the difference between latitude and longitude. She can be taught to think about how "lat" rhymes with "flat" (that the lines appear flat or horizontal) and that "long" are the long, tall longitude lines that run north to south.

Once students with TBI have developed a strategy for retaining information, they need a process to recall the data. The steps to recall memory strategies include:

- Make a start, in which students write down what they are thinking to try to jog the memory. Example: A student needs to remember his address, so he begins by writing down what he does know: the name of the street.
- Relax, which may help students recall information.
- Form a habit for daily activities, or using routines to help recall information, such as always having the students place their homework in the same spot.
- Keep and display mementos, such as attaching a doctor's note in the students' planners.

Students who have sustained a TBI can also find it difficult to recall information after reading from text. To ease this burden, bypass strategies may help with memory recall. For example, students might use computer software to store and organize information, thus eliminating the burden of having to recall information. This can also include a strategy such as using notes for quizzes and tests.

Planning and Organizational Difficulties

Poor planning impacts behavior, goal setting, task completion, punctuality, and overall daily living skills. A student's TBI-related difficulty remembering and planning ahead may be frustrating for the student, teachers, and family members. While working with a student with TBI who suffers from difficulties with remembering and planning ahead, adults may be surprised that at times they need to state the obvious. For example, when giving an assignment involving multiple steps or directions, a teacher may need to go through each individual step/direction more than one time in order for the student to successfully complete the assignment or be able to ask clarifying questions. Some students need to be patiently coached through each step. Routines, scripts, picture schedules, and calendars with short- and long-range plans may all be helpful. Checklists on which students mark off the steps they've taken to complete a task give concrete reminders as well as a sense of accomplishment. Planning and goal-setting sheets may be organized into a small notebook, delineating the number of steps in a task and the number of items to be completed (for examples of such forms, see the self-directed intervention planning forms on Intervention Central at http://www.jimwrightonline.com/mixed_files/montauk/Student_Self_Directed_Intvs_Planning_Sheet.pdf).

Difficulty Learning New Material

Students with TBI who have difficulty learning new material often benefit from longer viewing times and repeated viewing of new information. The direct instruction techniques discussed earlier in the chapter are particularly helpful for this area of deficit (for more information see Glang et al., 2008). Because students with TBI often have multiple difficulties following their injury, and because these often lead to a low level of frustration tolerance, feelings of being overwhelmed, and mental fatigue, the pace at which new material is presented to a student with TBI is important, especially in the early stages following the injury. Therefore, when presenting information teachers should present verbal information at a relatively slow pace, with appropriate pauses. In addition, the student should have frequent opportunities to respond, with high probability that those responses will be correct (see direct instruction above), and this verbal information should be reinforced with pictures or other images when appropriate. Advance organizers, including preteaching key words and concepts for lessons being taught, are also beneficial. Teachers should organize concepts from the concrete to the abstract and frequently summarize information as it is being taught as students with TBI, especially in the early stages of improvement, frequently have difficulty with the abstract.

Slow Processing Speed

Closely related to pacing is the issue of processing speed. In order to process information, it must first be retained in short-term memory. This becomes problematic for students with TBI who have damage to the areas of the brain involved with short-term memory. The key to assisting students with TBI who struggle with slow or inefficient processing speed is controlling the amount of information students receive at one time. Requiring frequent student responses allows the teacher to check for understanding and retention of new information. To help students experiencing short-term memory problems to retain new information and keep going until the work is complete, teachers should control the amount of information a student works with at one time (chunk assignments), allow rest breaks, give more time for students to respond, and/or allow additional time for work completion. Teachers and parents might also set targets for quantity of work. For example, instead of assigning a due date for an entire project, teachers could have students with memory deficits submit parts of the project across different dates. This helps these students complete work without overloading them with information, which could lead to fatigue, shutting down, or frustration. Additional review of previous segments can also be helpful.

Interventions for Communication and Academic Problems

Students with TBI often have difficulties with expressive and receptive language that are lessened by using evidence-based strategies for deficits in language or speech functioning (Laatsch et al., 2007; Lewandowski & Rieger, 2009). When students have TBI-related difficulty with language it is recommended that the school speech and language pathologist be consulted/involved in designing academic interventions. The following interventions may be helpful for these students.

Expressive Language

Classroom teachers may facilitate language improvement simply by providing students with TBI adequate time to complete their thoughts. Open-ended questions—rather than questions that might be answered with a "yes" or "no"—should be asked whenever possible. This encourages students to put thoughts into words and gives them the opportunity to practice responses. If students have difficulty with word or information retrieval, the teacher may provide initial sound cues, multiple-choice assessments, or key words for fill-in-the blank items.

Receptive Language

Students with TBI experiencing difficulties with receptive language often benefit from extra time to process verbal information and questions. Teachers may also find it helpful to repeat instructions in a different order or ask the student to repeat the instructions back to ensure understanding.

Social Language

Roleplays of conversations and social situations are often beneficial for students with TBI as it allows for instructional repetition and practice of important social language/ concepts. Helpful interventions may include teaching appropriate expressions and giving opportunities to practice these or practicing staying on-topic, taking turns speaking, sustaining conversation, and avoiding interrupting.

Difficulty with Reading, Writing, and Math

When selecting reading interventions for a student with TBI, members of the school team must first pinpoint where in the reading process the student experiences difficulty. Students who have difficulty with the "input" aspect of reading (i.e., visual) may benefit from books on tape, large-print books, or slant boards to modify a book's angle on the desk. If students have difficulty focusing on written words, a line marker or a piece of cardstock with a window cut out show only small sections of text at a time. The teacher may also provide preteaching or build on the student's previous knowledge, linking new learning to an established knowledge base. With TBI, previously learned material will generally be easier to recall than newly learned information. Preteaching can occur through advance guiding questions, an outline to fill out, or definitions of key vocabulary words. If a student has difficulty demonstrating knowledge, that student might benefit from having tests adapted. For example, instead of an essay test, the student might do fill-in-the blank responses or answer multiple-choice questions. For students with comprehension difficulties, a teacher or assistant might provide guided notes so the students learn how to identify the most salient details in a passage. For the student with TBI-related motor difficulties, assistive technology may help with production of written language. These students may also benefit from simply having more time to complete written tasks or dictating their own thoughts into a recording device prior to writing. Finally, teachers might help with written expression by providing headings, bullet points, or outlines.

Math difficulties for students with TBI may be minimized if teachers introduce concepts using concrete objects that can be manipulated, such as counters or pie pieces. They may also create functional activities to allow students to practice math concepts, such as purchasing items from a mock store or practicing word problems with pictures and stories. Compensatory aids, such as calculators, help students solve multiset problems. If students have difficulty focusing on one problem at a time, teachers might use a paper with a window cut out to display problems one at a time.

Guidelines for Writing and Implementing Educational Plans

Individualized Education Programs (IEPs) are designed to meet the needs of individual students who meet the IDEIA 04 eligibility criteria for special education services under a TBI classification. Like IEPs for all disability categories under IDEIA 04, the IEP for students with TBI will be highly individualized; however, the IEP will need to be reviewed and modified more frequently because of rapid skill level changes that typically occur during the improvement stages following injury. Also unique to students with TBI, the student may have skills one day but not the next. In fact, the IEP may need to be rewritten every few months to meet these students' changing needs. In addition, the student with TBI may be impacted more than other students by fatigue, stress, physical or sensory deficits, cognitive load from other activities, and dynamic biochemical changes during recovery.

Stages of Improvement

Soon after a student sustains a TBI, teachers may need to address in an IEP the safety of the student and ways of responding to any continued pain or other nonacademic needs the student may be experiencing. In fact, academic goals may not be a focus at this time. Safety needs are critical because if the student is still symptomatic, a second injury could lead to more severe or long-term impairment. The healing brain is more vulnerable to insult because of the myriad biochemical changes occurring during the brain's healing process and if the student has exacerbated symptoms at school, they may indicate he/she has returned to school too soon or that the cognitive load is too much for the student during the early recovery period. As a result, a reduction in cognitive load may be recommended. Safety interventions may include letting the student leave class late or early to avoid congested hallways or require a higher level of supervision on the playground.

Many students return to school following TBI taking prescribed medications (see chapter 14). When this happens, medication levels may still be under evaluation; therefore, academic performance and behavior may be quite unstable. Some medications may cause the student to become lethargic or fatigue easily and thus require accommodations for frequent breaks, rest periods in the nurse's office, or a shortened school day. At the early healing stage, the student may still be very sensitive to external stimuli and require a quiet, dim, calm environment that does not overstimulate.

At this stage, the IEP team should also be sensitive to the fact that the family (and teachers) may need a high level of support. The degree of TBI severity, the level of family resources, and the presence of injuries in other family members may mean the family has to deal with many competing needs. Depending upon severity, families may be experiencing emotional distress, confusion, anxiety, posttraumatic stress disorder, or recovery from a potentially life-threatening event. This will have a direct effect on a student's and family's ability to take in new information, have difficulty scheduling meetings, or be less active participants in the intervention process. These issues may also cause the student to perseverate on home issues while at school and affect his/her ability to study in the home environment and/or concentrate on academic tasks. The school team must therefore be mindful of the family situation and develop IEP goals that are clearly written and articulated.

In the middle stage of healing following TBI, students' skills can be steadily changing; therefore, frequent meetings are required to modify IEPs accordingly. In the later stages of healing, skills and needs become more predictable and tend to plateau. However, during this stage students may still have difficulty processing large amounts of information, be easily distractible, have self-regulation difficulties, and have trouble with depression or anxiety, so IEP goals should be monitored during this time.

Type of Goals

IEP goals for students with TBI should be functionally oriented and outcome-based. Because many students with TBI have areas of strength (intact areas of functioning), it may be helpful to base annual goals on student strengths paired with student need. The website contains sample IEP lists, goals, and objectives for Josiah (Case Study 6.1—Josiah; Moderate TBI), a student in first grade.

Location of Services

When considering location of services, it is important to keep in mind that many students with TBI best regain academic skills when intervention is conducted in the context of their regular classroom, with familiar teachers and peers and known routines. Therefore, if academic services are provided on a prolonged basis at home, as is often the case with severe TBI, it is possible that behavior problems will appear or increase because family members frequently are stressed and not properly trained to handle outbursts. In addition, because home instruction is generally focused on skills maintenance—not skills enhancement—with home instruction the student may fall behind academically. In addition, absence from school frequently increases anxiety about returning to school. Once back in school, if a student is provided an IEP, the team may assume that the intensity of services requires placement in a separate special education classroom. While a quiet, separate classroom may be beneficial for some students, or while it may particularly work for taking tests, temporary placement in a special education classroom could be a source of emotional stress for the student; it could also be a source of inappropriate modeling for students with TBI who are trying to regain social skills. All of these factors should be considered in placement decisions and the writing of IEP goals.

Progress Monitoring Strategies

As discussed in the previous chapter on behavioral interventions (chapter 12), it is important to implement appropriate and frequent academic progress monitoring strategies in order to assess intervention effectiveness. This yields more objective data in informing the school-based evaluation team of a student's progress compared to pre- and postinjury levels, and it helps indicate whether interventions should increase in intensity, decrease in intensity, or be altered. Progress monitoring of IEP goals, therefore, is essential. The team member carrying out the intervention should apply decision rules for changing interventions as needed, based on analysis of progress-monitoring data. Such data may include self-monitoring tallies; teacher or parent tallies; behavioral ratings for target academic behaviors (e.g., organization, work completion, remaining on-task); review of work products; curriculum-based measurement (CBM) of academic fluency; evidence of increase in correct answers or decrease of errors in a fixed time period; or evidence of any increased or decreased frequency of desired behavior. Data-based decision making for students with TBI should include visual analysis of charted data and calculations of effect size and Goal Attainment Scaling (see Hunley & McNamara, 2010). As with behavioral strategies, a crucial part of progress monitoring is evaluating treatment integrity and treatment acceptability. This will have a direct effect on a student's and family's ability to take in new information, schedule meetings, and be active participants in the intervention process.

14 Monitoring Pharmacological Interventions

TBI can result in attention problems, depression, anxiety, seizures, sleep problems, persistent headaches, and more. Further, TBI can exacerbate preexisting issues, such as attention deficit hyperactivity disorder (ADHD) or mood disorders. Therefore, medication may be prescribed in order to help manage the symptoms associated with TBI consequences. Some medications may be prescribed short-term during the acute and subacute phases (hospital and rehabilitation) while others may continue on a long-term basis during the chronic phase. For some individuals with TBI the onset of consequences may not appear for months following injury (e.g., depression) at which time medication will be prescribed. Because of the heterogeneity of TBI and TBI-related consequences, therapeutic response to medications is highly individualized and difficult to study in clinical trials.

Many students with TBI will reenter school settings with one or more prescribed medications. Thus, school professionals are well-positioned to gather multimethod and multisource data that may be shared with community-based health professionals responsible for providing pharmacological treatment.

Chapter Overview

This chapter provides basic information about commonly prescribed TBI treatment medications and information about side effects. It also contains guidelines for collaborating with medical professionals and parents in school-based monitoring of prescribed medications. The sections include information on:

- common medications for TBI;
- side effects of TBI treatment medications;
- educational implications of pharmacological treatments;
- collaboration with medical professionals and families; and
- ethical and legal issues for schools.

Common Medications for TBI

In the acute phase of treatment, students with TBI may be given a variety of pharmaceuticals—the most common being mannitol to control brain swelling (Shawkat, Westwood, & Mortimer, 2012). Other medications can include antiseizure medications and medications that induce comas. Individuals who sustained a moderate to severe TBI may be at risk for seizures during the first weeks after injury and antiseizure medications are sometimes prophylactically administered to reduce the likelihood during this acute/subacute timeframe and to help avoid additional brain damage that might be caused by seizures. Beyond that time, additional antiseizure treatments are generally used only if posttraumatic epilepsy occurs or epilepsy was a pre-injury factor. It should be noted that some antiseizure medications may also have beneficial effects on mood and behavioral regulation in the brain-injured child and may be prescribed for those reasons and not seizure control. During hospitalization after a moderate to severe TBI, physicians sometimes use medications to temporarily induce comas because a comatose brain needs less oxygen to function. This also has the potential to be helpful if blood vessels are compressed by increased pressure in the brain and are unable to deliver sufficient oxygen and nutrients to brain cells.

Although pharmacological management of symptoms is common following TBI, evidence to guide this practice beyond the acute phase is sparse. Studies to date have yielded minimal evidence that following TBI medication enhances function, memory, or behavior—particularly with pediatric populations (Chew & Zafonte, 2009). In addition, a recent review of the use of dopamine agonists in the intensive care unit, including methylphenidate, amantadine, and bromocriptine, failed to establish that these medications augment or accelerate cognitive recovery and rehabilitation or that they are safe to use (Frenette et al., 2012). The authors also reported a major concern that important sources of bias were present in the reviewed studies.

Cholinesterase inhibitors (e.g., donepezil), which have been shown to benefit the treatment of Alzheimer's disease, may show some positive results with TBI patients, particularly in the area of memory improvement; however, compelling evidence is lacking until further clinical trials can be conducted (Chew & Zafonte, 2009). This is particularly true in children. SSRIs (e.g., Sertraline) may help alleviate depressive symptoms in some students with TBI. Again, however, larger clinical trials are required (Chew & Zafonte, 2009). Antipsychotics, particularly those with strong dopamine blockade, may decrease symptoms of aggression and agitation; however, they have shown some adverse cognitive impact in animals and human subjects (Chew & Zafonte, 2009).

Finally, glutamate is one of the major excitatory neurotransmitters and has been shown to play an important role in mood and behavioral regulation. Amantadine is a glutamatergic antagonist that has shown some effectiveness in arousal from coma (Vargus-Adams, McMahon, Michaud, Bean, & Vinks, 2010) as well as some positive influence on mood and attention problems in children, including those with TBI (Hosenbocus & Chahal, 2013).

Side Effects of TBI Treatment Medications

For some students, unintended side effects of medications can be as troublesome as the original symptoms. Thus, the family and physician must carefully weigh benefits and drawbacks of various medications commonly prescribed to individuals with TBI, as due to ethical concerns, children and adolescents are not included in clinical drug trials. There are, however, many resources available that describe medication side effects in adult clinical populations.

Educational Implications of Pharmacological Treatments

At times, school personnel may be asked to dispense medication, keep records of medication administration, monitor medication effects, and educate school staff on medication side effects. One of the responsibilities of a school is the safeguarding of students during the school day. Thus, school personnel should obtain the appropriate training in the dissemination and storing of prescription medications. It is equally important that access to these medications be limited to those persons who have been properly trained. Furthermore, school district policies regarding dispensing prescription medication should be followed and permission to hold and dispense medications should be obtained from parents. This can help prepare school personnel to respond to requests that medication be taken during school hours and it also helps school professionals who work with the student (teacher, therapists). Some basic safety guidelines include

- ensuring there is signed permission on file from the legal guardian and the prescriber;
- reviewing information with the parent and prescriber about the medication, such as why it is needed, administration guidelines, possible side effects, and a termination date;
- having parents give medication to the school in the original, officially labeled container;
- safely storing and safeguarding the medication at school;
- documenting administration time and dosage;
- notifying the school of a plan by which refills will be provided;
- clearly identifying who is authorized to administer medication (e.g., school nurse, health aide, teacher, office staff); and
- creating a plan for how to deal with negative effects.

A sample form that can be used for monitoring administration of medication in the school setting is found on the website accompanying this book.

Those asked to provide feedback about medication effects should be familiar with the effects of the specific medication a student is taking. For example, effects of some medications may wane between administrations. Physicians typically provide families and school personnel with information about when the strongest effects are likely to occur and whether "withdrawal" symptoms or "rebound effects" (e.g., increased irritability or inattentiveness as medication effects wear off) might be observed in the waning period. School personnel should seek this information if it is not provided. School staff should also understand that in the early stages of treatment, dosages may vary until the right amount for a particular student is determined.

School personnel can provide feedback about medication effects to families and medical professionals using direct observations, interviews, and/or teacher rating forms. Structured direct behavior observation instruments, such as the Behavior Observation System for Students (BOSS; Shapiro, 2010) provide concrete data on off-task behaviors and academic engagement, which may be impacted by psychotropic medication dosage levels. The BOSS has been found to be useful for evaluating medication efficacy (Power, DuPaul, Shapiro, & Kazak, 2003). Other effective monitoring techniques include review of permanent products, such as accuracy and completion of assignments (Power et al., 2003), interviews with teachers and caregivers, and the completion of behavior rating scales. Teacher rating methods, such as the Child Behavior Checklist (CBCL; Achenbach, 1991), administered before and after a medication is instituted, are frequently employed in school and clinical settings. Curriculum-based measurement (CBM; Deno, 1985; Fuchs & Fuchs, 1998) is also an effective method for determining the response to medication. CBM is a method teachers use to find out how students are progressing in basic academic areas such as reading, writing, math, and spelling. It provides current, regular information on a child's progress within the curriculum. Previous research has indicated CBM is sensitive to changes in dosages of methylphenidate to treat symptoms of ADHD (Stoner, Carey, Ikeda, & Shinn, 1994).

To alleviate the burden of paperwork, a simple medication feedback form can be used, provided written parental consent for staff provision of the feedback is on file. The website contains a sample of such a feedback report.

Because students may be embarrassed about their medication or dislike the way it makes them feel, feedback information on medication should also include observations of the student's feelings about taking the medication. These psychological reactions can influence the apparent effects of the medication or even lead to students only pretending to take medication.

Collaboration with Medical Professionals and Families

Research on collaboration between pediatricians and school personnel indicate pediatricians would like more information regarding medication effects from school personnel. For example, in a study by Haile-Mariam, Bradley-Johnson, and Johnson (2002), 81% of pediatricians reported wanting direct observations from the school on medication efficacy and 45% wanted information on medication side effects; however, only 9% reported receiving this information.

Researchers have identified the school psychologist as a professional uniquely suited for collaboration with medical providers, such as physicians, to enhance the outcomes for children who are prescribed psychotropic medications (Power, DuPaul, Shapiro, & Parrish, 1995; Wodrich & Landau, 1999). School psychologists are well-suited to assist in medication monitoring in part because of the following skills: (a) training in data-based decision-making; (b) training in systematic problem solving from an ecological perspective; (c) ability to monitor progress using methods sensitive to small changes in performance; and (d) ability to observe students in the school environment (DuPaul & Carlson, 2005). Progress monitoring in the school environment can prove valuable to a treatment team because a child's behavior in a clinical setting may not accurately indicate functioning within an educational environment (Pelham et al., 2000). Behaviors occurring in the natural setting can provide valuable information, particularly when the data is provided by an individual with specific training in assessing and observing behavior, such as the school psychologist.

Given these, communication among school personnel, community-based professionals (e.g., pediatricians, psychiatrists), and families regarding pharmacological dosage changes, side effects, and effectiveness is crucial. Because impaired self-awareness may be an ongoing issue for a student with TBI, he/she may not be a reliable reporter of how well a medication is working or associated problems. In addition, it is human nature for parents to want to see improvement in their child when/where it does not exist; especially following a severe TBI. Unfortunately, this phenomenon is supported when popular media reports a case of miraculous, but unsubstantiated, "full recovery" following a severe TBI. Thus, collaborative consultation enhances the accurate reporting of improvement, related medication effects, and level and continuity of care.

The school can help ensure that the student and family understand medications that have been prescribed and why. School personnel can also help make sure that explanations are provided to students in a way they can understand. Because there are questionable overall benefits of medications for students with TBI, school personnel—in collaborative communication with physicians and psychiatrists—can help the student and family understand that medication is only one part of the overall intervention plan. They can also collaborate on documentation and reporting of side effects, ensuring continuous monitoring of medication and dosages.

Sulkowski, Jordan, and Nguyen (2009) describe guidelines set forth by the American Academy of Child and Adolescent Psychiatry (2004) to support collaborative efforts between prescribing physicians and school psychologists. The authors suggest school psychologists can

- help prescribing physicians better understand school systems and the feasibility of specific adaptations that can be made, such as decreased task demands or assigning a peer helper;
- take leadership roles in school systems by creating district-wide consultation with local pediatricians and psychiatrists; and
- forge alliances with physicians to promote district-wide services such as providing pharmacological consultations and in-service trainings on psychotropic medication management.

Ethical and Legal Issues for Schools

School personnel must only practice within their scope of professional training. Thus, they need to exercise caution when discussing recommendations with families, when dispensing medication, and when communicating with community-based care providers about student outcomes and needs (Carlson, Thaler, & Hirsch, 2005). In consequence, school personnel cannot mandate or even recommend that a student be placed on medication. In fact, state and federal legislation limits the role of school personnel in recommending or requiring that students take psychotropic medication as a condition of participating in school. For example, the 2004 reauthorization of IDEA includes provisions for each state to develop policies and practices prohibiting public school personnel from recommending parents seek prescriptions for controlled substances as a condition for school attendance (IDEIA 04).

Access to school nursing services is limited in many school systems, particularly in rural areas, which can increase the probability of medication administration errors. That is, due to a lack of access to trained medical professionals, nonmedical school personnel, such as secretaries and instructional aides, are increasingly asked to dispense medication to students during the school day, with little or no supervision (DuPaul & Carlson, 2005).

As previously mentioned, best practice dictates that school-based professionals have parents sign a district-approved consent form to allow school-based professionals to monitor medication efficacy and communicate with physicians regarding the student's performance and needs. Many districts and medical facilities will require their own forms; thus, school personnel must consult with district administrators and attorneys about any documentation or medication-related issues that might be unique to their state or district.

15   TBI Prevention and Policy

Every year in the United States, needless numbers of children and adolescents sustain a TBI. With collaborative effort, many of these injuries can be prevented. This can be done with protective equipment and educational programs, as well as legislation and policies that are designed to protect people from accidents, violence, and environmental risks.

Chapter Overview

This chapter will describe specific head injury prevention initiatives that can be carried out in the school setting. A sample Microsoft PowerPoint presentation and links to handouts are provided on the accompanying website. This chapter will present information on

- protective equipment;
- violence prevention;
- safe driving;
- safe living spaces;
- education programs;
- legislative initiatives; and
- future directions.

Protective Equipment

Protective equipment provides no guarantee that a person will not sustain a TBI, especially in the case of significant inertial force closed head injuries or penetrating head injuries. However, in many milder cases it can significantly reduce the amount of damage to the brain; there are even times when equipment can prevent TBI, as when a helmet worn by a construction worker deflects a falling object. Following are examples of protective equipment that can directly or indirectly help prevent TBI or reduce damage to the brain:

Seat Belts/Air Bags

Seat belts can help prevent the head from hitting the windshield or dashboard in a car accident. The lap portion keeps the individual in the car and the shoulder strap prevents forward movement, thereby keeping one from smacking the steering wheel in a quick stop.

Car Seats

Because children lack sufficient body mass for seat belts to be effective, the use of car seats is mandated by state law. By design, when properly installed, car seats are designed to prevent children from becoming airborne during an automobile accident. Children therefore should be buckled into the car using a safety seat, booster seat, or seat belt (when old enough). The Centers for Disease Control and Prevention (CDC, 2013j) has guidelines for safety seat recommendations based on children's height, weight, and age (www.cdc.gov/traumaticbraininjury/prevention.html). The CDC recommends that children younger than 13 years ride in the backseat, because air bags can injure or kill young children riding in the front seat. Correct child safety car seat use can reduce the risk of head injury by more than 75% (Muszynski, Yoganandan, Pintar, & Gennarelli, 2005).

Helmets

Helmets can reduce impact of forces to the head by displacing inertial energy; bicycle helmet use has been shown to decrease risk of head injury by 85% and risk of brain injury by 88% (Nagel, Hankenhof, Kimmel, & Saxe, 2003). However, helmets may not offer the level of protection expected by parents, athletes, and coaches. While helmets have reduced head injuries in sports like bicycling, hockey, horseback riding, and football, they do not all effectively reduce craniofacial injuries. Further, helmets reduce mortality and morbidity in motor vehicle-related accidents (e.g., motorcycle-car accidents); however, significant brain injury still occurs in these types of accidents (Lezak et al., 2012). Helmets provide protection for the skull, but the movement of the brain within the skull can still cause shearing and "mechanical deformation" of the brain (Lezak et al., 2012, p. 181).

Taken together, there is clear support for the use of helmets; however, it is also possible that wearing a helmet contributes to students' sense of invulnerability, particularly in adolescents. This might lead students in sports and recreational activities to increase their risk-taking or aggression against other players. It can be beneficial for educational professionals to discuss this with students during prevention efforts. Newer helmet technology seems to offer promising protection, but further research is needed to determine newer helmets' efficacy in reducing risk of TBI. All helmets should be assessed to meet requirements of the National Operating Committee on Standards for Athletic Equipment (Halstead et al., 2010). Further, they should be checked for appropriate fit on both individual athletes and nonathletes participating in recreation (e.g., children learning to ride bicycles). Children tend to wear helmets that are too loose or tilted back on the head, instead of covering the forehead. This offers insufficient protection to the most vulnerable part of the head in an accident or collision. According to the CDC (2013k), helmets should be worn for the following activities:

- riding a bike, motorcycle, snowmobile, scooter, or all-terrain vehicle;
- playing a contact sport, such as football, ice hockey, or boxing;
- using inline skates or riding a skateboard;
- Batting and running bases in baseball or softball;

- Riding a horse; or
- Skiing or snowboarding.

Protective Headgear

Protective headgear is increasingly worn on the soccer field, particularly by female athletes. Protective headgear is effective in providing some protection from contact force injuries and from lacerations and contusions to soft tissue of the head and face. However, most studies show limitations in their potential for reducing concussions (Halstead et al., 2010).

Mouthguards

Some believe mouthguards absorb some of the energy of a collision and can be an important part of TBI prevention. While mouthguards protect against oral and dental injury and may help keep athletes focused on thinking about prevention, there is no evidence that mouthguards minimize risk of TBI (Daneshvar et al., 2011).

Violence Protection

Traumatic brain injuries can result from acts of violence, including Shaken Baby Syndrome (SBS), child abuse, adolescent dating violence, assault, and the use of weapons, including firearms. Violence prevention can take many forms, including increasing awareness of the problem, initiating education programs, and advocating for laws and policies that involve clear consequences for offenders. According to the CDC, SBS is a form of abusive head trauma (AHT) and inflicted traumatic brain injury (ITBI); it is a preventable and severe form of physical child abuse (http://www.cdc.gov/concussion/headsup/sbs.html). It results from violently shaking an infant by the shoulders, arms, or legs; the whiplash effect can cause bleeding within the brain or the eyes. SBS victims generally suffer serious health consequences. At least one of every four violently shaken babies die from this form of child maltreatment (Ashton, 2010). Shaken Baby Syndrome education is often part of childbirth training seminars and information given to new parents at hospital discharge after delivery and may be required for childcare providers and daycare licensing. Prevention efforts can take the form of public service announcements regarding how to manage infant crying (e.g., soothing techniques, parent stress management skills).

Other effective violence prevention efforts to decrease TBI can include increasing availability of programs that support parents who may be at risk for injuring their child. If children are returned to abusive homes, they are at high risk of continued abuse or being killed. It is not uncommon for caregivers to fail to report a history of abuse, either because they are unaware of the abuse (it was inflicted by someone else) or because they want to protect themselves or the abuser. Thus, prevention efforts can be geared toward more thorough interviews and record reviews, considering the possibility of TBI as a result of abuse, and ensuring all school-based professionals are educated in identifying signs of abuse and methods of reporting suspected abuse to child protective services. Such reporting is mandatory in most states (Child Welfare Information Gateway, 2010).

Individuals with TBI may also be at risk for victimization as a result of their disability. This can involve physical violence, sexual abuse, emotional abuse, neglect, or financial harm. It may be perpetrated by family members, caregivers, intimate partners, or other people with disabilities. Students with TBI may be particularly at risk because of their difficulty with anger management, which can cause others to use undue force or unnecessary medication (Kim, 2002). Cognitive problems associated with TBI may also make it difficult for victims to remember, understand, or accurately perceive risky or harmful situations. TBI may also be related to disinhibition or substance use that can be associated with risky sexual behavior or episodes of victimization (additional information on victimization of people with TBI or other disabilities can be found at: http://www.cdc .gov/traumaticbraininjury/pdf/VictimizationTBI_Fact%20Sheet4Pros-a.pdf). In such cases of victimization of students with TBI, it is important for school personnel to be empowered with information on community resources and to have developed relationships with local law enforcement agencies.

Adolescent intimate relationship violence (IRV) can be a cause of TBI; students with TBI are also at risk for being victims of adolescent IRV because of some of the same factors above. Factors that can ameliorate an adolescent's propensity for engaging in acts of dating violence or being a victim of dating violence include having intact or violence-free households, a history of childhood stability, and religious affiliation (Brown & Bulanda, 2008). Additional protective factors include social support, particularly parental support (Holt & Espelage, 2005), high self-esteem, and success in school (O'Keefe, 1998). While school personnel are not in a position to impact all of those factors, they can be mindful of promoting self-esteem and success in school, particularly in students who lack the other ameliorating factors. Further, federal and statewide policies related to violence prevention can help address this issue. For example, several years ago Ohio passed a bill mandating education about adolescent dating violence and healthy relationships to all students in grades 7–12 (Ohio Domestic Violence Network, 2010). This bill also requires school staff members to be trained in recognition and prevention of various forms of dating violence.

TBI can also be caused by assault, physical fights, and weapons. Prevention efforts can focus on violence prevention and identifying gang activity in schools. Because many TBIs are caused by weapons, including firearms, school-based prevention efforts can educate parents about the importance of decreasing availability of weapons, storing firearms safely, and being aware of the possibility that their children may possess or be capable of creating hidden weapons.

Safe Driving

TBI incidence rates are high among adolescent drivers (Rice, 2003). New laws in many states are designed to protect teen drivers—and those who share the road with them— from dangerous and distracted driving, which cause 282,000 accidents a year (CDC, 2010). These laws include restrictions on new drivers' licenses, such as limits on who can be passengers, laws against texting and driving, limits to night driving, and increased number of supervised driving hours required prior to issuing a license. Avoiding driving while under the influence of drugs and alcohol—or when excessively fatigued—is another effective way of reducing accidents and thereby reducing risk of TBI. Parents can be educated about things they can do to promote their adolescents' safe driving, such as reducing access to drugs and alcohol and setting house rules, such as no driving with friends after dark, calling home for a ride if the driver had anything to drink, and so forth.

Safe Living Spaces

The rate of TBI in preschoolers is relatively high, largely due to falls and accidents. While it is important to allow preschoolers to explore their environment, a few simple steps can help make the living and learning environment secure. School personnel can share this information with families, while also evaluating early childhood education settings for safety standards. Old playground equipment, worn surfaces beneath monkey bars, and slippery staircases are just a few things that can make the school environment hazardous for young students. The following are a few ways living areas can be made safer for children:

- window guards that protect young children from falling out of open windows;
- safety gates at the top and bottom of staircases;
- shock-absorbing material on playground surfaces (e.g., mulch, sand);
- keep stairs clear of clutter;
- apply nonskid tape to slick steps;
- nonslip mat in the bathtub or shower;
- make sure area rugs are secure;
- do not permit children to play on fire escapes or balconies; and
- lock up firearms and do not let children know how to access them.

Education Programs

Education of TBI signs, symptoms, and risk factors is critical in order to build a community of care in schools. In sports, the simplest preventive measure appears to be rule changes, rule enforcement, and player and coach education about TBI (Cantu & Mueller, 2009). In addition to parents and students, all school personnel should be educated about TBI, including teachers, administrators, nurses, school psychologists, school counselors, educational aides/assistants, coaches, and athletic directors/trainers. This can be accomplished through a variety of ways including, but not limited to, in-service presentations to educational professionals and parents/guardians, school-wide safety campaigns (e.g., helmet awareness programs, concussion prevention), and newsletters.

School personnel would be wise to invest time in making connections and establishing relationships with members of the medical community, such as local sports medicine centers, in order to facilitate education initiatives. With some creative planning, school-based professionals might cultivate opportunities to speak about brain injury prevention at skate parks, local radio stations, or at Parent Teacher Organization (PTO) meetings, to name a few.

School-Based In-Service

It is important that teachers learn to identify students who may have sustained a TBI (Hooper, 2006b). In order for school personnel to learn about TBI, school-based in-services can be beneficial (Somers & Sikorova, 2002). Following the in-service, continued follow-up, consultation, and dissemination of information are recommended to help school personnel to retain the knowledge (Glang, Todis, Sublette, Brown, & Vaccaro, 2010).

Several factors impact the quality and efficacy of professional development training. It is essential that workshop or training leaders are role models and display knowledge in the area, provide inspiration, encourage teamwork, and provide individual support (Steyn, 2006). The leaders must communicate clearly and help participants understand the material and learn skills. Further, if the leaders are effective in their approach, attendees are more likely to change their practice as a result of the training.

Effective professional development also requires school personnel to practice their new skills in their environment (Yoon, Duncan, Lee, Scarloss, & Shapley, 2007) and receive consultation on the targeted skills (Fuchs & Fuchs, 1992). Professional development for TBI specifically should include evidence-based interventions; supervision with newly attained skills in the training site and classroom; and continued mentoring, feedback, and consultation in teachers' classrooms (Glang et al., 2010).

After an in-service or workshop, follow-up and consultation can reinforce the knowledge and skills that were taught. According to Davies & Ray (in press), knowledge and skills of traumatic brain injury were retained from a TBI workshop after the two-month follow-up; however, it dissipated by the one-year follow-up. This could be due to the lack of ongoing practice of skills, mentoring, feedback, and/or consultation that Glang et al., (2010) asserted is necessary.

While many school-based in-services target educators, they can also be designed for parents and members of the athletic community. Coaches, athletic trainers, parents, and athletes might learn that instruction on proper techniques for heading soccer balls can be beneficial due to the vulnerability of neck muscles, particularly in female athletes. Further, they might be reminded that many concussions are sustained on the soccer field by collisions between players and between players' heads and the ground. That is, the risk of concussion in soccer is not only from heading the ball.

School-Wide Safety Campaign

School personnel can take part in school-wide safety campaigns such as helmet awareness or concussion prevention initiatives. Some schools host a science night or safety fair. At these events, school-based mental or physical health professionals might present on brain safety by doing demonstrations with models of brains or showing how helmets might be worn incorrectly. Schoolchildren can learn about their frontal lobe while also learning how to protect it.

Students themselves can be some of our best allies in spreading the word about brain injury prevention. Students often are reminders to parents to reevaluate their own safety habits; the reminder may come in the form of a sweet voice from the backseat telling mom or dad to buckle up.

When carrying out a safety initiative, partnerships are encouraged between local schools, law enforcement, children's hospitals, pediatricians (including local chapters of the American Academy of Pediatrics), and family service agencies. State-level support can be provided through statewide brain injury associations (a list of these organizations can be found on the Brain Injury Association of America website at: www.biausa.org/state-affiliates.htm). Further, the CDC has a number of resources that can be accessed for a school safety campaign, including the "Heads Up" concussion toolkits for parents, coaches, clinicians, teachers, and school-based mental health providers, and "A-Head Check" steps for immediate head injury evaluation (see below). These resources are free at www.cdc.gov/traumaticbraininjury.

Following are examples of two school-wide safety campaigns, *Bike Helmet Awareness Week* (http://www.ohioaap.org/files/GAToolkit2013.pdf) and *Teen Driver Safety Week* (http://www.teendriversource.org/tools/teen and http://www.ridelikeafriend.org/). Sample presentations and materials can be found on these websites.

Bike Helmet Awareness Week

Besides cars, bicycles are tied to more childhood injuries than any other consumer product, including trampolines, ladders, and swimming pools, and are the top-ranked sports and recreation activity that accounts for the majority of nonfatal TBI-related HED visits under the age of 19 (CDC, 2011; Nagel et al., 2003). Events during a bike helmet awareness week focus on educating parents and children about the importance of wearing helmets. Activities undertaken by the school professional might include holding a bike rodeo, writing a letter to the editor of the local newspaper, helmet distribution, posting messages on social networking sites, distributing flyers, and encouraging involvement by statewide legislators. School professionals can also speak for a few minutes at a parent-teacher association meeting, encouraging parents to model wearing their bike helmets to increase the likelihood of a child wearing their helmet. The *General Assembly Outreach Toolkit* (http://www.ohioaap.org/files/GAToolkit2013.pdf) provides templates to help make getting involved easy, including sample press releases, sample social media posts, and pictures of proper versus improper helmet use.

Teen Driver Safety Week

Mid-October marks the National Teen Driver Safety Week, which was established by Congress in 2007 to find solutions to lower adolescent drivers' crash risks. Schools can tie a school-based campaign into this national initiative. Efforts include education of younger drivers, increasing seat belt use, and decreasing underage drinking. Parent-oriented activities might include efforts toward reducing adolescents' access to alcohol and drugs through parental responsibility and setting of house rules. They can also focus on parents modeling safe driving habits, as young drivers often learn bad driving skills from their parents. Materials adolescents can use to initiate safe driving activities within their schools can be found at TeenDriverSource (http://www.teendriversource.org). This site describes peer-to-peer school-based campaigns such as "Ride Like a Friend. Drive Like You Care," which focuses on the relationship between adolescent drivers and their passengers. The program helps raise awareness of crash risks and behaviors that promote safe driving. School-based mental health professionals can help older students access and promote these materials, thereby engaging them in an important brain injury prevention initiative.

Newsletters

Another means of education is through written newsletters. Outlets might include informational letters that are distributed (via paper copy or email) to teachers or parents; blurbs in school newsletters, websites, or social networking pages; or columns or letters to the editor in a local community press. Content can include safety tips, guidelines for responding to a suspected brain injury, resources for counseling and social support, information on smartphone applications that help with concussion identification, and so forth.

Legislative Initiatives

Policies and laws at the state and federal level, when well-constructed and enforced, can help prevent TBI. A few of these include high-visibility enforcement of driving under the influence and speeding, helmet legislation for motorized vehicles and appropriate sports, and policies for return-to-play of athletes who have sustained concussions.

Statewide Policies

Between 2009 and 2011, at least 34 states passed laws addressing TBI; in 2012, at least 15 states introduced some type of TBI legislation, the majority of which relate to youth sports concussions (National Conference of State Legislatures, 2012). For example, states may have enacted legislation requiring coaches of student athletes to complete a certain degree of training on head injuries, remove student athletes from play if they show signs of having sustained a concussion, and not permit return-to-play without written clearance from a licensed medical professional. Such statewide legislation might include requirements for refresher courses (e.g., once every five years) that are approved by the State Board of Education. In addition to recent concussion laws, the Insurance Institute for Highway Safety (http://www.iihs.org/laws/HelmetUseCurrent.aspx) reports that 21 states and the District of Columbia have bicycle helmet laws requiring various age groups to wear helmets.

Federal Legislation

The federal government has initiated several organizations and acts geared toward TBI prevention. In 1980, the Brain Injury Association of America (formerly the National Head Injury Foundation) was founded (Brain Injury Association of America, 2013). The BIAA has state affiliates, local chapters, and support groups, all aimed at offering information, advocacy, and support to individuals with TBI and their families. Sixteen years, later, the TBI Act of 1996 (amended in 2000 and reauthorized in 2008) created the Health Resources and Services Administration (HRSA) TBI Program, which oversees a system of state funding to develop TBI infrastructure.

The CDC has been very involved in TBI identification and prevention efforts. In 1999, the organization published a report to Congress detailing TBI prevalence, incidence, causes, severity, and associated disabilities, thus documenting that TBI is a significant public health issue. In 2003, the National Center for Injury Prevention and Control's

Mild Traumatic Brain Injury (MTBI) Work Group published *Report to Congress on Mild Traumatic Brain Injury in the United States: Steps to Prevent a Serious Public Health Problem.* This report described the significance of mTBI from a public health perspective and included recommendations for measuring the extent of the problem in the United States.

These initiatives helped increase awareness and knowledge of TBI, and also provided funding and other resources that ultimately benefit children and adolescents in the schools. Educational professionals can utilize these initiatives by soliciting free resources that are available from the CDC, including fact sheets, posters, magnets, and checklists on brain injury specifically designed for school professionals (http://www.cdc.gov/traumaticbraininjury; for more information, the reader is directed to: http://braininjuryeducation.com/Topics/Advocacy).

Future Directions

New research will continue to inform educators about effective brain injury prevention. This might include better safety equipment, more effective violence prevention initiatives, or better practices for brain injury education. The medical community continues to make advances that increase our understanding of brain injury risk factors and outcomes.

School-based professionals engaged in the prevention activities described in this chapter are encouraged to collect and share outcome data related to their efforts. This can help maintain awareness of various initiatives and encourage the sharing of resources.

References

Achenbach, T. M. (1991). *Integrative guide for the 1991 CBCL/4–18, YSR, and TRF profiles.* Burlington, VT: University of Vermont, Department of Psychiatry.

Adams, J. H., Doyle, D., Ford, I., Gennarelli, T. A., Graham, D. I., & McLellan, D. R. (1989). Diffuse axonal injury in head injury: Definition, diagnosis and grading. *Histopathology, 15,* 49–59.

Agnati, L. F., Zoli, M., Stromberg, I., & Fuxe, K. (1995). Intercellular communication in the brain: Wiring versus volume transmission. *Neuroscience, 69,* 711–726.

Agrawal, D., & Mahapatra, A. K. (2012). Biomechanics of head injury. In P. N. Tandon & R. Ramamurthi, (Eds.), *Ramamurthi & Tandon's textbook of neurosurgery* (pp. 314–318). London, England: Jaypee Brothers Medical Publishers.

Allen, T. R., Hulac, D., & D'Amato, R. C. (2005). The pediatric neurological examination and school neuropsychology. In R. C. D'Amato, E. Fletcher-Janzen, & C. R. Reynolds (Eds.), *Handbook of school neuropsychology* (pp. 145–171). Hoboken, NJ: Wiley.

Althouse, R. B., Jenson, W. R., Likins, M., & Morgan, D. P. (1999). *Get 'em on task software with manual.* Longmont, CO: Sopris West.

Alvarez, J. A., & Emory, E. (2006). Executive function and the frontal lobes: A meta-analytic review. *Neuropsychology Review, 16*(1), 17–42.

American Academy of Child and Adolescent Psychiatry. (2004). *Practice parameter for psychiatric consultation to schools.* Washington, DC: Author.

American Academy of Neurology. (1997). *Practice parameter: The management of concussion in sports: Summary statement.* Quality Standards Subcommittee of the American Academy of Neurology. Retrieved from http://www.aan.com/practice/guideline/index.cfm?fuseaction = home. view&guideline = 214

American Academy of Sleep Medicine. (2005). *International classification of sleep disorders (2nd ed.): Diagnostic and coding manual.* Westchester, IL: American Academy of Sleep Medicine.

Americans with Disabilities Act, 42 U.S.C. § 12101 et seq. (1990).

Anderson, D., Nashon, S. M., & Thomas, G. P. (2009). Evolution of research methods for probing and understanding metacognition. *Research in Science Education, 39*(2), 181–195.

Anderson, P. (2002). Assessment and development of executive function (EF) during childhood. *Child Neuropsychology, 8,* 71–82.

Andriessen, T. M. J. C., Jacobs, B., & Vos, P. E. (2010). Clinical characteristics and pathophysiological mechanisms of focal and diffuse traumatic brain injury. *Journal of Cellular and Molecular Medicine, 14,* 2381–2392.

Anthony, D. C., Couch, Y., Losey, P., & Evans, M. C. (2012). The systemic response to brain injury and disease. *Brain, Behavior, and Immunity, 26,* 534–540.

Arango-Lasprilla, J. C., & Kreutzer, J. S. (2010). Racial and ethnic disparities in functional, psychosocial, and neurobehavioral outcomes after brain injury. *Journal of Head Trauma Rehabilitation, 25,* 128–136.

Araque, A., & Navarrete, M. (2010). Glial cells in neuronal network function. *Philosophical Transactions of the Royal Society: Biological Sciences, 365,* 2375–2381. doi: 10.1098/rstb.2009.0313

Arroyos-Jurado, E., Paulsen J. S., Ehly, S., & Max, J. E. (2006). Traumatic brain injury in children and adolescents: Academic and intellectual outcomes following injury. *Exceptionality, 14,*125–140.

Ashley, M., O'Shanick, G., & Kreber, L. (2009). *Early vs. late treatment of traumatic brain injury.* A position paper of the Brain Injury Association of America. Vienna, VA: Brain Injury Association of America.

Ashton, R. (2010). Practitioner review: Beyond shaken baby syndrome: What influences the outcomes for infants following traumatic brain injury? *Journal of Child Psychology & Psychiatry, 51,* 967–980. doi:10.1111/j.1469-7610.2010.02272.x

Azevedo, F. A. C., Carvalho, L. R. B., Grinberg, L. T., Farfel, J. M., Ferretti, R. E. L., Leite, R. E., . . . Herculano-Houzel, S. (2009). Equal numbers of neuronal and non-neuronal cells make the human brain an isometrically scaled-up primate brain. *The Journal of Comparative Neurology, 513,* 532–541.

Azevedo, R. (2009). Theoretical, conceptual, methodological, and instructional issues in research on metacognition and self-regulated learning: A discussion. *Metacognition and Learning, 4,* 87–95.

Babbage, D. R., Yim, J., Zupan, B., Neumann, D., Tomita, M. R., & Willer, B. (2011). Meta-analysis of facial affect recognition difficulties after traumatic brain injury. *Neuropsychology, 25,* 277–285.

Bach-Y-Rita, P. (2003). Theoretical basis for brain plasticity after a TBI. *Brain Injury, 17,* 643–651.

Bakhos, L. L., Lockhart, G. R., Myers, R., & Linakis, J. G. (2010). Emergency department visits for concussion in young child athletes. *Pediatrics, 126,* e550–e556. doi: 10.1542/peds.2009-3101

Bandura, A. (1986). *Social foundations of thought and action: A social cognitive theory.* Upper Saddle River, NJ: Prentice Hall.

Barach, E., Tomlanovich, M., & Nowak, R. (1986). Ballistics: A pathophysiologic examination of the wounding mechanisms of firearms: Part 1. *The Journal of Trauma, 26,* 225–235.

Bargmann, C. I. (2012). Beyond the connectome: How neuromodulators shape neural circuits. *Bioessays, 34,* 458–465.

Barkley, R. A. (1989). Attention-deficit hyperactivity disorder. In E. J. Mash & R. A. Barkley (Eds.), *Treatment of childhood disorders* (pp. 39–72). New York, NY: Guilford Press.

Barth, J. T., Alves, W. M., Ryan, T. V., Macciocchi, S. N., Rimel, R. W., Jane, J. A., & Nelson, W. E. (1989). Mild head injury in sports: Neuropsychological sequelae and recovery of function. In H. Levin, H. Eisenberg, & A. Benton (Eds.), *Mild head injury* (pp. 257–275). New York, NY: Oxford University Press.

Baumann, C. R., Werth, E., Stocker, R., Ludwig, S., & Bassetti, C. L. (2007). Sleep-wake disturbances 6 months after traumatic brain injury: A prospective study. *Brain, 130,* 1873–1883.

Beaulieu-Bonneau, S., & Morin, C. M. (2012). Sleepiness and fatigue following traumatic brain injury. *Sleep Medicine, 13,* 598–605.

Beers, S. R., Goldstein, G., & Katz, L. (1994). Neuropsychological differences between college students with learning disabilities and those with mild head injury. *Journal of Learning Disabilities, 27,* 315–324.

Benedictus, M., Spikman, J. M., & van der Naalt, J. (2010). Cognitive and behavioral impairment in traumatic brain injury related to outcome and return to work. *Archives of Physical Medicine and Rehabilitation, 91,* 1436–1441.

Bennet, W. (1910). Some milder forms of concussion of the brain. In T. C. Allbutt and H. D. Rolleston (Eds.), *A system of medicine by many writers* (pp. 229–240). London, England: The Macmillan Company. Retrieved from http://www.archive.org/stream/systemofmedicine08al lbuoft/systemofmedicine08allbuoft_djvu.txt

Berg, J., Tagliaferri, F., & Servadei, F. (2005). Cost of trauma in Europe. *European Journal of Neurology, 12*(suppl. 1), 85–90.

Bigler, E. D. (2007). Anterior and middle cranial fossa in traumatic brain injury: Relevant neuro-anatomy and neuropathology in the study of neuropsychological outcome. *Neuropsychology, 21,* 515–531.

Bigler, E. D. (2012). Mild traumatic brain injury: The elusive timing of recovery. *Neuroscience Letters, 1,* 1–4. doi:10.1016/j.neulet.2011.12.009

Bigler, E. D., & Maxwell, W. L. (2012a). Neuropathology of mild traumatic brain injury and its relationship to neuroimaging findings. *Brain Imaging and Behavior, 6,* 108–136. doi:10.1007/s11682-011-9145-0

Bigler, E. D., & Maxwell, W. L. (2012b). Understanding mild traumatic brain injury: Neuropathology and neuroimaging. In J. Vasterling, R. Bryant, & T. Keane (Eds.), *PTSD and mild traumatic brain injury* (pp. 15–36). New York, NY: Guilford Press.

Blakemore, S. J., & Choudhury, S. (2006). Development of the adolescent brain: Implications for executive function and social cognition. *Journal of Child Psychology and Psychiatry, 47,* 296–312.

Boake, C., & Diller, L. (2005). History of rehabilitation for traumatic brain injury. In W. M. High, A. M. Sander, M. A. Struchen, & K. A. Hart (Eds.), *Rehabilitation for traumatic brain injury* (pp. 3–13). New York, NY: Oxford University Press.

Bowen, J. M. (2005). Classroom interventions for students with traumatic brain injuries. *Preventing School Failure, 49*(4), 34–41.

Braga, L. W., DaPaz, A. C. J., & Ylvisaker, M. (2005). Direct clinician-delivered versus indirect family-supported rehabilitation of children with traumatic brain injury: A randomized controlled trial. *Brain Injury, 19,* 819–831.

Brain Injury Association of America. (2013). *About us. BIAA: Brain Injury Association of America.* Retrieved April 22, 2013, from http://www.biausa.org/About-Us/about-brain-injury-association.htm

Bransford, J. D., & Stein, B. S. (1993). *The IDEAL problem solver: A guide for improving thinking, learning, and creativity* (2nd ed.). New York, NY: W. H. Freeman.

Brasure, M., Lamberty, G. J., Sayer, N. A., Nelson, N. W., MacDonald, R., Ouellette, J., . . . Wilt, T. J. (2012). *Multidisciplinary postacute rehabilitation for moderate to severe traumatic brain injury in adults.* (Prepared by the Minnesota Evidence-based Practice Center under Contract No. 290-2007-10064-I.) AHRQ Publication No. 12-EHC101-EF. Rockville, MD: Agency for Healthcare Research and Quality. Retrieved from http://www.effectivehealthcare.ahrq.gov/reports/final.cfm.

Bray, T. J. (2001). Design of the northern Nevada orthopaedic trauma panel: A model, level-II community-hospital system. *The Journal of Bone and Joint Surgery: American Volume, 83-A,* 283–289.

Brodal, A. (1981). *Neurological anatomy in relation to clinical medicine.* (3rd ed.). New York, NY: Oxford University Press.

Brown, S. L., & Bulanda, J. R. (2008). Relationship violence in young adulthood: A comparison of daters, cohabitation, and marrieds. *Social Science Research, 37,* 73–87. doi: 10.1016/j.ssresearch.2007.06.002

Bruininks, R., Woodcock, R., Weatherman, R., & Hill, B. (1996). *Scales of independent behavior—Revised.* Rolling Meadows, IL: Riverside.

Bryant, R. (2011). Post-traumatic stress disorder vs traumatic brain injury. *Dialogues in Clinical Neuroscience, 13,* 251–262.

Bunge, S. A., & Zelazo, P. D. (2006). A brain-based account of the development of rule use in childhood. *Current Directions in Psychological Science, 15,* 118–121.

Cantu, R. C., & Mueller, F. O. (2009). The prevention of catastrophic head and spine injuries in high school and college sports. *British Journal of Sports Medicine, 43,* 981–986.

Carlson, J. S., Thaler, C. L., & Hirsch, A. (2005). Psychotropic medication consultation in schools: An ethical and legal dilemma for school psychologists. *Journal of Applied School Psychology, 22,* 29–41.

Carmen, D. W., Proctor, B. D., & Smith, J. C. (2010). *Income, poverty, and health insurance: Coverage in the United States: 2010,* U.S. Census Bureau, Current Population Reports, P60-239. Washington, DC: U.S. Government Printing Office.

Carpenter, M. B., & Sutin, J. (1983). *Human anatomy* (8th ed.). Baltimore, MD: Williams & Wilkins.

Carroll, L. (1872). *Through the looking-glass, and what Alice found there.* London, England: McMillan.

Catroppa, C., Anderson, V., & Muscara, F. (2009). Rehabilitation of executive skills post-childhood traumatic brain injury (TBI): A pilot intervention study. *Developmental Neurorehabilitation, 12,* 361–369.

Centers for Disease Control and Prevention. (2010). Youth Risk Behavior Surveillance—United States, Surveillance Summaries, 2009. *MMWR, 59* (No. SS-5).

Centers for Disease Control and Prevention. (2011). Nonfatal traumatic brain injuries related to sports and recreation activities among persons aged <19 years—United States, Surveillance Summaries, 2001–2009. *MMWR, 60,* 1337–1342.

Centers for Disease Control and Prevention. (2013a). *National Center for Health Statistics. National Hospital Ambulatory Medical Care Survey (NHAMCS).* Retrieved from http://www.cdc.gov/nchs/ahcd.htm

Centers for Disease Control and Prevention. (2013b). *Concussion: What are the signs and symptoms of concussion?* Retrieved from http://www.cdc.gov/concussion/signs_symptoms.html

Centers for Disease Control and Prevention. (2013c). *Heads up on concussion.* Retrieved from http://www.cdc.gov/concussion/

Centers for Disease Control and Prevention. (2013d). *Heads up: Brain Injury in Your Practice.* Retrieved from http://www.cdc.gov/concussion/clinician.html

Centers for Disease Control and Prevention. (2013e). *Heads up: What to Expect After Concussion.* Retrieved from http://www.cdc.gov/concussion/clinician.html

Centers for Disease Control and Prevention. (2013f). *Facts about Concussion and Brain Injury: Where to Get Help.* Retrieved from http://www.cdc.gov/concussion/clinician.html

Centers for Disease Control and Prevention. (2013g). *Updated Mild Traumatic Brain Injury Guidelines for Adults.* Retrieved from http://www.cdc.gov/concussion/clinician.html

Centers for Disease Control and Prevention. (2013h). *Growth charts.* Retrieved from http://www.cdc.gov/growthcharts/

Centers for Disease Control and Prevention. (2013i). *Injury prevention & control: Traumatic brain injury.* Retrieved from http://www.cdc.gov/traumaticbraininjury/statistics.html

Centers for Disease Control and Prevention. (2013j). *Injury prevention & control: Motor vehicle safety. Child passenger safety.* Retrieved from http://www.cdc.gov/Motorvehiclesafety/Child_Passenger_Safety/index.html

Centers for Disease Control and Prevention. (2013k). *Prevention: What can I do to help prevent traumatic brain injury?* Retrieved from http://www.cdc.gov/traumaticbraininjury/prevention.html

Cernich, A., Reeves, D., Sun, W., & Bleiberg, J. (2007). Automated neuropsychological assessment metrics sports medicine battery. *Archives of Clinical Neuropsychology, 22*(Suppl 1), S101–S114.

Chaudhuri, A., & Behan, P. O. (2000). Fatigue and basal ganglia. *Journal of the Neurological Sciences, 179,* 34–42.

Chen, J. W. Y., Ruff, R. L., Eavey, R., & Wasterlain, C. G. (2009). Posttraumatic epilepsy and treatment. *Journal of Rehabilitation Research & Development, 46,* 685–696.

Chew, E., & Zafonte, R. D. (2009). Pharmacological management of neurobehavioral disorders following traumatic brain injury: A state of the art review. *Journal of Rehabilitation Research and Development, 46,* 851–878.

Child Welfare Information Gateway. (2010). *Mandatory reporters of child abuse and neglect: Summary of state laws.* Retrieved from http://www.childwelfare.gov/systemwide/laws_policies/statutes/manda.pdf

Childs, L. A. (2010). Assessing vestibular dysfunction. Exploring treatments of a complex condition. *Rehab Management, 23*(6), 24–25.

Christensen, J. (2012). Traumatic brain injury: Risks of epilepsy and implications for medicolegal assessment. *Epilepsia, 53*(suppl. 4), 43–47. doi: 10.1111/j.1528–1167.2012.03612.x

Cole, C. L., & Bambara, L. M. (1992). Issues surrounding the use of self-management interventions in the school. *School Psychology Review, 21*(2), 193–201.

Collins, M. W., Lovell, M. R., Iverson, G. L., Ide, T., & Maroon, J. (2006). Examining concussion rates and return to play in high school football players wearing newer helmet technology: A three-year prospective cohort study. *Neurosurgery, 58*, 275–286.

Cooper, J. O., Heron, T. E., & Heward, W. L. (2007). *Applied Behavior Analysis* (2nd ed.). Upper Saddle River, NJ: Pearson.

Coronado, V. G., McGuire, L. C., Faul, M., Pearson, W., & Sugerman, D. (2012). Epidemiology and Public Health Issues. In N. Zasler, D. Katz, & R. Zafonte (Eds.), *Brain injury medicine* (pp. 84–100). New York, NY: Demos Medical Publishing.

Coronado, V. G., McGuire, L. C., Sarmiento, K., Bell, J., Lionbarger, M. R., Jones, C. D., . . . Xu, L. (2012). Trends in traumatic brain injury in the U.S. and the public health response: 1995–2009. *Journal of Safety Research, 43*, 299–307.

Corrigan, J. D., Selassie, A. W., & Orman, J. A. (2010). The epidemiology of traumatic brain injury. *Journal of Head Trauma Rehabilitation, 25*, 72–80.

Coutinho, S. (2008). Self-efficacy, metacognition, and performance. *North American Journal of Psychology, 10*(1), 165–172.

Cramer, S. C., Sur, M., Dobkin, B. H., O'Brien, C., Sanger, T. D., Trojanowski, J. Q., . . . Vinogradov, S. (2011). Harnessing neuroplasticity for clinical applications. *Brain, 134*, 1591–1609.

Crone, D. A., & Horner, R. H. (2003). *Building positive behavior support systems in schools.* New York, NY: Guilford Press.

Daneshvar, D. H., Baugh, C. M., Nowinski, C. J., McKee, A. C., Stern, R. A., & Cantu, R. C. (2011). Helmets and mouth guards: The role of personal equipment in preventing sport-related concussions. *Clinics in Sports Medicine, 30*(1), 145–163. doi: 10.1016/j.csm.2010.09.006

Davies, S. C. (2013). School psychology programs: Graduate preparation in traumatic brain injury. *Trainers' Forum, 31*(2), 5–16.

Davies, S. C., Jones, K., & Rafoth, M. A. (2010). Effects of a self-monitoring intervention on children with traumatic brain injury. *Journal of Applied School Psychology, 26*, 308–326.

Davies, S. C., & Ray, A. M. (in press). Traumatic Brain Injury: The Efficacy of a Half-Day Training for School Psychologists. *Contemporary School Psychology.*

Davis, A. S., & D'Amato, R. C. (2005). Evaluating and using contemporary neuropsychological batteries: The NEPSY and the Dean-Woodcock Neuropsychological Assessment System. In R. C. D'Amato, E. Fletcher-Janzen, & C. R. Reynolds (Eds.), *Handbook of school neuropsychology* (pp. 264–286). Hoboken, NJ: Wiley.

Davis, A. S., & Dean, R. S. (2010). Assessing sensory-motor deficits in pediatric traumatic brain injury. *Applied Neuropsychology, 17*, 104–109.

Davis, A. S., Johnson, J. A., & D'Amato, R. C. (2005). Evaluating and using long-standing school neuropsychological batteries: The Halstead-Reitan and the Luria-Nebraska Neuropsychological Batteries. In R. C. D'Amato, E. Fletcher-Janzen, & C. R. Reynolds (Eds.), *Handbook of school neuropsychology* (pp. 236–263). Hoboken, NJ: Wiley.

Davis, G. A., & Purcell, L. K. (2013). The evaluation and management of acute concussion differs in young children. *British Journal of Sports Medicine.* Advance online publication. doi:10.1136/bjsports-2012–092132

Davis, K. (2011, April). *Deductibles, and coinsurance percentages for employer-sponsored health insurance in the private sector, by industry classification* (Statistical Brief No. 323). Rockville, MD: Agency for Healthcare Research and Quality. Retrieved from http://www.meps.ahrq.gov/mepsweb/data_files/publications/st323/stat323.pdf

Davis, P. C. (2007). ACR appropriateness criteria: Head trauma. *American Journal of Neuroradiology, 28,* 1619–1621.

Dean, R. S., & Woodcock, R. W. (2003). *Dean-Woodcock Neuropsychological Battery.* Itasca, IL: Riverside.

DeFina, P., Fellus, J., Polito, M. Z., Thompson, J. W. G., Moser, R. S., & DeLuca, J. (2009). The new neuroscience frontier: Promoting neuroplasticity and brain repair in traumatic brain injury. *The Clinical Neuropsychologist, 23,* 1391–1399.

De Jesus, O. N. (2012). Differentiated instruction: Can differentiated instruction provide success for all learners? *National Teacher Education Journal, 5*(3), 5–11.

Deno, S. L. (1985). Curriculum-Based Measurement: The emerging alternative. *Exceptional Children, 52,* 219–232.

Dennis, M., Simic, N., Bigler, E. D., Abildskov, T., Agostino, A. L., Taylor, H. G., . . . Yeates, K. O. (2013). Cognitive, affective, and conative theory of mind (ToM) in children with traumatic brain injury. *Developmental Cognitive Neuroscience, 5,* 25–39.

Dennis, M., Simic, N., Taylor, G. H., Bigler, E. D., Rubin, K., Vannatta, K., . . . Yeates, K. O. (2012). Theory of mind in children with traumatic brain injury. *Journal of the International Neuropsychological Society, 18,* 908–16. doi: 10.1017/S1355617712000756

Dikmen, S., Machamer, J., Fann, J. R., & Temkin, N. R. (2010). Rates of symptom reporting following traumatic brain injury. *Journal of the International Neuropsychological Society, 16,* 401–411.

Donders, J., & Strom, D. (1997). The effect of traumatic brain injury on children with learning disability. *Pediatric Rehabilitation, 1,* 179–184.

Douglas, J. M. (2010). Relation of executive functioning to pragmatic outcome following severe traumatic brain injury. *Journal of Speech, Language, and Hearing Research, 53,* 365–382.

Drew, L. B., & Drew, W. E. (2004). The contrecoup-coup phenomenon: A new understanding of the mechanism of closed head injury. *Neurocritical Care, 1,* 385–390.

Ducharme, J. M. (1999). Subject review: A conceptual model for treatment of externalizing behavior in acquired brain injury. *Brain Injury, 13,* 645–668.

Duhaime, A. C., Holshouser, B., Hunter, J. V., & Tong, K. (2012). Common data elements for neuroimaging of traumatic brain injury: Pediatric considerations. *Journal of Neurotrauma, 29,* 629–633.

DuPaul, G., & Carlson, J. S. (2005). Child psychopharmacology: How school psychologists can contribute to effective outcomes. *School Psychology Quarterly, 20,* 206–221.

Education for All Handicapped Children Act, 20 U.S.C. § 1400 et seq. (1975).

Erdogan, E., Gonul, E., & Seber, N. (2002). Craniocerebral gunshot wounds. *Neurosurgery Quarterly, 12*(1), 1–18.

Ernst, W. J., Trice, A. D., Gilbert, J. L., & Potts, H. (2009). Misconceptions about traumatic brain injury and recovery among nursing students. *Journal of Head Trauma Rehabilitation, 24,* 213–220.

Ettlinger, M., Margulis, E. H., & Wong, P. C. M. (2011). Implicit memory in music and language. *Frontiers in Psychology, 2,* 1–10. Retrieved from http://www.frontiersin.org/Journal/10.3389/fpsyg.2011.00211/full

Evans, C. C., Sherer, M., Nick, T. G., Nakase-Richardson, R., & Yablon, S. A. (2005). Early impaired self-awareness, depression, and subjective well-being following traumatic brain injury. *Journal of Head Trauma Rehabilitation, 20,* 488–500.

Evans, R. W. (2010). Persistent post-traumatic headache, postconcussion syndrome, and whiplash injuries: The evidence for a non-traumatic basis with an historical review. *Headache, 50,* 716–724.

Falleti, M. G., Maruff, P., Collie, A., & Darby, D. G. (2006). Practice effects associated with the repeated assessment of cognitive function using the CogState battery at 10-minute, one week and one month test-retest intervals. *Journal of Clinical and Experimental Neuropsychology, 28,* 1095–1112.

Family Educational Rights and Privacy Act (FERPA) of 1974, 20 U.S.C. § 1232g; 34 CFR Part 99, U.S. Department of Education, Final Rule (1974). Retrieved from https://federalregister.gov /a/2011–30683

Farkas, O., & Povlishock, J. T. (2007). Cellular and subcellular change evoked by diffuse traumatic brain injury: A complex web of change extending far beyond focal damage. *Progress in Brain Research, 161,* 43–59.

Farmer, J. E., & Johnson-Gerard, M. (1997). Misconceptions about traumatic brain injury among educators and rehabilitation staff: A comparative study. *Rehabilitation Psychology, 42,* 273–286.

Farmer, J. E., Kanne, S. M., Haut, J. S., Williams, J., Johnstone, B., & Kirk, K. (2002). Memory functioning following traumatic brain injury in children with premorbid learning problems. *Developmental Neuropsychology, 22,* 455–469.

Faul, M., Xu, L., Wald, M. M., & Coronado, V. G. (2010). *Traumatic brain injury in the United States: Emergency department visits, hospitalizations and deaths 2002–2006.* Atlanta. GA: Centers for Disease Control and Prevention, National Center for Injury Prevention and Control.

Fay, T. B., Yeates, K. O., Wade, S. L., Drotar, D., Stancin, T., & Taylor, H. G. (2009). Predicting longitudinal patterns of functional deficits in children with traumatic brain injury. *Neuropsychology, 23,* 271–282.

Feeney, T. J., & Ylvisaker, M. (2003). Context-sensitive behavioral supports for young children with TBI: Short-term effects and long-term outcome. *Journal of Head Trauma Rehabilitation, 18,* 33–51.

Fellin, T. (2009). Communication between neurons and astrocytes: Relevance to the modulation of synaptic and network activity. *Journal of Neurochemistry, 108,* 533–544.

Fingelkurts, A. A., Fingelkurts, A. A., & Kahkonen, S. (2005). Functional connectivity in the brain—is it an elusive concept? *Neuroscience and Biobehavioral Reviews, 28,* 827–836.

Flashman, L. A., & McAllister, T. W. (2002). Lack of awareness and its impact in traumatic brain injury. *Neurorehabilitation, 17,* 285–296.

Formisano, R., Bivona, U., Catani, S., D'Ippolito, M., & Buzzi, M. G. (2009). Post-traumatic headache: Facts and doubts. *Journal of Headache & Pain, 10,* 145–152.

Foster, M., Tilse, C., & Fleming, J. (2004). Referral to rehabilitation following traumatic brain injury: Practitioners and the process of decision-making. *Social Science & Medicine, 59,* 1867–1878.

Frank, E. M., Redmond, K. E., Ruediger, T. L., & Scott, W. K. (1997). Preparedness of educational speech-language pathologists to provide services to students with traumatic brain injury. *Journal of Children's Communication Development, 18*(2), 49–63.

Frenette, A. J., Kanji, S., Rees, L., Williamson, D. R., Perreault, M. M., Turgeon, A. F., . . . Fergusson, D. A. (2012). Efficacy and safety of dopamine agonists in traumatic brain injury: A systematic review of randomized controlled trials. *Journal of Neurotrauma, 29,* 1–18. doi: 10.1089/ neu.2011.1812.

Fuchs, D., & Fuchs, L. S. (1992). Limitations to a feel good approach to consultation. *Journal of Educational and Psychological Consultation, 3,* 93–97.

Fuchs, L. S., & Fuchs, D. (1998). Treatment validity: A unifying concept for reconceptualizing the identification of learning disabilities. *Learning Disabilities Research and Practice, 13,* 204–219.

Fulton, J. B., Yeates, K. O., Taylor, H. G., Walz, N. C., & Wade, S. L. (2012). Cognitive predictors of academic achievement in young children 1 year after traumatic brain injury. *Neuropsychology, 26,* 314–322.

Funk, P., Bryde, J., Doelling, J., & Hough, D. (1996). Serving students with traumatic brain injury. *Physical Disabilities: Education and Related Services, 15,* 49–64.

Galynker, I., Cohen, L., Salvit, C., Miner, C., Phillips, E., Focseneanu, M., & Rosenthal, R. (2000). Psychiatric symptom severity and length of stay on an intensive rehabilitation unit. *Psychosomatics, 41,* 114–120.

Gamm, L. D., Hutchison, L. L., Dabney, B. J., & Dorsey, A. M. (2010). *Rural and healthy people 2010: A companion document to healthy people 2010: Volume 1.* College Station, TX: The Texas A&M University System Health Science Center, School of Rural Public Health, Southwest Rural Health Research Center. Retrieved from http://srph.tamhsc.edu/centers/rhp2010/survey.html?redirect_to = http://srph.tamhsc.edu/centers/rhp2010/Volume1.pdf

Ganesalingam, K., Yeates, K. O., Taylor, H. G., Walz, N. C., Stancin, T., & Wade, S. (2011). Executive function and social competence in young children 6 months following traumatic brain injury. *Neuropsychology, 25*, 466–476.

Gardner, R. M., Bird, F. L., Maguire, H., Carreiro, R., & Abenaim, N. (2003). Intensive positive behavioral supports for adolescents with acquired brain injury: Long-term outcomes in community settings. *Journal of Head Trauma Rehabilitation, 18*, 52–74.

Gennarelli, T. A., & Graham, D. I. (2005). Neuropathology. In J. M. Silver, T. W. McAllister, & S. C. Yudofsky (Eds.), *Textbook of traumatic brain injury* (pp. 27–34). Arlington, VA: American Psychiatric Publishing.

Gentry, L. R. (1994). Imaging of closed head injury. *Radiology, 191*, 1–17.

Gharahbaghian, L., Schroeder, B., Mittendorff, R., & Wang, N. E. (2011). *Pediatric traumatic brain injury: Epidemiology, pathophysiology, diagnosis, and treatment.* AHC Media L.L.C. HighBeam Research. Retrieved from http://www.highbeam.com

Gioia, G. A., Isquith, P. K., Guy, S. C., & Kenworthy, L. (2000). *Behavior Rating Inventory of Executive Function.* Lutz, FL: PAR.

Glang, A., Dise-Lewis, J., Tyler, J., & Denslow, P. (2006). Identification and appropriate service delivery for children who have TBI: Abstracts from the 2nd Federal Interagency Conference on Traumatic Brain Injury. *Journal of Head Trauma Rehabilitation, 21*, 408–436.

Glang, A. Todis, B., Sublette, P., Brown, B. E., & Vaccaro, M. (2010). Professional development in TBI for educators: The importance of context. *Journal of Head Trauma Rehabilitation, 25*, 426–432.

Glang, A., Todis, B., Thomas, C. W., Hood, D., Bedell, G., & Cockrell, J. (2008). Return to school following childhood TBI: Who gets services? *NeuroRehabilitation, 23*, 477–486.

Gogtay, N., Giedd, J. N., Lusk, L., Hayashi, K. M., Greenstein, D., Catherine, A., . . . Thompson, P. M. (2004). Dynamic mapping of human cortical development during childhood through early adulthood. *Proceedings of the National Academy of Sciences of the United States, 101*, 8174–8179. doi: 10.1073/pnas.0402680101

Golden, C. J. (1987). Screening batteries for the adult and children's versions of the Luria Nebraska neuropsychological batteries. *Neuropsychology, 1*(2), 63–66. doi: 10.1037/h0091755

Golden, C. J., Hammeke, T. A., & Purisch, A. D. (1978). Diagnostic validity of a standardized neuropsychological battery derived from Luria's neuropsychological tests. *Journal of Consulting and Clinical Psychology, 46*, 1258–1265.

Goldsmith, W., & Plunkett, J. (2004). A biomechanical analysis of the causes of traumatic brain injury in infants and children. *The American Journal of Forensic Medicine and Pathology, 25*, 89–100.

Gottshall, K. (2011). Vestibular rehabilitation after mild traumatic brain injury with vestibular pathology. *Neurorehabilitation, 29*, 167–171.

Gottshall, K., Drake, A., Gray, N., McDonald, E., & Hoffer, M. E. (2003). Objective vestibular tests as outcome measures in head injury patients. *The Laryngoscope, 113*, 1746–1750.

Gouick, J., & Gentleman, D. (2004). The emotional and behavioural consequences of traumatic brain injury. *Trauma, 6*, 285–292.

Gould, K. R., Ponsford, J. L., Johnston, L., & Schonberger, M. (2011). The nature, frequency and course of psychiatric disorders in the first year after traumatic brain injury: A prospective study. *Psychological Medicine, 41*, 2099–2109.

Granacher, R. P. (2008). *Traumatic brain injury: Methods for clinical and forensic neuropsychiatric assessment.* Boca Raton, FL: Taylor & Francis.

Greenwood, R. (2002). Head injury for neurologists. *Journal of Neurology, Neurosurgery, & Psychiatry, 73*, i8-i16.

Guilmette, T. J., & Paglia, M. F. (2004). The public's misconceptions about traumatic brain injury: A follow up survey. *Archives of Clinical Neuropsychology, 19*, 183–189.

Gupta, A., & Taly, A. B. (2012). Functional outcome following rehabilitation in chronic severe traumatic brain injury patients: A prospective study. *Annals of Indian Academy of Neurology, 15*, 120–124.

Hagen, C., Malkmus, D., & Durham, P. (1972). *Rancho Los Amigos Level of Cognitive Functioning.* Downey, CA: Rancho Los Amigos Medical Center.

Haile-Mariam, A., Bradley-Johnson, S., & Johnson, C. (2002). Pediatricians' preferences for ADHD information from schools. *School Psychology Review, 31*, 94–105.

Hajek, C. A., Yeates, K. O., Taylor, H. G., Bangert, B., Dietrich, A., Nuss, K. E., . . . Wright, M. (2010). Relationships among post-concussive symptoms and symptoms of PTSD in children following mild traumatic brain injury. *Brain Injury, 24*, 100–109.

Halstead, M., Walter, K., & The Council on Sports Medicine and Fitness (2010). Clinical report: Sport-related concussion in children and adolescents. *Pediatrics, 126*, 597–615.

Harcke, H. T., Levy, A. D., Getz, J. M., & Robinson, S. R. (2008). MDCT analysis of projectile injury in forensic investigation. *American Journal of Roentgenology, 190*, W106-W111. doi: 10.2214/AJR.07.2754

Harris, K. R., & Pressley, M. (1991). The nature of cognitive strategy instruction: Interactive strategy construction. *Exceptional Children, 57*, 392–404.

Hart, T., Vaccaro, M. J., Hays, C., & Maiuro, R. D. (2012). Anger self-management training for people with traumatic brain injury: A preliminary investigation. *Journal of Head Trauma Rehabilitation, 27*, 113–122.

Harvey, J. M. (2006). Best practices in working with students with traumatic brain injuries. In A. Thomas & J. Grimes (Eds.), *Best practices in school psychology* (Vol. 4, pp. 1433–1446). Bethesda, MD: National Association of School Psychologists.

HCUP Kids' Inpatient Database. (2006). *Healthcare Cost and Utilization Project (HCUP).* Rockville, MD: Agency for Healthcare Research and Quality. Retrieved from http://www.hcup-us.ahrq.gov/kidoverview.jsp

Healthcare Cost and Utilization Project. (2003). *Overview of the HCUP Kids' Inpatient Database (KID), 2000.* Rockville, MD: Agency for Healthcare Research and Quality.

Health Insurance Portability and Accountability Act of 1996, 42 U.S.C. § 1320d-9 (2010).

Heartland Area Education Agency. (2005). *Special Education Procedures Manual.* Johnston, IA: Heartland AEA 11.

Heitger, M. H., Jones, R. D., Macleod, A. D., Snell, D. L., Frampton, C. M., & Anderson, T. J. (2009). Impaired eye movements in post-concussion syndrome indicate suboptimal brain function beyond the influence of depression, malingering or intellectual ability. *Brain, 132*, 2850–2870.

Henry, L. C., Tremblay, J., Tremblay, S., Lee, A., Brun, C., Lepore, N., . . . Lassonde, M. (2011). Acute and chronic changes in diffusivity measures after sports concussion. *Journal of Neurotrauma, 28*, 2049–2059.

Herculano-Houzel, S. (2011). Scaling of brain metabolism with a fixed energy budget per neuron: Implications for neuronal activity, plasticity, and evolution. *PLoS ONE, 6*(3), 1–9, e17514. doi:10.1371/journal.pone.0017514

Herrup, K., & Kuemerle, B. (1997). The compartmentalization of the cerebellum. *Annual Review of Neuroscience, 20*, 61–90.

Hesdorffer, D. C., Benn, E. K. T., Cascino, G. D., & Hauser, A. (2009). Is a first acute symptomatic seizure epilepsy? Mortality and risk for recurrent seizure. *Epilepsia, 50*, 1102–1108.

High, W. M., Boake, C., & Lehmkuhl, L. D. (1995). Critical analysis of studies evaluating the effectiveness of rehabilitation after traumatic brain injury. *Journal of Head Trauma Rehabilitation, 10*, 14–26.

High, W. M., Roebuck-Spencer, T., Sander, A. M., Struchen, M. A., & Sherer, M. (2006). Early versus later admission to postacute rehabilitation: Impact on functional outcome after traumatic brain injury. *Archives of Physical Medicine and Rehabilitation, 87,* 334–342.

Hoffman, J. M., Lucas, S., Dikmen, S., Braden, C. A., Brown, A. W., Brunner, R., . . . Bell, K. R. (2011). Natural history of headache after traumatic brain injury. *Journal of Neurotrauma, 28,* 1719–1725.

Holck, P. (2005). What can a baby's skull withstand? Testing the skull's resistance on an anatomical preparation. *Forensic Science International, 151,* 187–191. doi:10.1016/j.forsciint.2004.12.038

Holt, M. K., & Espelage, D. L. (2005). Social support as a moderator between dating violence victimization and depression/anxiety among African American and Caucasian adolescents. *School Psychology Review, 34,* 309–328.

Hooper, S. R. (2006a). Myths and misconceptions about traumatic brain injury: Endorsements by school psychologists. *Exceptionality, 14,* 171–182.

Hooper, S. R. (2006b). Traumatic brain injury: Preface. *Exceptionality, 14,* 121–123.

Hosenbocus, S., & Chahal, R. (2013). Amantadine: A review of use in child and adolescent psychiatry. *Journal of the Canadian Academy of Child and Adolescent Psychiatry, 22,* 55–60.

Hunley, S., & McNamara, K. (2010). *Tier 3 of the RTI model: Problem solving through a case study approach.* Bethesda, MD: National Association of School Psychologists.

Hunter, J. V., Wilde, E. A., Tong, K. A., & Holshouser, B. A. (2012). Emerging imaging tools for use with traumatic brain injury research. *Journal of Neurotrauma, 29,* 654–671.

Hux, K., Walker, M., & Sanger, D. D. (1996). Traumatic brain injury: Knowledge and self-perceptions of school speech-language pathologists. *Language, Speech, and Hearing Services in Schools, 27,* 171–184.

Individuals with Disabilities Education Act, 20 U.S.C. § 1400 et seq. (1990).

Individuals with Disabilities Education Improvement Act of 2004 [IDEIA 04], P.L. 108–446, §601 et seq., 118 Stat. 2647 (2005).

Institute of Medicine. (2011). *Cognitive Rehabilitation Therapy for traumatic brain injury: Evaluating the evidence.* Washington, DC: The National Academies Press.

International Classification of Headache Disorders, 2nd edition. (2004). *Cephalagia, 24* (suppl. 1), 1–160.

Iselin, G., Le Brocque, R., Kenardy, J., Anderson, V., & McKinlay, L. (2010). Which method of posttraumatic stress disorder classification best predicts psychosocial function in children with traumatic brain injury? *Journal of Anxiety Disorders, 24,* 774–779.

Ivancevic, V. G. (2009). New mechanics of traumatic brain injury. *Cognitive Neurodynamics, 2,* 281–293.

Iyer, S. G., Saxena, P., & Kumhar, G. D. (2003). Growing skull fractures. *Indian Pediatrics, 40,* 1194–1196.

Jang, S. H. (2009). Review of motor recovery in patients with traumatic brain injury. *NeuroRehabilitation, 24,* 349–353.

Jantz, P. B., & Bigler, E. D. (in press). *Neuroimaging and the school-based psychoeducational assessment of traumatic brain injury. NeuroRehabilitation.*

Jantz, P. B., & Coulter, G. A. (2007). Child and adolescent traumatic brain injury: Academic, behavioural, and social consequences in the classroom. *Support for Learning, 22,* 84–89.

Johansen-Berg, H., & Rushworth, M. F. S. (2009). Using diffusion imaging to study human connectional anatomy. *Annual Review of Neuroscience, 32,* 75–94.

Johnston, L. D., O'Malley, P. M., Bachman, J. G., & Schulenberg, J. E. (2011). *Monitoring the future: National results on adolescent drug use: Overview of key findings, 2011.* Ann Arbor, MI: Institute for Social Research, The University of Michigan.

Johnstone, B., Price, T., Bounds, T., Schopp, L. H., Schootman, M., & Schumate, D. (2003). Rural/urban differences in vocational outcomes for state vocational rehabilitation clients with TBI. *NeuroRehabilitation, 18,* 197–203.

Jones, J., & Curtin, M. (2010). Traumatic brain injury, participation, and rural identity. *Qualitative Health Research, 20,* 942–951.

Karver, C. L., Wade, S. L., Cassedy, A., Taylor, H. G., Stancin, T., Yeates, K. O., & Walz, N. C. (2012). Age at injury and long-term behavior problems after traumatic brain injury in young children. *Rehabilitation Psychology, 57,* 256–265.

Kayani, N. A., Homan, S., Yun, S., & Zhu, B. P. (2009). Health and economic burden of traumatic brain injury: Missouri, 2001–2005. *Public Health Reports, 124,* 551–560.

Kazim, S. F., Shamim, M. S., Tahir, M. Z., Enam, S. A., & Waheed, S. (2011). Management of penetrating brain injury. *Journal of Emergencies, Trauma and Shock, 4,* 395–402. doi: 10.4103/0974–2700.83871

Kennedy, M. R. T. (2004). Self-monitoring recall during two tasks after traumatic brain injury: A preliminary study. *American Journal of Speech-Language Pathology, 13,* 142–154.

Keow, L. K., Ng, I., & Ti, A. B. (2008). Common misconceptions about traumatic brain injury (TBI) among mild TBI patients and their immediate family members. *Singapore Nursing Journal, 35,* 18–26.

Kern, R. S., Hartzell, A. M., Izaguirre, B., & Hamilton, A. H. (2010). Declarative and nondeclarative memory in schizophrenia: What is impaired? What is spared? *Journal of Clinical and Experimental Neuropsychology, 32,* 1017–1027.

Kharatishvili, I., & Pitkanen, A. (2010). Posttraumatic epilepsy. *Current Opinion in Neurology, 23,* 183–188.

Kim, E. (2002). Agitation, aggression, and disinhibition syndromes after traumatic brain injury. *NeuroRehabilitation, 17,* 297–310.

Kim, J. J., & Gean, A. D. (2011). Imaging for the diagnosis and management of traumatic brain injury. *Neurotherapeutics, 8,* 39–53.

Kimberley, T. J., Samargia, S., Moore, L. G., Shakya, J. K., & Lang, C. E. (2010). Comparison of amounts and types of practice during rehabilitation for traumatic brain injury and stroke. *Journal of Rehabilitation Research & Development, 47,* 851–862.

Kiraly, M. A., & Kiraly, S. J. (2007). Traumatic brain injury and delayed sequelae: A review—Traumatic brain injury and mild traumatic brain injury (Concussion) are precursors to later onset brain disorders, including early onset dementia. *The Scientific World Journal, 7,* 1768–1776.

Korkman, M., Kirk, U., & Kemp, S. (1998). *NEPSY: A developmental neuropsychological assessment manual.* San Antonio, TX: Psychological Corporation.

Kotter, R., & Stephan, K. E. (1997). Useless or helpful? The limbic system concept. *Reviews in the Neurosciences, 8,* 139–145.

Kronkosky Charitable Foundation. (2012). *Brain Injury (Research Brief).* San Antonio, TX: Author. Retrieved from http://kronkosky.org/

Kuhtz-Buschbeck, J. P., Hoppe, B., Golge, M., Dreesmann, M., Damm-Stunitz, U., & Ritz, A. (2003). Sensorimotor recovery in children after traumatic brain injury: Analyses of gait, gross motor, and fine motor skills. *Developmental Medicine & Child Neurology, 45,* 821–828. doi:10.1017/S001216220300152X

Kumar, A., & Loane, D. J. (2012). Neuroinflammation after traumatic brain injury: Opportunities for therapeutic intervention. *Brain, Behavior, and Immunity, 26,* 1191–1201. doi:10.1016/j.bbi.2012.06.008

Laatsch, L., Harrington, D., Hotz, G., Marcantuono, J., Mozzoni, M., Walsh, V., & Hersey, K. (2007). An evidence-based review of cognitive and behavioral rehabilitation treatment studies in children with acquired brain injury. *Journal of Head Trauma Rehabilitation, 22,* 248–256.

Lah, S., Epps, A., Levick, W., & Parry, L. (2011). Implicit and explicit memory outcome in children who have sustained severe traumatic brain injury: Impact of age at injury (preliminary findings). *Brain Injury, 25,* 44–52.

Lane-Brown, A. T., & Tate, R. L. (2011). Apathy after traumatic brain injury: An overview of the current state of play. *Brain Impairment, 12,* 43–53.

Lange, R. T., Iverson, G. L., & Franzen, M. D. (2009). Neuropsychological functioning following complicated vs. uncomplicated mild traumatic brain injury. *Brain Injury, 23,* 83–91.

Lange, W. (1975). Cell number and cell density in the cerebellar cortex of man and some other mammals. *Cell and Tissue Research, 157,* 115–124.

Lee, L. K. (2007). Controversies in the sequelae of pediatric mild traumatic brain injury. *Pediatric Emergency Care, 23,* 580–583.

Levin, H. S., O'Donnell, V. M., & Grossman, R. G. (1979). The Galveston orientation and amnesia test: A practical scale to assess cognition after head injury. *Journal of Nervous and Mental Disease, 167,* 675–684.

Lew, H. L., Lin, P. H., Fuh, J. L., Wang, S. J., Clark, D. J., & Walker, W. C. (2006). Characteristics and treatment of headache after traumatic brain injury: A focused review. *American Journal of Physical Medicine & Rehabilitation, 85,* 619–627.

Lewandowski, L. J., & Rieger, B. (2009). The role of a school psychologist in concussion. *Journal of Applied School Psychology, 25,* 95–110. doi:10.1080/15377900802484547

Lezak, M. D. (1995). *Neuropsychological assessment* (3rd ed.). New York, NY: Oxford University Press.

Lezak, M. D., Howieson, D. B., Bigler, E. D., & Tranel, D. (2012). *Neuropsychological assessment* (5th ed.). New York, NY: Oxford University Press.

Lowenstein, D. H. (2009). Epilepsy after head injury: An overview. *Epilepsia, 50*(Suppl. 2), 4–9.

Lucas, S., Hoffman, J. M., Bell, K. R., Walker, W., & Dikmen, S. (2012). Characterization of headache after traumatic brain injury. *Cephalalgia, 32,* 600–606.

Luria, A. R. (1979). *The making of mind: A personal account of Soviet psychology* (M. Cole Trans.). Cambridge, MA: Harvard University Press.

Maddocks, D. L., Dicker, G. D., & Saling, M. M. (1995). The assessment of orientation following concussion in athletes. *Clinical Journal of Sport Medicine, 5,* 32–35.

Mainous, A. G., Diaz, V. A., Everett, C. J., & Knoll, M. E. (2011). Impact of insurance and hospital ownership on hospital length of stay among patients with ambulatory care-sensitive conditions. *Annals of Family Medicine, 9,* 489–495.

Marino, M. J. (2000). Special task force convened by the Brain Injury Association to address issues affecting children and adolescents after brain injury. *TBI Challenge, 4*(1), 18–19. Retrieved from http://www.biausa.org/brain-injury-publications.htm

Masson, F., Maurette, P., Salmi, L. R., Dartigues, J. F., Vecsey, J., Destaillats J. M., & Erny, P. (1996). Prevalence of impairments 5 years after a head injury, and their relationship with disabilities and outcome. *Brain Injury, 10,* 487–497.

Mathias, J. L., & Alvaro, P. K. (2012). Prevalence of sleep disturbances, disorders, and problems following traumatic brain injury: A meta-analysis. *Sleep Medicine, 13,* 898–905.

Max, J. E., Keatley, E., Wilde, E. A., Bigler, E. D., Levin, H. S., Schachar, R. J., . . . Yang, T. T. (2011). Anxiety disorders in children and adolescents in the first six months after traumatic brain injury. *Social Care & Neurodisability, 2,* 200–207.

Max, J. E., Keatley, E., Wilde, E. A., Bigler, E. D., Schachar, R. J., Saunders, A. E., . . . Levin, H. S. (2012). Depression in children and adolescents in the first 6 months after traumatic brain injury. *International Journal of Developmental Neuroscience, 30,* 239–245.

Mazaux, J. M., & Richer, E. (1998). Rehabilitation after traumatic brain injury in adults. *Disability and Rehabilitation, 20,* 435–447.

Mazurek, M., Johnstone, B., Hagglund, K., Mokelke, E., Lammy, A., & Yamato, Y. (2011). Geographic differences in traumatic brain injury and spinal cord injury rehabilitation. *International Journal of Therapy and Rehabilitation, 18,* 551–556.

Mazzeo, A. T., Beat, A., Singh, A., & Bullock, M. R. (2009). The role of mitochondrial transition pore, and its modulation, in traumatic brain injury and delayed neurodegeneration after TBI. *Experimental Neurology, 218,* 363–370.

McAvoy, K. (2012). Return to learning: Going back to school following a concussion. *Communique, 40*(6), 23–25.

McCarney, S. B., & Arthaud, T. J. (2005). *Behavior Evaluation Scale* (3rd ed.). Columbia, MO: Hawthorne Educational Services.

McClure, J. (2011). The role of causal attributions in public misconceptions about brain injury. *Rehabilitation Psychology, 56,* 85–93.

McCrea, M., Kelly, J., Kluge, J., Ackley, B., & Randolph, C. (1997). Standardized assessment of concussion in football players. *Neurology, 48,* 586–588.

McCrory, P., Meeuwisse, W., Johnston, K., Dvorak, J., Aubry, M., Molloy, M., & Cantu, R. (2009). Consensus statement on concussion in sport: The 3rd international conference on concussion in sport held in Zurich, November 2008. *British Journal of Sports Medicine, 43,* i76–i84.

McGinnis, E. (2011). *Skillstreaming the elementary school child: A guide for teaching prosocial skills,* (3rd ed.). Champaign, IL: Research Press.

McGrath, N. (2010). Supporting the student-athlete's return to the classroom after a sport-related concussion. *Journal of Athletic Training, 45,* 492–498.

Mendoza, J. E., & Foundas, A. L. (2008). *Clinical neuroanatomy: A neurobehavioral approach.* New York, NY: Springer.

Menon, D. K., Schwab, K., Wright, D. W., & Maas, A. I. (2010). Special communication: Position statement: Definition of traumatic brain injury. *Archives of Physical Medicine and Rehabilitation, 91,* 1637–1640.

Menon, V. (2011). Large-scale brain networks and psychopathology: A unifying triple network model. *Trends in Cognitive Sciences, 15,* 483–506.

Meschan, I. (1975). *An atlas of anatomy basic to radiology.* Philadelphia, PA: Saunders.

Micheloyannis, S., Pachou, E., Stam, C. J., Breakspear, M., Bitsios, P., Vourkas, M., . . . Zervakis, M. (2006). Small-world networks and disturbed functional connectivity in schizophrenia. *Schizophrenia Research, 87,* 60–66.

Milders, M., Ietswaart, M., Crawford, J. R., & Currie, D. (2008). Social behavior following traumatic brain injury and its association with emotion recognition, understanding of intentions, and cognitive flexibility. *Journal of the International Neuropsychological Society, 14,* 318–326.

Moser, R. S., & Schatz, P. (2012). A case for mental and physical rest in youth sports concussion: It's never too late. *Frontiers in Neurology, 3,* 1–7.

Munoz-Cespedes, J. M., Rios-Lago, M., Paul, N., & Maestu, F. (2005). Functional neuroimaging studies of cognitive recovery after acquired brain damage in adults. *Neuropsychology Review, 15,* 169–183.

Muszynski, C., Yoganandan, N., Pintar, F., & Gennarelli, T. (2005). Risk of pediatric head injury after motor vehicle accidents. *Journal of Neurosurgery: Pediatrics, 102,* 374–379.

Nagel, R. W., Hankenhof, B. J., Kimmel, S. R., & Saxe, J. M. (2003). Educating grade school children using a structured bicycle safety program. *Journal of Trauma, Injury, Infection and Critical Care, 55*(5), 920–923.

National Center for Injury Prevention and Control. (2003). *Report to Congress on mild traumatic brain injury in the United States: Steps to prevent a serious public health problem.* Atlanta, GA: Centers for Disease Control and Prevention.

National Conference of State Legislatures. (2012). *Traumatic brain injury legislation.* Retrieved from http://www.ncsl.org/issues-research/health/traumatic-brain-injury-legislation.aspx

Nelson, J. R., Smith, D. J., Young, R. K., & Dodd, J. M. (1991). A review of self-management outcome research conducted with students who exhibit behavioral disorders. *Behavior Disorders, 16,* 169–179.

Niemeier, J. P. (2010). Neuropsychological assessment for visually impaired persons with traumatic brain injury. *NeuroRehabilitation, 27,* 275–283.

Nieuwenhuys, R. (1996). The greater limbic system, the emotional motor system and the brain. In G. Hoslstege, R. Bandler, & C. B. Saper (Eds.), *Progress in brain research* (Vol. 107, pp. 551–580). New York, NY: Elsevier Science.

Nudo, R. J. (2006). Plasticity. *NeuroRx, 3,* 420–427.

O'Keefe, M. (1998). Factors mediating the link between witnessing interparental violence and dating violence. *Journal of Family Violence, 13,* 39–57.

Office of Technology Assessment. (1989). *Rural emergency medical services—Special report.* OTA Publ. No OTA-H-445. Washington, DC: U.S. Government Printing Office.

Ohio Domestic Violence Network. (2010). *Dating violence prevention education—House Bill 19.* Retrieved from http://www.education.ohio.gov/GD/Templates/Pages/ODE

Ono, M., Ownsworth, T., & Walters, B. (2011). Preliminary investigation of misconceptions and expectations of the effects of traumatic brain injury and symptom reporting. *Brain Injury, 25,* 237–249.

Ottens, A. K., Kobeissy, F. H., Golden, E. C., Zhang, Z., Haskins, W. E., Chen, S., . . . Denslow, N. D. (2006). Neuroproteomics in neurotrauma. *Mass Spectrometry Reviews, 25,* 380–408.

Pappadis, M. R., Sander, A. M., Struchen, M. A., Leung, P., & Smith, D. W. (2011). Common misconceptions about traumatic brain injury among ethnic minorities with TBI. *Journal of Head Trauma Rehabilitation, 26,* 301–311.

Peiniger, S., Nienaber, U., Lefering, R., Braun, M., Wafaisade, A., Borgman, M. A., & . . . Trauma Registry of the Deutsche Gesellschaft fur Unfallchirurgie. (2012). Glasgow coma scale as a predictor for hemocoagulative disorders after blunt pediatric traumatic brain injury. *Pediatric Critical Care Medicine, 13,* 455–460. doi: 10.1097/PCC.0b013e31823893c5

Pelham, W. E., Gnagy, E. M., Greiner, A. R., Hoza, B., Hinshaw, S. P., Swanson, J. M., . . . McBurnett, K. (2000). Behavioral versus behavioral and pharmacological treatment in ADHD children attending a summer treatment program. *Journal of Abnormal Child Psychology, 28,* 507–525.

Pershelli, A. (2007). Memory strategies to use with students following traumatic brain injury. *Physical Disabilities: Education and Related Services, 26,* 31–46.

Pham, H. L. (2012). Differentiated instruction and the need to integrate teaching and practice. *Journal of College Teaching & Learning, 9,* 13–20.

Pinto, P. S., Poretti, A., Meoded, A., Tekes, A., & Huisman, T. A. G. M. (2012). The unique features of traumatic brain injury in children. Review of the characteristics of the pediatric skull and brain, mechanisms of trauma, patterns of injury, complications and their imaging findings—Part 1. *Journal of Neuroimaging, 22,* e1–e17. doi: 10.1111/j.1552–6569.2011.00688.x

Posner, J. B., Saper, C. B., Schiff, N., & Plum, F. (2007). *Plum and Posner's diagnosis of stupor and coma* (4th ed.). New York, NY: Oxford University Press.

Power, T. J., DuPaul, G. J., Shapiro, E. S., & Kazak, A. E. (2003). *Promoting children's health: Integrating school, family, and community.* New York, NY: Guilford.

Power, T. J., DuPaul, G. J., Shapiro, E. S., & Parrish, J. (1995). Pediatric school psychology: The emergence of a subspecialization. *School Psychology Review, 24,* 244–257.

Prigatano, G. P., & Gale, S. D. (2011). The current status of postconcussion syndrome. *Current Opinion in Psychiatry, 24,* 243–250.

Proctor, M. R., & Cantu, R. C. (2000). Head and neck injuries in young athletes. *Clinical Sports Medicine, 19,* 693–715.

Putukian, M. (2011). The acute symptoms of sport-related concussion: Diagnosis and on-field management. *Clinics in Sports Medicine, 30,* 49–61.

Ramirez, J. J. (2001). The role of axonal sprouting in functional reorganization after CNS injury: Lessons from the hippocampal formation. *Restorative Neurology and Neuroscience, 19,* 237–262.

Rapoport, M. J. (2012). Depression following traumatic brain injury: Epidemiology, risk factors, and management. *CNS Drugs, 26,* 111–121.

Redpath, S. J., Williams, W. H., Hanna, D., Linden, M. A., Yates, P. & Harris, A. (2010). Health care professionals' attitudes towards traumatic brain injury (TBI): The influence of profession, experience, aetiology and blame on prejudice towards survivors of brain injury. *Brain Injury, 24,* 802–811.

Reitan, R. M., & Wolfson, D. (1993). *The Halstead-Reitan neuropsychological test battery: Theory and clinical interpretation* (2nd ed.). Tucson, AZ: Neuropsychological Press.

Reynolds, C. R., & Kamphaus, R. W. (2004). *Behavior assessment system for children* (2nd ed.). San Antonio, TX: Pearson.

Rice, T. M. Peek-Asa, C., Kraus, J. F. (2003). Nighttime driving, passenger transport, and injury crash rates of young drivers. *Injury Prevention, 9,* 245–250. doi:10.1136/ip.9.3.245

Riemann, B. L., Guskiewicz, K. M., & Shields, E. W. (1999). Relationship between clinical and forceplate measures of postural stability. *Journal of Sport Rehabilitation, 8,* 71–82.

Robinson, L. (2011). *Talking with parents: When a student has a brain injury.* Youngsville, NC: Lash & Associates Publishing/Training Inc.

Ross, D., & Frey, N. (2009). Real-time teaching: Learners need purposeful and systematic instruction. *Journal of Adolescent & Adult Literacy, 53,* 75–78.

Sady, M. D., Vaughan, C. G., & Gioia, G. A. (2011). School and the concussed youth: Recommendations for concussion education and management. *Physical Medicine Rehabilitation Clinics of North America, 22,* 701–719. doi: 10.1016/j.pmr.2011.08.008

Sander, A. M., Maestas, K. L., Sherer, M., Malec, J. F., & Nakase-Richardson, R. (2012). Relationship of caregiver and family functioning to participation outcomes after postacute rehabilitation for traumatic brain injury: A multicenter investigation. *Archives of Physical Medicine and Rehabilitation, 93,* 842–848.

Sandhaug, M., Andelic, N., Vatne, A., Seiler, S., & Mygland, A. (2010). Functional level during sub-acute rehabilitation after traumatic brain injury: Course and predictors of outcome. *Brain Injury, 24,* 740–747.

Schacter, D. L., Gilbert, D. T., & Wegner, D. M. (2010). *Psychology* (2nd ed.). New York, NY: Worth Publishing.

Schneier, A. J., Shields, B. J., Hostetler, S. G., Xiang, H., & Smith, G. A. (2006). Incidence of pediatric traumatic brain injury and associated hospital resource utilization in the United States. *Pediatrics, 118,* 483–492. doi: 10.1542/peds.2005-2588

Section 504 of the Rehabilitation Act of 1973, as Amended 29 U.S.C. § 794 et seq.

Sepulcre, J., Sabuncu, M. R., & Johnson, K. A. (2012). Network assemblies in the functional brain. *Current Opinion in Neurology, 25,* 384–391.

Shapiro, E. S. (2010). *Academic skills problem workbook* (4th ed.). New York, NY: Guilford Press.

Shapiro, E. S., & Cole, C. L. (1994). *Behavior change in the classroom.* New York, NY: Guilford Press.

Shawkat, H., Westwood, M., & Mortimer, A. (2012). Mannitol: A review of its clinical uses. *Continuing Education in Anaesthesia, Critical Care & Pain, 12,* 82–85. doi: 10.1093/bjaceaccp/mkr063

Shenton, M. E., Hamoda, H. M., Schneiderman, J. S., Bouix, S., Pasternak, O., Rathi, Y., . . . Zafonte, R. (2012). A review of magnetic resonance imaging and diffusion tensor imaging findings in mild traumatic brain injury. *Brain Imaging and Behavior, 6,* 137–192.

Sherer, M., Bergloff, P., Levin, E., High, W., Oden, K. E., & Nick, T. G. (1998). Impaired awareness and employment outcome after traumatic brain injury. *Journal of Head Trauma Rehabilitation, 13,* 52–61.

Sherer, M., Struchen, M. A., Yablon, S. A., Wang, Y., & Nick, T. G. (2008). Comparison of indices of traumatic brain injury severity: Glasgow Coma Scale, length of coma and post-traumatic amnesia. *Journal of Neurology, Neurosurgery, & Psychiatry, 79,* 678–685. doi:10.1136/jnnp.2006.111187

Shi, J., Xiang, H., Wheeler, K., Smith, G. A., Stallones, L., Groner, H. J., & Wang, Z. (2009). Costs, mortality likelihood and outcomes of hospitalized US children with traumatic brain injuries. *Brain Injury, 23,* 602–611.

Silver, J. M., McAllister, T. W., & Yudofsky, S. C. (Eds.). (2011). *Textbook of traumatic brain injury* (2nd ed.). Arlington, VA: American Psychiatric Publishing.

Slobounov, S., Gay, M., Johnson, B., & Zhang, K. (2012). Concussion in athletics: Ongoing clinical and brain imaging research controversies. *Brain Imaging and Behavior, 6,* 224–243.

Smith, D. H., & Meaney, D. F. (2000). Axonal damage in traumatic brain injury. *The Neuroscientist, 6*, 483–495.

Somers, J., & Sikorova, E. (2002). The effectiveness of one in-service education of teachers course for influencing teachers' practice. *Journal of In-Service Education, 28*, 95–114.

Sparrow, S., Cicchetti, D., & Balla, D. (2005). *Vineland adaptive behavior scales* (2nd ed.). San Antonio, TX: Pearson.

Spitz, G., Ponsford, J. L., Rudzki, D., & Maller, J. J. (2012). Association between cognitive performance and functional outcome following traumatic brain injury: A longitudinal multilevel examination. *Neuropsychology, 26*, 604–612.

Springer, J. A., Farmer, J. E., & Bouman, D. E. (1997). Common misconceptions about traumatic brain injury among family members of rehabilitation patients. *Journal of Head Trauma Rehabilitation, 12*, 41–50.

Stamas, P. (1997). Rural EMS: Who are you and what do you need? *Wisconsin Medical Journal, 96*(8), 14.

Stein, D. G. (1999). Brain injury and theories of recovery. In L. B. Goldstein (Ed.), *Restorative neurology: Advances in pharmacotherapy for recovery after stroke* (pp. 1–34). Hoboken, NJ: Wiley-Blackwell.

Stewart-Scott, A. M., & Douglas, J. M. (1998). Educational outcome for secondary and postsecondary students following traumatic brain injury. *Brain Injury, 12*, 317–331.

Steyn, G. M. (2006). A qualitative study of the aspects influencing the implementation of invitational education in schools in the United States of America. *Journal of Invitational Theory and Practice, 12*, 17–36.

Stiles, J., & Jernigan, T. L. (2010). The basics of brain development. *Neuropsychology Review, 20*, 327–348.

Stoner, G., Carey, S. P., Ikeda, M. J., & Shinn, M. R. (1994). The utility of curriculum based measurement for evaluating the effects of methylphenidate on academic performance. *Journal of Applied Behavior Analysis, 27*, 101–113.

Strauss, I., & Savitsky, N. (1934). Head injury: Neurologic and psychiatric aspects. *Archives of Neurology and Psychiatry, 31*, 893–955.

Sulkowski, M., Jordan, C., & Nguyen, M. (2009). Current practices and future directions in psychopharmacological training and collaboration in school psychology. *Canadian Journal of School Psychology, 24*, 237–244.

Sundstrom, A., Nilsson, L. G., Cruts, M., Adolfsson, R., van Broeckhoven, C., & Nyberg, L. (2007). Fatigue before and after mild traumatic brain injury: Pre-post-injury comparisons in relation to apolipoprotein E. *Brain Injury, 21*, 1049–1054.

Supekar, K., Musen, M., & Menon, V. (2009). Development of large-scale functional brain networks in children. *PLOS Biology, 7*, e1000157. doi:10.1371/journal.pbio.1000157

Sweet, J. J., & Westerveld, M. (2012). Pediatric neuropsychology in forensic proceedings: Roles and procedures in the courtroom and beyond. In E. M. S. Sherman & B. L. Brooks (Eds.), *Pediatric forensic neuropsychology* (pp. 3–23). New York, NY: Oxford University Press.

Tang-Schomer, M. D., Patel, A. R., Baas, P. W., & Smith, D. H. (2010). Mechanical breaking of microtubules in axons during dynamic stretch injury underlies delayed elasticity, microtubule disassembly, and axon degeneration. *FASEB Journal, 24*, 1401–1410.

Taylor, H. G., Swartwout, M. D., Yeates, K. O., Walz, N. C., Stancin, T., & Wade, S. L. (2008). Traumatic brain injury in young children: Postacute effects on cognitive and school readiness skills. *Journal of the International Neuropsychological Society, 14*, 734–745.

Teasdale, G., & Jennett, B. (1974). Assessment of coma and impaired consciousness: A practical scale. *Lancet, 2*, 81–84.

Technical Assistance Coordination Center. (2011). Child count. Retrieved from http://tadnet .public.tadnet.org/pages/712

Tedesco, A. M., Chiricozzi, R. R., Clausi, S., Lupo, M., Molinari, M., & Leggio, M. G. (2011). The cerebellar cognitive profile. *Brain: A Journal of Neurology, 134,* 3672–3686.

Todis, B., & Glang, A. (2008). Redefining success: Results of a qualitative study of postsecondary transition outcomes for youth with traumatic brain injury. *Journal of Head Trauma Rehabilitation, 23,* 252–263.

U.S. Consumer Product Safety Commission. (2013). *National electronic injury surveillance system–All Injury Program (NEISS–AIP).* Retrieved from http://www.cpsc.gov/library/neiss.html

U.S. Department of Education. (2010). *Section 504: Guidelines for educators and administrators for implementing Section 504 of the Rehabilitation Act of 1973-Subpart D.* Washington, DC: U.S. Department of Education.

U.S. Department of Education/U.S. Congress. (1992). *Federal Register. Definition of traumatic brain injury, 57, 189, p. 44802.* Washington, DC: Federal Register.

U.S. Department of Health and Human Services. (2011). *The value of health insurance: Few of the uninsured have adequate resources to pay potential hospital bills.* ASPE Research Brief, Office of the Assistant Secretary for Planning and Evaluation, Office of Health Policy. Retrieved from http://aspe.hhs.gov/health/reports/2011/ValueofInsurance/rb.shtml

U.S. Department of Health and Human Services. (2013). *Healthcare cost and utilization project (HCUP),* Agency for Healthcare Research and Quality. Retrieved from http://www.ahrq.gov/research/data/hcup/index.html

U.S. Federal Register. (2006). *Part II: Department of Education: 34 CFR Parts 300 and 302, Assistance to States for the Education of Children With Disabilities and Preschool Grants for Children With Disabilities; Final Rule, 71, 156.* Washington, DC: Federal Register.

Vagnozzi, R., Signoretti, S., Cristofori, L., Alessandrini, F., Floris, R., Isgro, E., . . . Lazzarino, G. (2010). Assessment of metabolic brain damage and recovery following mild traumatic brain injury: A multicentre, proton magnetic resonance spectroscopic study in concussed patients. *Brain, 133*(11), 3232–3242, doi:10.1093/brain/awq200

Vakil, E. (2005). The effect of moderate to severe traumatic brain injury (TBI) on different aspects of memory: A selective review. *Journal of Clinical and Experimental Neuropsychology, 27,* 977–1021.

van den Heuvel, M. P., Mandl, R. C. W., Stam, C. J., Kahn, R. S., & Hulshoff Pol, H. E. (2010). Aberrant frontal and temporal complex network structure in schizophrenia: A graph theoretical analysis. *The Journal of Neuroscience, 30,* 15915–15926.

van der Naalt, J., van Zomeren, A. H., Sluiter, W. J., & Minderhoud, J. M. (1999). One year outcome in mild to moderate head injury: The predictive value of acute injury characteristics related to complaints and return to work. *Journal of Neurology, Neurosurgery and Psychiatry, 66,* 207–213.

Vargus-Adams, J. N., McMahon, M. A., Michaud, L. J., Bean, J., & Vinks, A. A. (2010). Pharmacokinetics of amantadine in children with impaired consciousness due to acquired brain injury: preliminary findings using a sparse-sampling technique. *PM&R, The Journal of Injury, Function and Rehabilitation, 2,* 37–42.

Vespa, P. M., McArthur, D. L., Xu, Y., Eliseo, M., Etchepare, M., Dinov, I., . . . Hovda, D. (2010). Nonconvulsive seizures after traumatic brain injury are associated with hippocampal atrophy. *Neurology, 75,* 792–798.

Wade, S. L., Carey, J., & Wolfe, C. R. (2006). The efficacy of an online cognitive-behavioral, family intervention in improving child behavior and social competence following pediatric brain injury. *Rehabilitation Psychology, 51,* 179–189.

Wade, S. L., Cassedy, A., Walz, N. C., Taylor, H. G., Stancin, T., & Yeates, K. O. (2011). The relationship of parental warm responsiveness and negativity to emerging behavior problems following traumatic brain injury in young children. *Developmental Psychology, 47,* 119–133.

Wagner, M., Newman, L., Cameto, R., & Levine, P. (2005). *Changes over time in the early postschool outcomes of youth with disabilities.* A report of findings from the National Longitudinal Transition

Study (NLTS) and the National Longitudinal Transition Study-2 (NLTS2). Menlo Park, CA: SRI International. Retrieved from www.nlts2.org/reports/2005_06/nlts2_report_2005_06_complete.pdf

Watts, D. J., & Strogatz, S. H. (1998). Collective dynamics of 'small-world' networks. *Nature, 393,* 440–442.

Wilde, E. A., Hunter, J. V., & Bigler, E. D. (2012a). Pediatric traumatic brain injury: Neuroimaging and neurorehabilitation outcome. *NeuroRehabilitation, 31,* 245–260.

Wilde, E. A., Hunter, J. V., & Bigler, E. D. (2012b). A primer of neuroimaging analysis in neurorehabilitation outcome research. *NeuroRehabilitation, 31,* 227–242.

Wilde, E. A., Ramos, M. A., Yallampalli, R., Bigler, E. D., McCauley, S. R., Chu, Z., . . . Levin, H. S. (2010). Diffusion tensor imaging of the cingulum bundle in children after traumatic brain injury. *Developmental Neuropsychology, 35,* 333–351.

Williams, C., & Wood, R. L. (2010). Alexithymia and emotional empathy following traumatic brain injury. *Journal of Clinical and Experimental Neuropsychology, 32,* 259–267.

Williams, J. M., Ehrlich, P. F., & Prescott, J. E. (2001). Emergency medical care in rural America. *Annals of Emergency Medicine 38,* 323–327.

Wodrich, D., & Landau, S. (1999). School psychologists: Strategic allies in the contemporary practice of primary care pediatrics. *Clinical Pediatrics, 38,* 597–606.

Woodcock, R. W., McGrew, K. S., & Mather, N. (2001a). *Woodcock-Johnson III tests of achievement.* Itasca, IL: Riverside.

Woodcock, R. W., McGrew, K. S., & Mather, N. (2001b). *Woodcock-Johnson III tests of cognitive abilities.* Itasca, IL: Riverside.

World Health Organization. (2006). *Neurological disorders: Public health challenges.* Geneva, CH: WHO Press.

Yan, C., & He, Y. (2011). Driving and driven architectures of directed small-world human brain functional networks. *PLoS ONE, 6,* e23460. doi:10.1371/journal.pone.0023460

Yeates, K. O., Gerhardt, C. A., Bigler, E. D., Abildskov, T., Dennis, M., Rubin, K. H., . . . Vannatta K. (2013). Peer relationships of children with traumatic brain injury. *Journal of the International Neuropsychological Society, 19,* 518–527.

Ylvisaker, M., & Feeney, T. J. (1998). School reentry after traumatic brain injury. In M. Ylvisaker (Ed.). *Traumatic brain injury rehabilitation: Children and adolescents* (2nd ed., pp. 369–388). Boston, MA: Butterworth-Heinemann.

Ylvisaker, M., Todis, B., Glang, A., Urbanczyk, B., Franklin, C., DePompei, R., . . . Tyler, J. S. (2001). Educating students with TBI: Themes and recommendations. *Journal of Head Trauma Rehabilitation, 16,* 76–93.

Yoganandan, N., Gennarelli, T. A., Zhang, J., Pintar, F. A., Takhounts, E., & Ridella, S. A. (2009). Association of contact loading in diffuse axonal injuries from motor vehicle crashes. *Journal of Trauma, 66,* 309–315.

Yoon, K. S., Duncan, T., Lee, S. W-Y, Scarloss, B., & Shaplay, K. L. (2007). *Reviewing the evidence on how teacher professional development affects student achievement.* National Center for Education Evaluation and Regional Assistance, Institute of Education Sciences, U.S. Department of Education.

Zaben, M., El Ghoul, W., & Belli, A. (2013). Post-traumatic head injury pituitary dysfunction. *Disability and Rehabilitation, 35,* 522–525.

Index